"Margaret Croyden's book is an absolute necessity for any reader interested in twentieth-century theater or interested in Peter Brook, one of the great artistic explorers of our time. A valuable book about an extraordinary artist! *Conversations with Peter Brook* is truly a meeting with a remarkable man."   —Andre Gregory

"I loved it. The interaction between Margaret Croyden and Peter Brook is amusing and not at all reverential and the revelations of Brook on his adventures in theater and in life are thrilling. A great life-inspiring story."
                                        —Harvey Lichtenstein

"What comes across in Margaret Croyden's *Conversations* is Peter Brook's warm, engaging search that touches all of us. Brook talks about ultimate matters with remarkable insights that reveal the spiritual need for the theater of our time. Margaret Croyden has done a brilliant job in catching the essential Peter Brook."   —Andrei Serban

"Margaret Croyden's sharp, provocative questions to Peter Brook and his brilliant responses make *Conversations with Peter Brook* a truly sophisticated book—not only about the theater, but about what a great artist thinks, how he works, and how he lives. It is a pleasure to read." —Ellen Stewart

"In *Conversations with Peter Brook,* Margaret Croyden has compiled a fascinating portrait of Brook—the director, the artist, the man—a book that will inspire theater people and all those who love the arts."   —Joseph Chaikin

Margaret Croyden

•

Conversations with Peter Brook, 1970–2000

MARGARET CROYDEN is a well-known critic, commentator, and journalist whose articles on theater and the arts have appeared in *The New York Times, The Village Voice, The Nation, The American Theater Magazine, Antioch Review, Texas Quarterly, Transatlantic Review,* and other publications. She is the author of *Lunatics, Lovers and Poets: The Contemporary Experimental Theater,* a seminal book tracing the development of the nonliterary theater, and a host for more than a decade on CBS-TV's *Camera Three,* an arts program where she interviewed and discussed the work of leading people in the theater.

Ms. Croyden, formerly a professor of English Literature at New Jersey City University, was educated at Hunter College and New York University and studied also at Oxford University and the Shakespeare Institute in Stratford-on-Avon, England. She has lectured widely on American and European theater and has been a featured speaker at international gatherings in the United States, Europe, the Middle East, and Japan. Her most recent publication is a memoir, *In the Shadow of the Flame: Three Journeys.* She is a regular critic and contributor to nytheatre-wire.com under the byline "Croyden's Corner."

Conversations with
Peter Brook
1970–2000

———————— • ————————

Margaret Croyden

FABER AND FABER
NEW YORK • LONDON

First published in 2003 by Faber and Faber, Inc.
an affiliate of Farrar, Straus and Giroux
19 Union Square, New York 10003
Published in the United Kingdom
by Faber and Faber Limited
3 Queen Square
London WC1N 3AU

Distributed in Canada by Penguin Books of Canada Limited
Printed in the United States of America
First edition, 2003

0 571 22172 6

Designed by Patrice Sheridan

1 3 5 7 9 10 8 6 4 2

To the memory of my dear friends
Jerzy Grotowski

and

Ryszard Cieslak

Contents

Introduction

Peter Brook, whose productions have captivated people all over the world, has often been referred to as the most important contemporary theater director in the West. His revolutionary *Marat/Sade* and *King Lear,* his airborne *A Midsummer Night's Dream* and untraditional *La Tragédie de Carmen,* his *The Man Who* and *The Tragedy of Hamlet,* and his masterwork, the nine-hour production of the Indian myth, *The Mahabharata,* place him in the forefront of those artists who can reach various audiences regardless of cultural boundaries. In an age when interest in theater arts has shifted from the stage to the screen, when the latest work of currently famous film directors, rather than plays, seem to offer vitality, Peter Brook continues to find his forum of expression primarily in the theater, through the interaction of actors and audience in live performances. To expand the range of his endeavors, he successfully developed a flexible, noninstitutionalized company (in 1970) at his International Center of Theater Research in Paris, which offered a fusion of cultures, temperaments, and styles—a theater that would express a certain freedom and variety, a melding of traditions, and a universal sensibility. During his years with his ensemble in Paris and, indeed, even before then, Brook became a symbol of the everlasting creativity of theater artists; he has shown what it is possible for an artist to achieve if he has the courage, the integrity of purpose, and the belief in the value of art that defines Brook's own life and work.

Today, after more than forty years in the theater and having directed more than eighty productions, many seen all over the world, Brook has not slowed down. His signature traits remain the iconoclastic approach and the belief in the power and value of art in all cultures. Possibly no other director in the West has had the confidence and daring to challenge conventional concepts as Brook has—and in the process influenced multiple generations of theater artists and excited theatergoers everywhere. His is an undaunted search for new meanings, for greater insights, and for what may be beyond the sight lines of the naked eye. Even before multiculturalism came into fashion in the West, Brook traveled to Africa and Asia to explore non-Western cultural traditions and reach local audiences. Always striving to find a more refined aesthetic to express the mysteries of the human spirit, Brook is unfazed by challenges and hardships. He actually rather fancies difficulties, for he has a clear vision, a strong belief in what he is doing, and the genius to fulfill his goal.

From his youth, Brook has searched for new forms. A successful stage director at the age of twenty, he was appointed director of Covent Garden at twenty-four, where he created what was considered a scandalous *Salome* and an innovative *Boris Godunov.* He later directed every conceivable type of play, ranging from Arthur Miller's works to those of Jean-Paul Sartre and Jean Genet, from Tennessee Williams's to Shakespeare's and George Bernard Shaw's, not to mention Broadway musicals, television shows, and films. When he became one of the directors of the newly organized Royal Shakespeare Company in the 1960s, Brook revolutionized Shakespeare productions with a bold, austere *King Lear,* which served as a model for reexamining conventional concepts of staging Shakespeare. He was also the first director in London to work experimentally with a group of actors from the RSC that was interested in exploring the techniques of Brecht and Artaud. Then came the renowned production of *Marat/Sade,* a study in revolution and madness, an artistic milestone that integrated radical concepts of acting and audiences, staging and space, and design and material with revolutionary politics, followed by the joyous *A Midsummer Night's Dream,* which captivated critics and the public alike.

In 1968, after embarking on an experimental project in Paris with an international company (an enterprise interrupted by the student uprising), Brook decided to form a group of his own. It was a time for adventure, for a break with the past, not only politically but artistically. Radical groups were organizing: The Living Theatre and the Open Theater in New York were engaging audiences all over the world, and the phenomenon of Jerzy Grotowski and his brilliant nonlinear productions prompted a reevaluation of basic theater work. Something was happening—and Peter Brook was in the middle of it all.

Excited by all the new developments, Brook went back to Paris in 1970 to organize his permanent group: the International Center of Theater Research, an organization that would focus on both research and production. The Vietnam War had reached a critical stage, and rebellious young artists were fed up with traditional concepts, with what they considered double-talk, and with everything the establishment represented. Various theater groups gave voice and credence to this disgust with political and social corruption. Thus, two camps were forming in the theater: that of traditional naturalism, represented by the dominance of the playwright and the staging of conventional productions, and the experimental nonliterary theater of images and nonverbal behavior, represented by the counter-culture groups that were flourishing in basements, studios, and storefronts. Although some of the latter groups fell apart by the late 1970s, Brook and his newly formed company persevered and flourished. What was the secret of this success?

From the beginning, Peter Brook has always had an iconoclastic, almost revolutionary streak. When he was directing in the West End in his twenties, he was an enfant terrible, unafraid to attempt all sorts of plays. His revolutionary fervor, however, doesn't come entirely from political theory or social upheavals, although he was influenced by the times and still is; instead, it stems from an extreme singularity, a special sensibility that allows him to remain open to all possibilities and the implications of contemporary events that makes him unwilling to be bound by commercial needs alone. It is this zest for creation and his capacity for living, combined with an extraordinary energy, that defines Brook's individuality. It was therefore logical for him to organize a group of his own, to be his own master, to disengage from the commercial world, in which he had been extremely successful, so that he could emerge as a truly unique, independent artist.

In creating his International Center of Theater Research, Brook was able to establish an audience of students, intellectuals, and neighborhood people who supported his productions regardless of criticism or controversy. A great piece of luck was the discovery of an ideal venue for his work—Les Bouffes du Nord, a dilapidated old vaudeville house that had somehow maintained its original beauty despite its increasing shabbiness; it has remained the home of all Brook's productions since the seventies. Brook's survival was also linked to his having already built an international reputation, which enhanced his prestige and made him attractive to the French. Parisians were happy to support him and his creative efforts, for they regarded it as a privilege to do so. It was also no doubt a source of pride that France was instrumental in supporting some of the most brilliant theater work to be seen on the Continent.

The most important aspect of Brook's character and of his artistry is that he is a searcher—a rare phenomenon in the theater. Theater directors stage plays; they are engaged for several weeks and leave for another job; there is no continuity and very little rehearsal time. Most directors have little concept of ensemble work, having had little chance to work with a permanent company. Nor do many directors have a point of view or express themselves through the plays they direct. Brook, by contrast, has a signature, a philosophy, a raison d'être. He chooses material because he wants to say something through the work—he is an auteur, although few who are called auteurs truly are.

And as an auteur, Brook is a questioner, a teacher; he is forever posing problems. In *The Mahabharata,* for example, an essential issue is raised about the forces of destruction and one's role in the battle between good and evil. What position should one take? In *The Conference of the Birds,* a similar question arises: Does one have the strength to make sacrifices to achieve enlightenment, or would one rather live without the experience? In *La Tragédie de Carmen,* different questions come to the fore: What is the nature of obsessional love? And what is the price to be paid for it?

Then there is the power of his personality, his enormous knowledge, and his boundless energy. He always looks at the world with fresh eyes, almost as a child would, but his perceptions are highly sophisticated. When he speaks, he is totally involved with what he is saying and with whom he is speaking. His focus never seems to waver. The gaze from his incandescent blue eyes is uncanny—penetrating and fiercely attentive. And he has a brilliant gift for conversation, for explanations, for telling stories at any time of the day or night, and he can talk at great length, as this compilation of our many conversations through the years will show. Although I often did not agree with him about many of his explorations, he remained undaunted, stood his ground, and offered more explanations, for he liked being challenged.

In my interchanges with Brook from 1970 to 2000, he talked freely about his major works, such as *A Midsummer Night's Dream;* the establishment of the Paris Center; his Persian and African experiences; his foray into opera with *La Tragédie de Carmen;* his return to the Royal Shakespeare Company for *Antony and Cleopatra;* his monumental *Mahabharata,* as well as *The Tempest, The Man Who,* and *The Tragedy of Hamlet;* and his filming of *Meetings with Remarkable Men.* Included also are random conversations—

reminiscences and bits and pieces about such disparate subjects as sex, politics, fathers, and philosophy.

In each segment, Brook discusses his artistic aims and concepts, as well as his theatrical choices and the rationale behind them. In the course of the conversations, one can easily trace his artistic development and the effect of his directorial method on various productions. As a lifetime searcher, he speaks about what this means and its effect on his lifestyle and artistic quest. He defines his directorial techniques, what he expects from actors, and his longtime effort to forge a genuine relationship between actors and audience. Storytelling and its relation to ethnic cultures have always been of fundamental interest to him, and he speaks about the importance of his travels to Persia, Africa, and India in this regard. But it is his love of Shakespeare, who, he claims, has always been his model, that is at the heart of his work. His building of the International Center of Theater Research and a company came from the idea, he has said, of producing theater that would be comic and tragic, political and frivolous, rough and holy—similar to what was achieved in Elizabethan times.

My meetings with the remarkable Peter Brook and knowing him all these years have been rewarding and meaningful experiences. He has been a dear friend, a mentor, and a guide—a truly uncommon human being, and, for me, a consummate artist.

New York City, May 2002

Conversations with Peter Brook
1970–2000

One

A Midsummer Night's Dream

Peter Brook burst into New York in 1971 with *A Midsummer Night's Dream,* five years after his *Marat/Sade* appeared on Broadway. *Dream* had received unanimous raves in London and was shortly to garner unqualified acclaim when it opened on Broadway. Critics and audiences embraced Brook's radical approach to a surprising degree, and soon *Dream* became a landmark in Shakespearean production. Departing from his dark period of *King Lear* and *Marat/Sade, Dream* was a joyous celebration that created pride in performance and a newfound delight in theater itself for all who either performed in it or saw it. In its break with tradition, Brook's production, in all its visual beauty, opened up new possibilities for producing Shakespeare, and, in fact, it encouraged new and daring work by others.

Through the years, *A Midsummer Night's Dream* has meant dancing fairies, green woodlands, and gossamer wings—Oberon, Titania, and Puck flitting about, casting their magic spells with sweet sentimentality. From David Garrick to Max Reinhardt, directors had leaned heavily upon this tradition of cloying romanticism, and few had had the temerity to break it. Finally, Peter Brook did. His *Midsummer Night's Dream* was a deliberate departure from convention—contemporary in design, Freudian in tone, and, at the same time, faithful to the Shakespearean text. Here are no winged fairies, fake moons, or silver sequins, but a pristine and sensuous vision—a joyful tribute to Shakespeare's "the poet, the lunatic, the lover."

Brook staged *Dream* on a brightly lighted, open white stage with galleries running around the top, a setting reminiscent of Shakespeare's Globe, but one in which the fairies, dressed in nondescript gray satin slacks and shirts, played Richard Peaslee's atonal music on bongo drums, tubular bells, and Elizabethan guitars, creating sound effects on washboards and metal sheets, as in the Chinese theater. On the side of the walls were fireman's ladders, on which actors ran, jumped, and played.

Here the forest was not a place where "the wild thyme grows"; this forest had trees with white metal coils cast down from the galleries like fishing nets by capricious beefy male fairies to entangle the two pairs of Athenian lovers, who were dressed in tie-dyed pink-and-blue mod outfits.

Without makeup and wearing white satin cloaks, the entire company of players—dashing, energetic, and proud—started the play to the sound of drums; as each made his entrance, he bowed to the audience to signify the beginning of the ceremony. Under the bright lights, the magic was made visible. Oberon and Puck were not earthbound, but flew through the air on trapezes—like sudden lightning flashes of yellow and purple, the colors of their costumes—dispensing their love juice from a silver plate spinning on a juggler's stick. Titania, in striking green satin, was on a scarlet ostrich-feather bed that levitated in space like a swing. There the burly Ass with a Bert Lahr clown's nose, string undershirt, and worker's clogs would bed the glamorous Queen like a fighter going into the ring. And at this climactic point, phallic jokes and ironic stage business were introduced to mark the union of this bizarre pair.

The ultimate magic was the sight of Oberon and Puck swinging through the air, throwing their magic western flower—a disk—to each other from the height of about thirty feet. At another point, Puck walked on stilts, and Oberon swung on a long rope suspended from the ceiling, his purple satin gown billowing in the air to celebrate the union of his queen with the Ass, while most of the rest of the company, to the tune of Mendelssohn's "Wedding March," pelted the entire wedding party with confetti and paper plates, leaving the mischievous Puck to clean up the mess with broom and shovel.

This *Dream* revealed the ambiguities of love, the uncertainties of sexual desire, the grotesque subconscious images, the lunacy and obsession of love. "What fools these mortals be" is, to be sure, an integral part of the play, but so is "what visions have I seen," which underscores the essence of this amazing production.

In an interview in his handsome Paris apartment in 1971, Peter Brook, lounging in his stocking feet on a low orange couch and flanked on one wall by a stunning Afghan tapestry and on the other by his then four-year-old child's crepe-paper collage, recalled when he and Sally Jacobs, the set and costume designer, started work on *Dream*.

•

Q: How did the *Dream* project begin?

PB: Sally Jacobs and I started in New York. We said we were going to make a theatrical space in which theatricality could be celebrated. And that nothing was going to impose an actual shape on the story, nor would any of the costumes impose an interpretation on the actors. It would all be purely functional, in a theatrical way. The place had to be somewhere that told no story but enabled very difficult theatrical actions to be seen. So we had a place like a gymnasium, which told no story—it had to be white—in which people could be on wires, could be on the ground, could be in the air, could leap, swing, hang, fly, jump, and run. And that was the space.

Q: I understand that you always start work on a bare stage and that you sometimes want to keep it that way.

PB: Well, yes, we thought that. What would be wrong with a bare stage? Why should we put anything on it at all? And why should we have any costumes? Sally is the first person—although she's a brilliant designer of costumes and scenery—to use, if this is what's right, "working clothes." In *US*—an experimental work about Vietnam—she scrapped a whole set of costumes in favor of jeans. So that at the dress rehearsal, actors, in working clothes, were closer to the basic reality of Vietnam, the subject of the piece. Here, we did start with a bare stage, and actors in working clothes, and we said, What's wrong with that? Actors in jeans and sweaters. We rejected this in *Dream* for a very simple reason. Because there was nothing wrong with it, except that it was not joyful. The bare stage, the Stratford hall, was a rather negative statement. The actors in their own clothes—this was not the starting point of a celebration. We were making a celebration in *Dream*. We didn't want that great, stark, spare, empty desert. We wanted a small place. And we wanted a small luminous place. So we made a box.

Q: How did the rest of it fit in—the trapezes and all that?

PB: We wanted certain facilities in the box. We were not certain how it was going to be used, but they had to be there for people to jump and spin. So the instruments came into it. We used a million props in rehearsal, which we threw out, one by one, until we simplified it down to these few sticks. And then for the costumes, we said we did not want bare clothes, but brilliant and joyful clothes . . . Actors dress up because you can do more brilliant movements if you have a flying cloak; you can fly through the air more dazzlingly if you know that you are a streak of yellow moving through the air. Yet we didn't want any of those things to indicate, before we started, that this was the character of Puck, or this was the character of Titania. So, in fact, Titania was bright green, and Oberon was purple, and Puck was a streak of yellow. They were working clothes for performers trying to perform, proud of what they were—that is, performers enjoying performing in front of other people.

Q: But whose idea was it working the actors as if they might be on a trapeze in a circus?

PB: I didn't do it as a circus. It has nothing to do with the circus. It worked quite the other way around. What I wanted to do came from the elimination of impossible alternatives. You have a play that contains elements of magic and fantasy. It's about acting. It's about illusion. And it is a joyous play. It is a celebration for actors, to be performed by actors, and, in one respect, it is a celebration of the arts of the theater, of the performing arts. Therefore, the options to be eliminated were the restrictive ones of doing it, in the form of, say, Victorian theater, or of the illusionist theater, because that would be a poor, weak, and decayed way, by which no real magic or illusion could be produced. If you take all that away, you are left with the basic, unchanging, joyous, and essential elements of pure theater; you are, at once, in a bright light, with performers performing as performers. Now, performers performing as performers are immediately in a world of acrobatics, of virtuosity, of dexterity, of vast physical movement for the pleasure of it, for the sheer pleasure of doing difficult things. Which means that you rapidly come into the area of the musical circus, or popular theater. My basic decision was that this should be theater that celebrates theater and therefore it had to be theatrical. Which is quite different from wanting to use the circus as a metaphor, or something like that. Which I wouldn't dream of doing.

Q: What are you looking for when you do Shakespeare in this way?

PB: I wrote in my book *The Empty Space* that the theater has to go forward. It can't live in the past or even the present. And that it must go forward to Shakespeare. And that going to Shakespeare is a movement forward because, whether one likes it or not, the phenomenon of Shakespeare is like the carrot in front of the donkey. It is always ahead and never behind. When you read the plays of Shakespeare, you find two very striking facts. One: Shakespeare is extremely difficult to turn into an autobiographical author, although scholars by the millions search desperately through his plays to evolve autobiographical theories, and to try to write about him the way you write about Alfred Hitchcock. The fact remains that it is virtually impossible; never has somebody's personal identity been so hidden, and submerged by the torrential outpouring of a greater reality, than Shakespeare. In fact, the man is not present with his own personal obsessions anywhere. If you put all the works together—with the enormous range of subject matter—and try to find what are the few obsessional themes of Shakespeare, you will find that they are everything you can think of. One of the striking things is that he is non-autobiographical.

The second striking feature is that while he is accepted by everyone as being beyond any other playwright in quality, he is, at the same time, the most open in terms of form. In music, for instance, the greatest musicians are, for the sake of argument, Mozart and Bach. The greater the composer, the more precise his work. You find in Mozart and Bach a quite unbelievable and almost inhuman exactness. In Mozart, conductors burst into screaming fits with singers or musicians who are one semiquaver off the beat. To realize Mozart perfectly, everything has to be exactly as he laid it down.

Q: And to play Shakespeare?

PB: To play Shakespeare right is the exact reverse. Everything Shakespeare wrote is open-ended. If you take the writing of lesser playwrights, you find that they put brackets on how a line should be spoken and give directions for a stage set. In Shakespearean theater, you can turn the lines around. With Shakespeare, you can genuinely turn the play inside out. You can put the first scene last. You can cut out lines, as John Barton has done very successfully [in *The Wars of the Roses*]; you can write lines in.

Q: Why? Wouldn't it distort the meaning?

PB: It doesn't make any difference. This is part of the reality of Shakespeare—that, because it is like the real world, it has a looseness, an openness, which goes far beyond the vanity of strict form—strict form in which the right word is stressed, as in Racine, for example, where he imposes his own, narrow, private world.

Q: What is the difference between the two?

PB: Shakespeare doesn't do this; he was not working as most authors do. He produces dynamic, very concentrated material; he doesn't produce a finished product. Nothing of Shakespeare's exists until it's performed. That's why the whole question of contemporary and non-contemporary Shakespeare doesn't really exist, because his plays are as old-fashioned, or as contemporary, as making love or eating an apple. Because the juice, or the sperm, or however you want to put it, emerges where and when the act takes place. Perhaps, along with making love or eating an apple, there would be a third example, which is perhaps even clearer. Shakespeare's plays are like a pack of cards.

A pack of cards was invented at a certain period in history. Millions of other things invented have fallen away, but a pack of cards has such a logic, such a dead-right, concentrated exactness in the way each card was originally defined, that all through history playing with a deck of cards has become an operation in the present. And whether today you are playing poker or telling a fortune, you are not doing an old-fashioned, historical enterprise. A deck of cards becomes a brand-new vehicle the moment you start to cut, shuffle, and deal. A deck of cards has an infinite number of permutations, and yet every one of the permutations belongs to the reality of the deck, as well as to the reality of the people playing the game. If you and I now start playing poker, we're using the elements of poker that have served for the last five hundred years. But the reality is nobody else's reality. It is ours as we play it.

Q: How does this apply to Shakespeare specifically?

PB: Shakespeare can be understood as a vast human deck of cards that has total identity, card for card, total concentration, but yet can be shuffled and redealt in endless permutations in each place, in each context, in each period of history. This understood, then one is approaching something of the nature of Shakespeare's works.

Now, if you say what is the result of dealing out this deck, if it is done by a group of people searching for one thing only—the re-creation of a complete miniature world observed by members of a larger world (this is a basic function of the theater)—you can see that there is no deck like Shakespeare's. The end result of using that deck rightly is, in fact, a contemporary exercise.

Q: Did you think that *Dream* as you have done it is, more than any other of Shakespeare's plays, an example of a contemporary exercise? Or would you say that any one of the plays would have the same effect?

PB: I'd say that there always have to be points of contact, that a play comes to life through individuals. And so the points of contact have to be human, and that means passionate. And so for myself at that moment, *Dream* meant passion that enabled me to work in that way. But that's a personal thing. Somebody else, at exactly the same moment, could have found the same elements in another play. I personally found those elements in *Titus Andronicus* ten years ago, not in *Dream*. But the potential is there in all the plays.

Q: Was *Dream* an outgrowth of your experiment in 1968 of *The Tempest*?

PB: Oh yes. But it's out of a lot of previous work, and *Tempest* was very definitely a first sketch, a first exploration of all the things.

Q: In *Dream,* you kept very much to the text, unlike your work in *Tempest,* which was actually a deconstruction.

PB: Yes.

Q: There didn't seem to be any manipulation of the text in *Dream*.

PB: One word.

Q: You changed something?

PB: Yes. This was because in *Dream*, there are certain extraordinary values that come from the interweaving of themes in a particular order that are actually in the text. Let me put it this way: One of the great needs in the theater to produce explosive results is

that there has to be friction. You can't get any com-
bustion, nothing can burst into flame, without an element of friction. And one of the great weaknesses,
for instance, in improvisation, or in improvised theater, is that although it can produce a great liberation,
up to a certain point, eventually improvisation fails to
go as far as we often want because you're not fighting against anything. Everything is flowing in one direction, and there's no element of a real fight. The
moment you have a real struggle with your material,
you can make great discoveries. If, for instance, you
can cut the play around to suit your purpose, you gain
a great freedom. This often can lead to great results.
On the other hand, if you take a play of sufficient
quality and make a point of not changing anything,
that gives you a completely different sort of challenge.
In *Dream,* this was one of the basic things we decided to do: we would struggle with the material to
find our proper relation to it.

Q: In other words, you stuck to the text, which was
quite different from what you did in *The Tempest.*

PB: Certainly. Yes . . . take any position in which there
are not two sides to it. There is more than one aspect
to everything. And I certainly wouldn't ever say that
there is a right, or a wrong, or a good, or bad way.
And saying that you can't chop a masterpiece to
pieces is rubbish, because you don't do any harm.
The masterpiece remains there in its covers, and can
be put together the next day by anyone who wants
to. Of course you can take a play of Shakespeare,
and if you want to turn it inside out, you turn it inside out. And people like it, or dislike it. You take a

play and you treat it reverently, and you don't change a word, and you may lose a lot, and you may gain a lot. And in this case, we decided to do without changing the text—having done the opposite in *The Tempest*.

Q: I'm interested in the play within the play in *Dream*. Has that particular section always been done like that? It is played so realistically and seriously, even though it has always been seen as a comic interlude.

PB: No. That is not the way it has usually been done.

Q: Is there a traditional way? The day I was there, a bunch of schoolchildren and I were sitting right in the middle of the theater. It was really quite an experience, because the children's eyes were popping out. They were quite enthralled.

PB: Well, the play within the play was perhaps the start of the whole production. Because, traditionally, it's considered that actors acting badly is a funny joke. And this is something that has rarely, if ever, been questioned. The play within the play has been treated as something very silly. And because it's treated as nonsense, the basis of it is that the actors are bad. They are so bad that they are to be laughed at for being bad. And so, once you start on that, the play has developed away from reality into something that's zany and sometimes extremely funny in surrealist terms. It is developed for the sake of great vaudeville gags of all that goes wrong in an amateur performance. So all the actors are funny because they're bad, and the worse they are, the funnier they are. The traditional business is the actors forgetting their lines, and getting lines wrong, and doing things that no actor would possibly do. So this is always a knock-about farce climax of the play.

Q: What attitude did you work for? It is, in fact, farcical.
How did you get around that?

PB: In *A Midsummer Night's Dream,* there are no grounds
for taking a condescending nineteenth-century upper-
class view that peasants, who try to do a play, must
be comic. That is a pure nineteenth-century snobbish
view of the world, in which servants are always
comic characters. If you just naïvely read what was
written, you see that a group of underclass, small ar-
tisans are trying to do a play, and then you actually
see the play they do. If one follows this, say, with the
realistic logic of Chekhov, it's like when Nina acts in
Konstantin's play in *The Sea Gull*—a bad play, and
yet, is this comic because it is bad? It may be comic,
and yet it is very moving because it is also true that,
at a certain age, a romantically inspired girl should
believe in that material. And so you enter a very rich,
subtle, and complex relationship with it. It's neither
good nor bad, but all those things at once. It's the
same with *Pyramus and Thisby.* The play they present is a mixture, done with love and respect by these
men trying to act. To me, what the whole of *Midsummer Night's Dream* is about, amongst other
things, is acting—and illusion.

Q: But is it also about role-playing?

PB: Yes, about role-playing and love. And one sees
where the two go together: Men with no skill, but
with a capacity for a certain form of love, can reach,
in their own way, a truth which goes beyond illusion.
Because in direct terms, an audience sees for itself
how you can be laughing at a clumsy actor. Yet the
next second, when Thisby does her ridiculous lament
over a character called Pyramus, whom you're not

taking seriously, a simple feeling comes through because of the boy's identity with the role. Therefore, what he actually believes in comes true. You certainly realize that Thisby's suicide—ridiculous though it is—is also serious. And you're forced at that moment to wonder about the whole nature of what you believe, and what you don't believe. And even then, you're forced to wonder: Are you believing in the actor? Whom are you believing in? Are you believing in yourself? What makes it work is that the audience, which is laughing a minute before, is suddenly silent when Pyramus, a gawky country, small-town sort of boy, is suddenly sinking to the ground, having pretended to kill himself. And you know that everything about it is unreal, and yet at the moment it is reality. Out of this comes what is talked about during the play, which is that what's real depends on what you bring to it, as much as what your dream is.

Q: And is everyone in everyone's dream?

PB: Well, yes. When Theseus says, at the end, "The best in this kind"—meaning from the best of all acting, the finest and the best are the chatterers, and the worst is no worse if imagination is brought to it. And the Queen says sharply, "It must be your imagination, then." And he says [in essence], Yes, that's what it's all about.

Q: Is that also the metaphor for your production as well as a metaphor for the actual play? A metaphor as well for acting and creativity? Does the the play within the play express this?

PB: Why I talked about the actors making a theater, and the actors making a world, is because when you create something that has any element of reality about it, each person can read true things in different ways. A three-dimensional object hasn't only three sides. It's got any number. A two-dimensional object has only one view. But a three-dimensional object—there's no end.

Q: But there wasn't an end. Everybody's in everybody's dream and the final removal of the clothes shows that they are real people. You have the same actor playing Oberon and Theseus and the same actress playing Titania and Hippolyta. What was your point? Are you interweaving the world of the fairies and the nobles as if they were all part of the same dream?

PB: Well, yes. Theseus and Hippolyta, the nobles, are trying to forge a complete and true relationship. Before their wedding, an almost identical couple appears— Oberon and Titania, the fairies, who have had a dispute and need to bring about a "concord" out of the "discord." In that way, the two couples resemble each other, as if Oberon and Titania could be sitting inside the minds of Theseus and Hippolyta.

There's no end to the levels of this play. At the same time, the whole play is a wedding celebration, and is given, therefore, through the language of a celebration—the celebration of a wedding. Which means a celebration of the actor making love, and under what conditions that making love can be most auspicious. That's the only real blessing you can bring to a wedding. Say a wedding goes wrong; love may not produce love, so let's make a wedding a ceremony of celebration in which love is taken apart. Love as an illusion is one theme. Now the illusion is all part of one theme. You can't have love without people making love. And you can't have people making love without their playing parts. And you can't have them play parts without elements of illusion.

Q: Add to that elements of ambiguity, as well.

PB: There are lots of different layers, and that's why you can peel them off. It is an exploration of all the different aspects of making love, and being in love, including this extraordinary and almost demonic notion of Oberon. Oberon is clearly depicted as being the equivalent of Titania's husband. As her husband, he decides that he's going to have his wife screwed by the most physically repellent object possible—an ass—and just sits by and watches it. Nothing in Strindberg, or way-out modern novels, or in the contemporary cinema—in Luis Buñuel, for example— goes beyond that as a basic situation. He, Oberon, is genuinely doing this, not out of cynicism, or out of a warped sense of humor, not out of brutality, or sadism; he is genuinely doing it as a true expression of true love. The truest act of love that an all-loving, all-compassionate husband can do for his wife is to take her out and have her screwed by the largest truck driver he can find, to put it in contemporary terms.

Q: I don't quite follow this. I don't know what you mean by that, the "truest act of love." That hardly seems plausible to me. Are you saying that Oberon does this out of love for her? Isn't that a warped way to express love?

PB: He is doing it to make possible their final and total reconciliation.

Q: I'm not sure I see how that follows.

PB: That's why it relates to Theseus and Hippolyta, where Theseus is shown [to be] somebody of enormous love and compassion. If you take the play, which is one of a million ways you can look at it, as being like the wedding-night dream of Theseus and Hippolyta, her being pushed into the arms of Bottom is an action that leads to a fulfillment, the ultimate coming together of the couple in total harmony. This is clearly my interpretation—that at the end of the Oberon-Titania plot, they are reconciled in a way that they haven't been. She says at the very beginning that there is this deep parental gap between them that can't be healed. In her first long speech, she says that they are the parents of this deep clash between two forces in the world. So you really see a situation where nothing can be resolved. And yet, by the end, it is totally resolved. They are in total love. And he, with his eyes open, has brought it about—not to punish her, and make her a submissive woman, but to arrive at a full, balanced, harmonious expression of their love. That's why I said that he, out of objective love, pushes his wife into bed with a truck driver. And there's not one neurotic flicker in this whole activity. Try [to find] an author that can match that.

Q: I don't know if it's neurotic or not. But your idea of their reunion through this unappealing act is certainly far-fetched. And actually almost absurd.

PB: There's nothing neurotic in *A Midsummer Night's Dream*. Do you think that's a neurotic play?

Q: I am not saying that the play is neurotic. I am only saying that the idea you're talking about is a bit peculiar, to put it mildly. I don't see how, if a husband arranges that his wife sleep, as you say, with a truck driver, that the couple would then be united in true love. Sounds almost comic.

PB: But . . . would you call the play a neurotic play?

Q: No. It is your conception of it that's a bit, how shall I say, peculiar.

PB: That's what happens. Those are the events, presented in such a manner that one finds the conclusion totally satisfying. If the conclusion is satisfying and the events are what they are, then there's nothing neurotic. Because were it neurotic, the conclusion would be disharmonious. Neurosis breeds neurosis.

Q: I'm afraid it is you who are harping on this neurotic business. I have not said that *A Midsummer Night's Dream* is neurotic, or that any play in itself can be neurotic; people are neurotic, not plays. I only maintain that while I loved your production of the play, I do not agree with what you are postulating right now. Or believe it. Now, to the next question. How much did the actors contribute? Or were you the brains behind it all?

PB: That's not the way I work.

Q: No, I didn't think you did, but I would like to hear more about it.

PB: In the play, one sets out to discover a play in a most intimate relationship with a group of actors. And this long, difficult, and ever-changing communal work is aimed at reaching a revelation of the material in the play that can only be tapped through the work of the actors. This means that the actors are bringing forth their full talent, including their intelligence, critical faculty, and their imagination. Everything they have is brought to bear. So of course the development of the form is what the rehearsal period is for. Difficult things.

Q: One of the actors told me that you did a lot of improvisations. Do you usually work that way?

PB: Yes, in a particular way. I suppose all methods have strengths and dangers. You can't use just any one. Just improvisation alone is not going to get you anywhere in Shakespeare. But there are different exercises and things that we do in combinations. I have a very set formula, which is to prevent anything from being set. That is a formula, as well.

Q: Now that *Dream* has opened and you have had this fantastic set of reviews, one wonders what do you want now.

PB: Nothing I've done has ever been complete. I have never just put on a play, collected the notices, and gone away. Each thing has been leading toward what I'm now working on in a more concentrated way. I've resolutely, from the first production that I did, switched ground—whether it be geographic, going from one country to another, whether it's been within the work that's being done, whether it's been commercial or noncommercial, from big plays to little plays, from contemporary to old plays, to musicals, or dramas, or whatever. I've done this rigorously for the simple reason that I've never believed in any theater sect, any theater line, or any theater theory whatsoever. And the first thing that I wanted to do in the theater, as outside the theater, was to explore myself in a nonsnobbish way. I have refused to believe that, at the start, a musical and a grand opera were better, or worse, than each other, or that television was better, or worse, than poetry. I have never believed in any of the snob levels of value, or any of the basic cultural values, which say that one form is better than another. So, yes, I try to get firsthand experience for the pleasure of it. There's nothing I enjoy more than changing scenes all the time. And that I have done all my life.

1970

Two

The Beginnings of
the International Center
of Theater Research

Peter Brook achieved enormous success with his *A Midsummer Night's Dream* but he was not a man to rest on his awards and honors. *Dream* went on its tour of the world, and Brook went his own way; clearly, he had other plans. In 1968, about the time of the outbreak of the student uprising in Paris, Brook had been invited by the French actor and director Jean-Louis Barrault to create a workshop with actors, writers, and directors from diverse backgrounds and cultures. He had already explored new ideas in the English theater, and he had now become greatly interested in investigating the possibilities that might arise from commingling different cultures and by the possibility of working with a group of artists that might be dedicated to researching the basic aims and fundamental aspects of theater. Although the project in Paris was cut short, owing to the student uprising, the experiment had had its effect:

Brook did not forget the experience. When he returned to London later that year, he staged an experimental deconstruction—a workshop, really—of *The Tempest* at the Roundhouse with a company of international actors. That production, after his experience in Paris, so whetted his appetite that two years later, in 1970, he teamed up with his producer friend Micheline Rozan and together they formulated the principles for a group of their own: the International Center of Theater Research. From that point on, Brook's life changed. He moved to Paris, returned infrequently to London, and set out on a brilliant adventure, which not only changed his career but affected numerous artists who were invited to the Center to work and study.

The Center became a hub, a vehicle for a group of international artists to participate in an exploration—through art—that was involved with human relationships, relationships with one another, and with the material and the audience. Brook hoped to develop a permanent group of actors and a permanent home where he could experiment, clarify, distill, and discard the ideas he had accumulated through the years—to start from scratch, as it were. He hoped to develop a noninstitutionalized, mobile, permanent theater company that would offer a fusion of cultures, temperaments, styles, and backgrounds. He wanted to be released from absolute dogma, from the demands of trustees and boards of directors, and from buildings and stages that in themselves were incapable of allowing experimentation.

The idea for the Center took hold in 1970, and a certain excitement surrounded its activities. After meeting 150 actors, designers, and directors from many parts of the world, Brook selected people who came from various backgrounds and who had diverse theatrical training. There were four artists from La Mama in New York: Andrei Serban, Andreas Katsulas, Michelle Collison, and Lou Zeldis; one from Japan: Yoshi Oida; one from Africa: Malick Bowens; one from Germany: Miriam Goldschmidt; two from England: Bruce Myers and Natasha Parry; and one from France: François Marthouret. Later, others joined the Center; among them were the composers Richard Peaselee and Elizabeth Swados and the actress Helen Mirren.

The Center was supported at first by foundation grants, and the French Ministry of Culture provided a space in Paris in the Mobilier National, a former Gobelin tapestry factory on the Left Bank. It was an unadorned, prosaic room, one hundred feet long and one hundred feet high, with windowless walls and floors that were icy cold. But at exactly 10:00 a.m. each day, the work would begin. Brook would lead physical and vocal exercises and improvisations, as well as discuss specific problems and future projects. From time to time, various other artists were invited to participate: Moshe Feldenskrais, a master of body awareness; Joseph Chaikin, a director; Kristin Linklater, a voice teacher; and Cathy Berberian, a singer. The company studied acrobatics, tai chi chuan, Noh movements, and kathakali, and undertook special voice exercises led by a member of the Center, Yoshi Oida. Sometimes students and guests from all parts of the world came to observe and participate. One such group was the American National Theater of the Deaf, directed by David Hays, which did a three-week workshop. Sometimes directors like Harold Clurman came to observe, and writers showed up, as well. Brook had engaged the poet Ted Hughes to begin work on a new experimental piece—which turned out to be *Orghast*, the first original project to engage the company.

Soon Brook realized that a theater that he could call his own was needed. As luck would have it, in 1971 Micheline Rozan happened to find a century-old theater that was about to be demolished. Near the Gare du Nord, in a working-class section of Paris, the Théâtre des Bouffes du Nord had housed music-hall stars and been a venue for Ibsen productions at the turn of the century. But it was now a ruined hulk. Its floors were stained and its walls battered; the interior was unadorned except for the horse-shoe balcony, which had retained some of its past glory. But Brook and Rozan saw its possibilities, leased it, and got to work. The orchestra seats were replaced by wooden bleachers; the proscenium was ripped away to leave an open stage area. In various places, doors and crevices jutted out from peeling walls like open wounds. Cat-walks had been built on the stage, and actors used narrow passages for entrances and exits. But the peeling walls remained—a testament to the century that had passed.

In choosing the Bouffes, Brook deliberately rejected the decorative pomposity of most theaters and elected to stage productions within those decaying walls, debunking the notion that what is needed for good theater is a large house equipped with modern technology.

The Bouffes had a unique aura, the quality of a living, breathing entity—undefinable, strange, and mysterious—in itself a thing of beauty. So it was that this theater, which had shocked audiences that first saw it, became Brook's permanent home. There on that stage Peter Brook produced his most important and brilliant work.

At the time of this interview, Brook did not describe specifically all the work at the Center (he was to do that later); however, he was very clear in enunciating his goals: what he hoped to accomplish with the international group he had assembled, and what he thought the purpose of the theater should be. Our meetings took place over a period of several days; we met in his studio, in cafés and restaurants, and even during his lunch breaks at the Center. Brook was always ready to talk, no matter where.

——————————— • ———————————

Q: What is your idea in developing the International Center of Theater Research? What exactly are you planning?

PB: I want to take what was experimented with very simply in the *Tempest* project [1968] and develop it more fully, along more permanent lines. The *Tempest* project was a short-term experiment; we had the possibility, and the money, and everything else to run it for three months. However, we did it as a pilot, and, like lots of pilot experiments, it gave us a lot of information. Now I want to develop the organic element that was already there in the project—in other words, a center in which it is possible to do theater by bringing together actors and collaborators from many different countries and sources.

Q: Are you patterning yourself on Jerzy Grotowski?*

PB: I wouldn't think so at all, no. I think that all groups have certain things in common. But the aim of our group is toward a completely homogenous nature. It is definitely focused on a small group of people in one spot sharing the same intention, the same orientation, who would be working together away from

*The great avant-garde Polish director who created the Polish Laboratory Theater, which enjoyed a big success in New York and Europe.

an audience. This is very far from the *Tempest* project, which was based on bringing together actors from very different backgrounds, who were trying to relate to their work step by step. Here we would need some relation with an audience within the first three months. Exposing work, or incomplete work, to other people is a necessary stage in research, so I would say that it is a very different form of a project from the *Tempest* project.

Q: As a result of the *Tempest* project, did you come to any conclusions about the relationship between the audience and the actors?

PB: It confirmed my deep belief that in the theater, however much one may rehearse the work in stages, which can be divided up, you can also rehearse with an actor by himself, or with an actor in a group, and then eventually the whole group can meet an audience and call it a performance. In fact, none of these elements can be separated, but the relationship between the actor and the audience is the only theater reality. There is no theater, there is nothing that one can examine, or discuss, or feel, or think, or argue about except at the moment when the actor and the audience are related. The question of what makes this a satisfactory relationship is the deepest and perhaps the only question in the theater of our time.

Q: How would you know the exact moment when it is satisfying? How do you prepare a company to attain that relationship?

PB: You can look at preparation in many ways. Preparation in terms of literary theater means that one man has spent two years behind locked doors preparing his text. Preparation for nonliterary theater means that a group of actors working together for two years might reach a point of spontaneous creativity. In fact, working together for months and years continually results in a partnership of a telepathic sort, like Elaine May and Mike Nichols. Several years of preparation go into preparing for the point when they can actually work in public. Now, in each of those cases, one sees that all schools of theater expect preparation—massive preparation. You may be surprised [to know] that without this preparation, the material wouldn't be flexible enough to work.

When a play, or playwright, or actor, actually meets with an audience, we all expect that the most profound contact can somehow happen by itself. Every shade of theater in existence today—from the most traditional, to the most popular, to the most committed research theater—approaches this question as if it were secondary. In fact, it needs to be faced with the same intensity, the same understanding of the impossible difficulty that one encounters in other explorations. To me, this is where the question lies.

Q: Is your direction somewhat different, let's say, from that of Grotowski?

PB: Yes, from the very start, the basis of our relationship has been one in which there is a deep community view in certain directions and a difference in others. This is the question that we—Grotowski and I—often discussed together. I don't think we disagreed at all. I think we may take different directions. I think there is no more disagreement than there would be between two people sharing a theater in which one does opera and one does ballet, and working through different forms and different directions. He has said repeatedly that his interest, his concentration, his search is really based on the actor and that the audience is unnecessary. The link—the relation with the audience—in a sense, is secondary. This is where his purpose lies. So he, in fact, wishes to increase the distance between them.

Q:　Are you saying your purpose is exactly the opposite—that you are searching for a special contact with the audience?

PB:　He wishes, as it were, to put the actor on the roof of a very tall building—so that he could climb still higher and do something impossibly dangerous and, in a sense, reinforce the distance by his movements. The whole of his theater is based on the distance between the man on the roof and the people on the ground. And if that man can then scan the entire Empire State Building, people would stand aghast, looking up. Every action that the man does reminds the audience how far they are from him, and he is from them, and that is one conception.

Q:　And the opposite conception? Your conception?

PB:　The opposite of that would be a conception of mountaineering with rope, where somebody with a pick and irons climbs up the mountain but unfortunately is tied with cords to other people below him, and every step he takes on the rock, he is compelled to pull the people up behind him. So he moves up very slowly, but every bit he gains is at once matched by the people following him, and who come up that much more, so that as they go up and about, they go painfully and slowly upward, but they all go up, more or less in proportion. That's why there is a difference of direction.

Q: Isn't it also a question of your tradition, of the choices one makes? Grotowski's theater is based on what you would call "the holy theater." You seem to accept the "rough" theater, or is it a synthesis you are looking for?

PB: In my book *The Empty Space*,* I have made these categories for the purpose of conversation and for the purpose of writing about them. Having made this category of "holy" and "rough," I then try to show that in each case there is something incomplete, that the holy theater . . . that's a name, I don't think there is such a thing as holy theater or such a thing as popular theater. I don't think there is such a thing as popular theater in existence. I think there is a partially holy theater, which is true about everything we do. Nothing is complete.

Q: Why make all these definitions that seem inaccurate in the first place?

PB: By giving oneself a definition—holy theater—and going resolutely in that direction, eventually one doesn't get there. I think there is a truth to all human activities. You go almost all the way, but you don't get there.

Q: I still don't see why you need to categorize them.

PB: You then step away, which is what history does, and look and see why did that stop there. And you see that something was incomplete in that direction. Although the holy theater aims at capturing the richness of the invisible world, it has a tendency to make

*In *The Empty Space* (Atheneum, 1968), Brook refers to various types of theater—"deadly," "holy," "rough," and "immediate"—and analyzes each one.

its definition something that can't be broken. You asked about synthesis—I don't know if you can get that all through synthesis.

Q: Does anyone get it?

PB: In the whole work of Shakespeare, you see something very close to the whole life pouring through a man's creation. You then take what you call "holy theater" and you find that it's got all sorts of marvelous things—great intensity—but not the whole life. And when you find part of life left out, you say, Well, then, the holiness is slightly incomplete, because holiness must cover every single phase of activity. You then take the rough theater—Well, you say, we don't want any of this holiness, this sort of holy nonsense; we want life—life means everything that's noisy and rough. But what about quietness—is that less life than noise?

Q: Are you saying that synthesis would always lack some important life element?

PB: Let's turn back to what Grotowski would say—about the impulses. What is the impulse behind the search for the holy theater? I think if you look deeply enough, it is all the same impulse. It is the same impulse, which actually goes off in two directions. The impulse is to find something that you can only call a real life that goes through the event. It is something that the only person writing in the twelfth century about Noh theater talked about—what really happens when theater magic takes place, where something of total satisfaction is created in the theater. He called it the "flower." The reason he called it the "flower"—it isn't a word; there isn't a word for it, so you might just as well call it the "blue moment" or the "microphone." When a very precise master of the Noh theater said "flower," he meant the rare moment when what the actor is doing and what the audience is doing come to a point when there is a real flow of life—like the act of creation—when out of nothing something really is created. Therefore, you can't say it is more satisfactory for the actor than for the spectator, more satisfying for spectator A than for spectator B. All that vanishes. Something complete has actually happened. All of that is very rare.

Q: Is that what you are looking for?

PB: That is what all forms of theater are really searching for. What I was trying to do when I wrote my book *The Empty Space* was to follow without any dogma all the deep attempts that seem to branch off in different directions. But I don't think that any one of the directions is complete, because it really doesn't complete what the impulse, the root, is really calling for.

Q: Some time ago, you wrote a piece about whether the theater was necessary. How do you feel about that now?

PB: Anyone can see that for the maintenance of life, certain things are necessary. Air is a fundamental necessity, food is a fundamental necessity, and out of that grow elements of social patterns, some of which still remain deeply necessary and some of which remain utterly useless. At the moment of social crisis, like the one we are in, one really sees very clearly everybody going through a day using forms, half of which one may be perfectly willing to let go of if some new revolutionary government were to sweep them away, but half of which correspond to a deeper sense of necessity. It is very important to settle what is important and necessary, to know what one needs, what one has to have and what one can do without, what is really necessary deep down.

Q: To get to the point—why would theater be necessary or unnecessary?

PB: However you look at it, it is there in order to correspond to a psychic need in man. One sees that a theater that is unnecessary isn't much of a theater. If it isn't something that people in a community demand, that people feel they can't live without, without which people would feel deprived, as if you took the sunshine away—if theater doesn't evoke that same need, it is not a real theater. It's an interesting theater; it's amusing, like a show, a film that you'll go see, or not; it is not for you or against you; but it doesn't correspond to a deep need. It's very easy if you look at simple tribal customs to see the ceremony that is needed. Any anthropologist can do it. It's an easy trap to think that because people are dancing in a circle in a certain tribe, they are totally satisfied and wouldn't be able to live without that. You can equate that to urban life, and feel that dancing in a circle in New York City must therefore be a necessary ceremony. But, of course, that is not true.

Q: Well, what do you think is necessary?

PB: I saw something that was necessary last Thanksgiving [in New York City]. I went for a walk in the park on Thanksgiving Day. The town was quiet, empty, except for a few people wandering about peacefully and quietly in Central Park. There was a real silence over the whole town. It suddenly struck me, although I shouldn't think anybody was actually thinking of it, that by popular agreement, there are a small number

of days when the whole town stops—out of total necessity. Half the people, or more, don't care what
Thanksgiving is theoretically celebrating. What everybody in town is benefiting from is the sudden
break in the movement of the city—and the silence.
I was thinking that if you took away from New York—
a city near a breaking point and near hysteria—its
popular holidays, or even its Sundays, possibly that
would be the fine line upon which the other side of
madness would lie. The city would eventually burst
out, and crack up, and fall to pieces. That moment
of calm, whether the pretext for it is Christmas or
Thanksgiving—the deep need is for a hysterical place
just to shut up for a moment. That was, I felt, an actual organic necessity for the town. In fact, if some
new totalitarian government were to say that this town
needs compulsory silence, people would be very re-
sentful and would say the government is forcing
them into compulsory silence. In fact, that is what actually happened. People may not even know what
Thanksgiving is about, or why they are being thank-
ful. It doesn't matter. Units of compulsory silence are
a ceremony that makes life, which is almost intolera-
ble, just possible.

Q: How do you relate all this to the basic question—the
necessity of theater?

PB: If you look for a theater in a community that could
give those great intakes of breath to people, one
would have to find a model. Is there a model of that
in any Oriental theater art? No, I don't think you can
find in theater that source of life that a community
draws on. No theater does that.

Q: Well then, if no one does that . . .

PB: And yet, if you look at the work of Shakespeare just as a complete thing—perhaps this theater comes closer than any other in being all-rewarding on a multitude of levels. More people of more varied backgrounds over a longer period of time have drawn more deeply on this source called the Shakespearean theater than any other that we know about. It is because of this—not because we want to reconstruct a Shakespearean theater and do nothing but produce works of Shakespeare, which isn't a solution—but if there is a model that we can turn to—it is always useful to have a reference—there is nothing as rich, powerful, complex, and challenging as the achievement of the Shakespearean theater.

Q: Is there any contradiction in your taking Shakespeare as your model and, on the other hand, your discarding the language of Shakespeare, as you did in your deconstruction of *The Tempest*?

PB: Yes, I do see a contradiction. But you mustn't forget that what we did with *The Tempest* was incomplete. We made this very clear. We said that it was laboratory work, that it was useful to us, and may be useful to other people. We said, "Come, have a look at these experiments, and draw from them, what you want. This is quite a different situation than a performance. If I were to set out to do a production of *The Tempest,* I would search for the most complete and satisfying form possible.

Q: As a result of the *Tempest* experiment, are you interested in pursuing a nonverbal theater?

PB: I think it is a trap to think that experimentation never stops and never finishes, like a long TV program. I think that you have to talk a bit historically. When forms become rigid, when a certain type of theater becomes settled and established, there has to be a reaction against it. And over the last thirty or forty years, all sorts of people, in different ways and at different times, have been reacting against the nineteenth-century theater. Nobody has been reacting against every aspect of the nineteenth-century theater all at once, but what you'll find is that many reactions have been about one point only: a company doing conventional plays in a conventional manner. One reaction might be against the author; another group reacts against something else. But what is called experiment is, in most cases, a reaction to a movement in a different direction.

Q: So do you think that the reaction against the literary theater was inevitable?

PB: The only form the reaction against literary theater can take is in the opposite direction of nonverbal theater. Which opens up new grounds and new possibilities. When I did the original Theater of Cruelty experiments within the RSC, everyone was saying, Why are you doing nonverbal work? Does this mean that you want to maintain that there is no such thing as the word, and that we shouldn't be doing Shakespeare?

Q: Well, what *was* your point?

PB: The full energies of the RSC, day and night, are geared to doing verbal theater. The first step we had to take was obviously a refusal of the word, because none of our actors had any living experience of not going straight to the word. The first thing that they needed, the first thing that could be useful to them, even if you saw it only as a very therapeutic basis, was to step away from themselves and discover what a universe they carried within them—without words. This came as a surprise to actors who discovered that indeed there was a world within them that held enormous power without words.

Q: What is the significance of this? What does this mean in terms of performance?

PB: What this means is this: You're sitting here talking. I manage to capture your attention with my words. And not only with my words but with something physical. I can say that I have a certain percentage of your interest. But not every single fiber of you is riveted completely on our conversation. That wouldn't be true. To say I have none of you wouldn't be true, either. I have a certain amount, isn't that so, not more, not less? If, at this moment, I stopped talking, and began some physical exercises with you, I could get your muscles and your physical attention very involved. But the part that is in contact with me at this moment would not be so involved. The part of your intelligence and imagination that come into a conversation—that would be less involved, while your body would be more involved. Your body is sitting here at this moment, and is not heavily involved in our conversation, but could become very involved. And your mind could be so free that you could be standing here, and doing the exercises, but your mind might be thinking about something else—a phone call you've got to make, or something like that. You can see how rare it is for every single part of you to be involved in one and the same moment. Now, if one says that the "flower" only appears when the audience is alerted completely—in other words, when their bodies, their emotions, and their intelligence are all attuned together—it is at that moment that there is real life in the proceedings. And there isn't when the person is deeply moved emotionally but the mind has gone to sleep. Or under some very physical circumstances, where you are sexually aroused but afterward you realize you haven't been really touched. You look at the experiences and you see that they are partial. You can be highly involved sexually and still not be touched and still be contemptuous. The rarest thing that happens once in a lifetime is to be so involved that your total incandescence is more brilliant.

Q: How does this all apply to the theater?

PB: If you reach the point in a common service where everything is charged, then a rewarding experience begins to shape. This being the case, it really means that the whole act of theater is an appeal to the whole man. What it is is very hard to define; what it isn't is very easy to define. Therefore, if you take something like the nonverbal theater and you ask me if I am for or against it, I would refuse to answer in those terms.

Q: Well, what *would* you say about the nonverbal theater?

PB: As long as nonverbal theater did not exist, it was a vital necessity for this to be opened up. Once it is opened up, then one has to see it for what it is. It is an enriching of certain things, no more, no less, like the invention of baseball: It is what it is. A nonverbal theater can explore a number of areas: It can bring something very vital to the theater, but not everything that we are looking for, however. What the nonverbal theater has done, which is essential, is challenge verbal theater to the roots. It shows that two thousand years of verbal theater hasn't really gotten very far and isn't really much good, and it really makes everyone go back to the start and say, What is one word? What are two words? What are five words? Through continually looking at them, one can see that there is obviously a place for the word, but what the place is has to be discovered and rediscovered. What is valuable is that at some point, at every cycle of human development, there is a moment when a word becomes necessary. That big step is of enormous importance.

Q: Do you think there's any special revulsion against the word at this particular time?

PB: Yes, it's being cheapened out of existence. Wherever you turn, the word is pouring out and is used more to cover up, to cheat, than to help or to create. So many vast disasters can be linked to the deception created by the word. I read somewhere the other day that never in history has the prestige of politicians been so low. There has never been so large a number of people in the world who think that all politicians are crooks and liars. The cause of this is very clear. The number of promises betrayed through public speech has been tremendous—and that means everybody in top office: the Pope, priests, leaders of every sort. The mass media is so prevalent that obviously it must be the prime suspect, for it is mass media that has to carry the word. The word is one thing, and the use it is put to is another.

Q: Let's talk again about the audience. What is the significance of the audience's total connection to the performance? What does that do for them? Is it going to change their lives, or will they become radicalized? Or is it just enough for people to have an experience?

PB: If the experience corresponds to what really concerns you, then something quite different operates. One can only find analogies in simple things like falling in love. One person meets dozens of persons a day, each one of whom can represent different levels of interest and different levels of experience. None of those may be a deep experience. If somebody falls in love, if somebody has a baby—each is a quite different sort of experience. If you're so touched by another person that everything is turned upside down, that is another kind of experience. You meet someone at a party and the phenomenon of falling in love is a natural thing, but ten years or twenty after that, it stops working. What is in question here is the quality of experience. If you lump together all experience and say that all experience is valuable—well, that's just rubbish. One thing that is clear, however, is that there are experiences of different qualities. At a certain point in life, every experience is useful, but that doesn't go on all through life.

Q: Joe Chaikin, the founder of the Open Theatre, says that his theater is a personal theater, that his theater deals with his own crisis. Jerzy Grotowski's theater is based on the actor's confrontation with life; he has nothing to do with the audience. If you happen to be on their wave length, then you're okay. Now, what does this mean for the audience? You have all kinds of people in the audience who may not be interested in Chaikin's personal crisis, or Grotowski's confrontation with Dostoyevsky. Everyone may be interested in the artistry of Grotowski's theater, but what is he actually saying with it? You talked about *Lear* in one of your books. You said that *Lear* changed with the audiences. Does that mean you control the audience? Are you going to select your audience? In Europe, it's one thing; in New York, it's another. Whom do you want to reach—just the people who feel the way you do and relate to your particular experience or are you interested in a larger audience and a larger experience?

PB: I think the highest-quality audience in life is larger than any personal group, larger than politics. The most intense experience is when, at some point in their lives, people can experience something totally satisfying—and in every way larger than themselves—and different from experiences in his or her everyday life. An experience of this quality is very hard to come by but can be reached by the concerted efforts of a group.

Q: Is that the basic thing you are searching for? And hope, through your work with the Center, you will ultimately find?

PB: Yes, of course.

Three

In the Hills of Iran: *Orghast*

The first production that resulted from Brook's work at the Center took place not in Paris but in the ruins of Persepolis. There, in close collaboration with the noted British poet Ted Hughes and a group of twenty actors, directors, and designers from twelve different countries, Peter Brook undertook, in 1971, a new and daring production. Staged in the sand and mountains of ancient Persia (now Iran), the experimental piece, *Orghast,* was written in a completely new language devised by Ted Hughes, a language that is itself called Orghast.

This time, the setting was not the bare white walls and trapezes symbolic of Shakespeare's forest on a London or New York stage, but the culture, climate, history, and topography of a country viewed by Brook as the meeting place of the Occident and the Orient. In a series of performances that were part of the annual Festival of Arts in

Shiraz, Brook, Hughes, and the company sought to create a unique fusion of drama and environment that could not be achieved elsewhere.

To experience Brook's experiment, one had to cope with the environment first. That meant riding in a bus or car for an hour from the provincial city of Shiraz to Persepolis. The road was bumpy, hot, and dusty, and en route, one met with donkeys, flocks of sheep, and peasants carrying provisions on their backs. Black-eyed children squatted in the ditches and young women peeped out from under their veils.

Then—suddenly—the mighty ruins of one of the most sophisticated wonders of the world appeared: Persepolis, once the imperial capital of Persia, conceived by Darius, completed by Xerxes, and destroyed by Alexander. The remains of the city of Persepolis stand in all their symmetry and grace, revealing the splendor of ancient Persia: exquisitely sculptured staircases, dozens of abraded fluted columns, statues of winged bulls on fifteen-foot pedestals, tablets, mounds, friezes, cuneiform inscriptions—silent witness to what was once the most powerful empire in the world.

The performance of *Orghast* was not staged in the ruins, but at the top of the mountain overlooking them, the Mountain of Mercy. To get there required a twenty-minute climb on foot up a winding, steep road full of rock, gravel, debris, and sand. By then, it would be dusk, with the only illumination coming from dozens of fire lamps along the road. Now one paused to look down upon those broken columns, to watch the other climbers, who formed a design against the undulating path of fire, to gaze in wonder upon a mise-en-scène that no theatrical designer in the world could match.

At the top of the peak was Brook's "theater"—an open

space in front of the huge tomb of King Artaxerxes III. The tomb is surrounded by four columns, which support an intricate carving of the king facing the three emblems of divinity: sun, fire, and the Zoroastrian god of wisdom. The front edge of the open space looks down upon the ruins of Persepolis and, in the far distance, the lights of Shiraz. During the performance, two faint spotlights shone down from the cliffs that rose still higher above the tomb; later, they would be replaced by fire and moonlight.

Before the tomb sat the actors in yoga position. They wore their own native clothing: American jeans, Persian robes, African dashikis. Suddenly, one's attention was drawn to the highest point of the cliff. There, seventy feet above the open space where the audience sat, stood an actor illuminated by the faint spotlight. Bare-chested, arms outstretched, he was chained to the rocks. There he would remain for the rest of the evening—Prometheus, who, having stolen Zeus's precious fire to give to mankind, was punished for eternity. On another high cliff stood a woman. (The actress Natasha Parry.) Her long robe billowed in the breeze, her slender body silhouetted against the sky, the curve of the mountain, and the rising moon. Slowly, one spied other actors stationed on various ledges of the cliffs, as if to watch over the sacred mountain where Prometheus was being sacrificed.

Then there was a soft drumming, followed by silence. The woman wailed out strange words—Ted Hughes's Orghast language—and the actors sitting on the level ground and the men on the mountaintops echoed her cries. Perhaps it was the legendary nightingale of Persia calling us to life, or an expression of Prometheus's passion. Suddenly, there was a fantastic theatrical moment— an enormous ball of fire attached to a chain was lowered

from the peak near Prometheus. It was caught in a cauldron and carried to the edge of the open space. There an
actor—presumably Man—lighted a torch from the stolen
fire; the cauldron was quickly covered and the original
flame snuffed out. From his cliff, Prometheus looked down
in agony. With the end of the fire ritual—itself a link to the
worship of fire by the ancient Persian Zoroastrian religion—
Hughes's and Brook's *Orghast,* an experiment in pure
communication, unfolded.

Orghast has no linear plot (except for the Prometheus
myth) and few discernible characters. Hughes drew on ancient sources—abstractions from literary themes, allusions
to Greek and Roman myth, Zoroastrian rituals, and Oriental legends—and then melded them all into one "passion"
play. Murder, violence, and self-destruction, the slaughter
of the innocents, the revenge of the women, the archetypal conflict of father and son for the possession of
power, and, of course, the Prometheus sacrifice—man's re-
ceiving light, only to remain among the dark forces—these
are the main aspects of *Orghast.* It is an evocative dramatic
poem, written entirely with a poet's tools—metaphor, image, and symbol—and aided immensely by the stunning
contrasts of moonlight, fire, and darkness, all evoking ancient ritual.

Using a language with no recognizable words, Hughes
and Brook forced the spectator to listen to the work as
they would listen to music, and to watch the action as if
it were a religious experience. The sound of the Orghast
language—its rhythms, tone, and texture as it reverberated
and echoed all over the mountains—was virile and austere, yet touched with pity and human suffering. The actors, speaking with totally new vocal techniques, produced
a symphony of sound and word that underscored their in-

ternational composition. Hard *or, gr,* and *tr* and soft *sh*
sounds—the five vowels sliding from one to the other to
mesh into one word—were intended to transport the lis-
tener to Oriental, African, Semitic, Greek, and Persian
worlds. Hughes used certain combinations—the *gr* sound,
for example—as root words. He interspersed ancient Greek,
Latin, Hindu mantras, and Asvestan, the dead language of
the Zoroastrian religion. Actors spoke in unpredictable in-
flections; they also chanted, incanted, wailed, cried, and
made the most extraordinary sounds, but always in combination with Orghast words, which defy literal analysis.

For some, the language and significance of *Orghast*
was by and large incomprehensible, and some wanted more
of a narrative plot. For others, the work depended upon
one's capacity to receive it on an emotional level. But one
thing was certain: Peter Brook's and Ted Hughes's daring
experiment to discover the magic in the word was a stunning experience for all those who saw *Orghast* and for all
those who were part of it.

——————————— • ———————————

Q: You've been very much criticized for attending the Shiraz Festival in Iran, because in many people's minds,
Iran is a very reactionary and repressive country. What
answer would you give them?

PB: An individual, in this respect, is like a government.
There are situations where you break off diplomatic
relations with another country. And situations where,
whatever your feelings about what goes on in the
country, you maintain relations. Now, every country
where one works has got a vast pile of social injus-
tices, which each person struggles with or fights

against in his own way, and continues, at the same
time, with his own field of work. Certain situations
become so extreme that, much like a country that
breaks off relations, one decides that this is a country into which one will not set foot. And that is, for
instance, a conclusion people have reached with
Greece. Some people reached this with South Africa.
And even then, it opens up a very complex question:
Is the intellectual who refuses to go into the country
right? And for the one who does go in, it becomes a
very complicated question. What I am saying is that
Iran is not a country that I've broken relations with.
It's a very complex country, with good and bad elements. In fact, you might say there are two Irans: an
Iran that one dreads and an Iran of great quality. One
positive quality is the fact that we were able to do
this piece, *Orghast,* at Persepolis within a particular
tradition, which was a necessary base for this stage of
our work. I couldn't say that we should work in England, France, or America and refuse to set foot in
Iran. If I can set foot in the United States, then I can
set foot in Iran. And this is one of the complexities of
living in our time.

Q: People may want to know what is it about the country that so attracted you. Perhaps if they saw *Orghast,*
they would immediately know why. But they are unable to fathom why you would elect to work in Iran,
of all places.

PB: We all agree that we live in a time of emotional
poverty. The word *emotion* is one that carries with it
all the finest feelings through which man has reached
a high level. The West lives off either poor emotions
or crude emotions. And in certain parts of the world,

there are certain forms, certain ways of life, or certain languages that are living relics of a different substance that goes under the same name "emotion." The arts and, in this particular case, the performing arts, have only one material that they live on, which is emotion. Historically, we're at a very important moment in a swing of the pendulum. A crude form of emotionalism has reached a certain pitch. The theater is there as food for higher perceptions. It's through the theater that the faculty for perceiving more vividly can be matched. There is a line in *King Lear* that says this very potently. After Gloucester goes blind he says, "I see it feelingly." To see feelingly is a quality of emotion that penetrates, that spreads light. To understand what that is can be understood when Ted Hughes [the poet and the writer of *Orghast*] says that inside every man, there is the key to be found that opens that feeling.

Q: But to get back to the question. Was there something very special that was found in Iran and couldn't be found elsewhere?

PB: One goes to certain sources in Persia because it is a particular meeting place, and has been, for Oriental and Occidental movements. It is not for nothing that Persepolis is there, and Alexander swept through it. And in Persepolis, you have a point where Eastern and Western influences meet. Now, the very qualities that are in the air in Persia can be made palpable. As you saw for yourself, one can actually make Persepolis a living theater. And through our work, we came to be influenced by it; we came to be absolved and be helped. This would not have taken the same form if we had been doing it—this work—in London or New York. Doing this for and in Persepolis, with its relation to these sounds that belong to this place, has enabled us to look into something that we couldn't have looked into elsewhere. And in this way, one sees in the actors a certain absence of theatricality. For instance, at the first performance, it was quite extraordinary to see a complete absence of any sort of first-act nerves. And it was because the surrounding framework and conditions had nothing to do with making it or not making it, doing it or not doing it within a theatrical context.

Q: Has this experience helped your future plans in theater? After all, you work in the city, be it London or Paris. Of what use is this exotic trip to the practical work in theater? Or how does it fit into your experimental work at the Center?

PB: In *Orghast,* we concentrated on one area only: the Prometheus fire myth and the particular emotions that belonged to that myth. We were exploring that in all its complexities, from ancient Persian fire myths through our own version today at Persepolis. The first step in experimental work is to separate elements. If you study a car, you take apart its pieces, first the engine, then the wheels, then the steering wheel. Not because you believe that eventually any of those work separately, but the research is there. The research is to discover what is going right and what's going wrong in each of these component parts before you can put the big machine together again. During our first year of experiments, the big emphasis was on sound and sound vibration, and this was directly related to the imagery of the subconscious, the imagery of myth.

Q: How did this lead to *Orghast*?

PB: The basis for this work, a mixture of existing myths, was regurgitated through Ted Hughes. The work was very concentrated, very intense, and the vibrations were powerful. We went into a country knowing that we were experiencing something that went beyond our city life in the West. We were wondering how is it that Artaud, trying to break through the confines of a narrow world, created a world in which cries, screams, howls, and writhing bodies were more acceptable than people in bowler hats, colored mustaches, and red noses. What we were looking for was something that could move freely in all directions.

Q: What were the essentials that would enable you to move freely in all directions?

PB: My essential raw material is always the author and the actor. We wanted to steer away from all the factors that condition the theater the way it is. All the factors that one normally talks about separately, like the building, the audience, and all that, are all parts of the whole. Ted, who has gone through a very considerable experience for himself as an artist, as a writer, is part of this development. The individual actors, coming here from different backgrounds, have been through an experience, not only of a special intensity but of a totally nontheatrical order. In other words, all of this has crystallized the group and its first public work. The fact that this first public work took place in a village of central Asia three weeks ago, and in Persepolis, means that the work is tipped in a different direction from what would have happened if the first public work had been in a loft or an attic in Paris or London. Perhaps very good and interesting work could have been done, and we might have received a marvelous response from the audience. But it would have crystallized a different silhouette than this one.

Q: What about the language that was created for the piece, and which no one understands? Did you work with the language in connection with the myth? Was the language devised through improvisation, so that the emotion and the language would coincide? Or was language attacked separately?

PB: Two things were going at once. Our improvisational language, which is quite separate, and which actors developed through a series of symbols entirely from their own language. Then there is a writer's language, and that's what Ted writes and the actors use—the way actors use language. Ted amends it and amends it. And you mustn't forget that this monumental task—like Joyce writing *Finnegans Wake*—is only three months old. We keep on saying that this is work in progress. Ted had been working on the task for three months.

Q: What has been the result? What have you discovered even if it is only three months that you've been working?

PB: We're beginning to see things; we're beginning to learn an enormous amount. The *Orghast* Ted is writing this week is radically different from the *Orghast* he was writing a month ago. We've done many experiments intertwining his language with modern words, with English. All those perspectives are just beginning to open up. Before we finish here, we're going to do two interesting experiments. We're going to play the piece in a village.

Q: Why in a village? What do you hope to accomplish?

PB: We are going to try an entirely different manner of communicating. Ted is writing a short scene for some actors, just to experiment. We want to try to express a non-mythological subject using the *Orghast* language.

Q: But I don't understand why you're trying to play in a village. Is this an attempt to bring culture to the Third World, so to speak, or to do something socially significant?

PB: It is important to make something that could take any form. The actor then may dress as he is—maybe he is a cop—so that the outer form is free; we want to bring *Orghast* into a modern context. We want to do this because new areas may open up, as Ted begins to master an incredibly technical and difficult task that he set for himself. We're just at the point where all these doors are opening.

Q: When Jerzy Grotowski, whom you admire so much, uses language, it comes concretely and organically from something internal—from the actors' impulses, from their bodies. But this language in *Orghast* seems superimposed.

PB: You've touched on what is central in my work. No man reveals his depth, or his truth, without a challenge. This is why freedom, if it's weakly conceived, like the freedom of doing your own thing, is always feeble in its result. If you put a man against a mountain, he'll climb it. If you give a man freedom in the face of a challenge, he will use the freedom to wrestle with the challenge. And between freedom and challenge, something powerful comes out. Give a man freedom and no challenge, and the freedom will just peter out. Where acting, directing, writing are concerned, where the creation of plays is concerned, if an actor is given a great part—Oedipus, Prometheus, Hamlet, or Lear—the incredible challenge of doing this will bring the best out of the man. I've seen actors transformed in the course of a season through playing Hamlet. Because the challenge to the imagination, to the spirit, to the emotions of having to understand Hamlet turns the man inside out, and challenges him to give his best. Let a man improvise Hamlet, and he won't even be true to himself. He'll only be true to what you call the top of his head.

Q: You speak of actors. Where does the director come into this? What is his role?

PB: An actor needs a director because the director is there to force what won't happen by itself. It's the challenge again. The director needs the challenge of actors to bring out what the director can do. It's in this way that the work I'm looking for is always based on two elements: the inner riches of a human group with its impulses, and the call coming from the outside, which is either the material or direction, but something has to be put into the challenge.

Q: How would you compare your approach to the work with that of Grotowski, who has also experimented with language and sound?

PB: Grotowski has always, up till now, insisted on material. Although he has never used new material, he has never made a performance *without* material. What he has always done is wrestle with an existing piece. Directing a work like *The Constant Prince,* Grotowski found that it didn't correspond to today, nor to the actors of today, and this gave him something to fight about. His use of existing material is valid because the quality of the material he chose is worthy to wrestle with. In a sense, I used Shakespeare this way—as material to wrestle with. For example—if you are a sculptor, you have to work in stone or in wood. If you work in plastic or in water, you can't get anywhere. The good sculptor respects the hardness. He likes a piece of granite because he knows that he has a challenge. That's why one likes Shakespeare—the challenge—and that is why Grotowski has taken plays with bones in them to fight with. As long as one stays within that solution—using existing material—one can do a great deal of work. If you say we're using an existing play because we have not got anything else—well, this isn't the real solution. Say we take a play and chop it up and redo it. That's sort of makeshift, and that, too, is not a solution. So we have to create our own material.

Q: That seems to be a tall order. Creating your own material may not result in anything very interesting. How would you avoid that?

PB: The creation must come from a clash between the raw material inside the actor and the material coming toward him. And it is he—the actor—and it—the material—fighting together. To be sure, the author has to be there, and the author must work in the deepest harmony with the group; he must know what it's looking for. The author cannot act as a tape recorder, or as a kind of editor who sits at rehearsals, watches improvisations, and then edits the group's work; then he is in too passive a role. He isn't challenging anything if the author, in the traditional role, sits at home, invents his play, and says, Here it is; this is my play. That is a possibility, of course.

Q: Then what is Ted Hughes's role? How does he differ from the other writers you've just described?

PB: Ted is part of the group; he is present at every improvisation, at every function, absorbing the actors. Everything he's written has been written with the actors in mind, but not on that weak level of playing up to them, but by turning his work into a challenge. It is his line, even if it's "gradch um am oul"; they are shaped words that have come from Ted. That gives the actor a different challenge than if you say, "Here are four syllables: *ma ta fa da*. Arrange them in a way you want them." If you give an actor that freedom, he is less likely to reveal something deeply true to himself. When the line is open-ended, the actor stretches and strains until he suddenly finds a meaning, and one may accept many meanings. If he has found a meaning that is deeply his own, and yet it is Ted's, too, and the two come together—well, this can only happen through the dialectical movement between author and actor.

Q: But the language seems composed of sounds that are in themselves incomprehensible. What does it all mean? And how are these sounds put together to provide an understandable language without its being a form of Esperanto?

PB: The sounds are provoked by Ted's language on paper.

Q: How does this work out practically?

PB: Well, I'll tell you exactly. You know the line in *King Lear* when he speaks to the Fool about "Monster ingratitude"? Now, the sense of that line is very simple. But the line has electrifying weight and power. Now,

if you imagine Shakespeare's head—there he is, sitting, writing this particular line, and these words are
forming in Shakespeare's head at that moment. It's
like when you're waking up from sleep and there's a
moment before something is fully formed. In Shakespeare's mind, as a poet, he begins to look for something but is not quite sure what words he's looking
for. It's like a crossword: He knows roughly the pattern. He tries "monster monstrousness," and he tries
that over and over. There are the slots that are already prepared; he tries in his mind "horrendous ingratitude"—but that's a very bad phrase; that won't
do. And suddenly, as he thinks of monster, it falls
into its slots. And all that clicks into place and he
says, "That's it. I've got the line."

Q: Are you saying that Ted is working this way?

PB: Ted is actually writing with a clear image in his head
that he wants to reach. And so, with a very clear notion, he writes this image down and it emerges on
paper. This is what he gives an actor. An actor, given
this at first sight, would say, "It's just a collection of
letters." But an actor who is working into it already
looks at that and he reads "stch chchchcroooar," and
as he says it, he knows that it's not a love phrase. He
doesn't need to be told.

Q: Can you give a concrete example of how this works?

PB: An actor has got this beautiful song—singing, as he
comes down the ladder, of coming down the ladder.
For that role, Ted wrote a character called Farog. When
Ted gave the actor his part, the script said: "Farog
sings a song that starts with these sounds which have
no apparent meaning: 'Gralakagong.'" Now, you can
see that a song made out of these sounds would be

totally different from some of the other sounds, like "lohorn . . . lohorn." These sounds dictate or evoke his song. Ted's provided the atom from which a sound has emerged. The singing music is an extension, a development, of the implied vocal music.

Q: Don't you need to have some kind of collective understanding of the sound? Some common vocabulary? Otherwise, one might understand something entirely different by the sounds given to it.

PB: Oh, yes. That's why we've worked together.

Q: But didn't you need to decide that a specific sound means something concrete, because otherwise, it would mean that anything goes, any kind of gobbledygook?

PB: Well, yes.

Q: So then would the actors need to learn the alphabet of specific sounds or a combination of sounds?

PB: Yes. Everyone has been through many stages together to get to a collective way of thinking about the problem.

Q: Did you finally come up with some collective understanding of sounds?

PB: Yes.

Q: Did you need a vocabulary that everyone would agree with?

PB: Well, it's been worked out. It's evolved.

Q: Are you saying that once you had some group understanding in place, then Ted Hughes actually wrote phrases in this strange language?

PB: Oh, yes. As a tool. A working tool.

Q: When he gave the actors the script with these words—if they are words—or sounds, did he tell the actors what they meant?

PB: At the beginning, yes. He'd give them the words and then actors would work on them, trying to discover what they meant. And at a certain point, he would reveal what the words meant to him, and then there would be a meeting on that. Gradually, as he developed his style more and more freely, he did that less and less. His meaning and the word had come together more and more, so that rational explanation was not right for him, or for the actors.

Q: Why did you say this piece was like Calderon's *Life Is a Dream*? Did you use Calderon's work or his philosophy in your production?

PB: Well, *Life Is a Dream* is the basic Promethean situation: A father chains up his son because he is potentially too dangerous. Prometheus is dangerous because he has given away fire. He is either rightly chained up, because all the disasters come from fire, and that worries mankind, or he is wrongly chained up, because all mankind's development comes from fire. So the question that can never be resolved is whether Zeus, in taking the father's tyrannical revenge, is doing what he thinks is right, or whether he should have taken the rebellious son and punished him. Whether he is saving the order in the world, or, on the contrary, destroying man's possibility of development, is the Prometheus story.

Q: What exactly from Calderon did you use?

PB: Calderon wrote two plays called *Life Is a Dream*. One is a story play and one is a church play. Both have the same title. The story play has action. And a narrative. The church play is a complete morality play, with only symbolic characters like Light and Darkness, and has no action, no story whatsoever. But both have the same theme. The narrative play *Life Is a Dream* is a story of a king who locks his son out and keeps him in a cave. The son grows up not knowing who he is. The father repents and one day has him drugged and brought back into the palace. When the boy comes around and is told that he has always been a prince, he goes mad with violence and proves to the father that, in fact, he has a dangerous nature and he was better off being locked up. That is sort of the essential story. The two versions take a different form, but they bear a great relationship with the Promethean story. And so, in fact, we did use these elements.

Q: What other rituals or myths did you use? There are various sacrificial killings in the piece. Which myths or rituals were they based on?

PB: By taking an essence of myth, you've already come to ritual. For instance, the myth behind all those killings is related to two myths, in fact. One is the Hercules myth. He is a man going through a series of labors, and having to undertake greater and greater tasks. Having successfully completed all the labors, you would think he is a fulfilled man. But, in fact, he is mad and murders all his children. In this terrible twist of the Hercules story, you don't go in a straight path to wisdom, but when you get to the top, that's when you fall off a cliff. There, at that moment, Hercules murders everyone.

Q: What about the Japanese influence? It seemed to me that your Japanese actor, Yoshi Oida, was acting out a certain myth. What was that about?

PB: It was this Japanese story that haunted Ted. It is a marvelous story about a samurai who spends a night in a ghost-ridden castle. And then in the morning, he finds that he has killed his whole family. Ted assimilated all that. And it became a form of ritual—a tyrant-figure material—that was refined and worked over. And it became the essence of a scene: a fight between a man and a flame, in which a man with a knife tries to destroy a flame and, in so doing, kills his family. That episode provided us with imagery we were looking for: a moment when two men, the African [the actor Malick Bowens] and the Japanese [the actor Yoshi Oida], confront each other with two fires during the night. This sort of imagery speaks to everyone. And everyone understands it. It's direct and cuts through class—it doesn't matter who the people are. Any village, or any sophisticated person, has the same reference to fire, and to two fires in a night.

Q: Does it matter that many people cannot link up with the Orghast language and, in fact, don't really know what the piece is about?

PB: One knows and one doesn't know. I think that this is the only honorable relation with an audience. Otherwise, whom are we to tell, and what are we to tell? We open something up together. We open it, the audience opens it, and we meet in the middle.

Q: Is it possible to do a piece like *Orghast,* with so many esoteric symbols and allusions, and still capture the attention of the audience?

PB: I think that there is a vast misunderstanding about what a symbol is. A symbol is not something that means something precise. For instance, say a man comes in with his hand outstretched and that you say that that symbolizes man's walking toward his salvation. But that is a very poor symbol. Because a real symbol is something that challenges you—opens you up to a lot of meanings, but without telling you what the meaning is. That's why I say that a meeting between a knife and a candle is a symbol, and has all the overtones of meaning that a person finds within himself.

Q: You said once that you worked on Shakespeare because there was really no poet equal to him.

PB: Yes.

Q: What have you found in this kind of work that rivals anything you have done with Shakespeare?

PB: I don't think that one can rival or do better than Shakespeare. And so in a sense, if I could do nothing but work in Shakespeare, I wouldn't need to explain, because one could never really get to the end of that richness in Shakespeare's material.

Q: Then why not just continue to explore that "richness"?

PB: Well, from another point of view, our responsibility working in the theater now is not to stop there and say, "Fine" and "That's it." We try to find what in actual terms one can do today. This is an obligation. This is work that has to be done. This will not stop me from doing, when the occasion presents itself, certain plays of Shakespeare. We always like to do what we do. But we need to try to discover what is a true theater language today, and we know that it cannot be based on any form of imitation of Elizabethan structures or methods. One has to absorb from what one knows of Shakespeare—that sense of possibility. We have to take a different path today to make a theater language for *today,* and that is what has to be done.

Q: There have never been such sounds onstage as there are in *Orghast*. But what have you accomplished with all this experimenting in sound? How will you use this in the future?

PB: There is only one answer, which is a question. Which is: What is a sound? One thinks that man's sound comes from a link between what's deepest in him, his body, his windpipe, his diaphragm, his throat, and his head, and that that link between the head and the stomach comes into play when he makes a sound. When you say that the making of sound is one of the most profound and the most intimate actions, then the moment you start approaching sound in that way, you can't fail to enter into a world of infinite qualities.

Q: How were the actors actually prepared for this work?

PB: We've spent many months in the Paris theater doing exercises on single letters, seeing how habitually one just uses a letter like *k* or a vowel like *o* just like that. And then one sees what is, in fact, the property of that letter. The moment you begin to see what is a *k* and what is an *o*, everything opens up. For instance, one of the reasons we work so much in Greek is that in Greek, you have words with five vowels, one after another. Now you begin to say five vowels, one after another, and you are involved.

Q: What kind of specific training was needed for this particular use of language?

PB: The training is using the words. The vocal exercise that we gave, the strongest vocal exercise, was just using words—I mean, using words is a vocal exercise.

Q: I'm interested in what happened when you played *Orghast* in a village in Iran. How did the people react to the sound and to the language? How were they affected by it?

PB: They were enormously gripped and impressed at the very beginning by the strange, powerful, primitive sounds of Orghast and the coming of the fire. It at once caught their imaginations. They didn't know what it was about, but they liked it. They were held by it. Later on, the girl who played the vulture stuck a stick in Prometheus's stomach, and they all laughed. This was very interesting for us, because it was a very healthy reaction: Nothing is funnier than to see an angry woman prod a naked man with a stick. The sophisticated audience, with a civilized approach to an artistic event, enters into set rules. They discovered after the first ten minutes that the work was very serious, and so they remained serious through to the end. But the natural audience, not knowing what this event was, was wide open in each direction. It was open to being impressed, and it was. It was open to being moved, and it was. And it was open, at a bat of an eyelid, to changing to honest laughter at what it thought was a farcical situation.

Q: What did you conclude from all this experience?

PB: Well, it was something akin to the richness of the Elizabethan theater, where the natural freedom of life is, and should be, present all the time. What we want are forms that not only speak directly, because that's our basic research, but that speak directly to anyone passing by who stops and looks and understands. Our aim is to find the forms that, because they speak directly, don't set up rules. If you laugh, if you cry, you can't have any feeling that you're doing the wrong thing. You are responding intensely to what you see; there can't be any wrong reaction. In other words, the living relationship is one that allows all possibilities.

Iran, August 30, 1971

Four

Experiments at the Center

After Brook's experience with the amazing production of *Orghast* in Iran, he returned to Paris to continue his experiments and to plan for his next project—the group's journey to Africa—a daring adventure that was to amaze the theatrical world. In the meantime, he had invited some groups and individuals to work with him at the Center and participate in improvisations that were done in various places in and around Paris, as well as for invited audiences. All the while, he and Ted Hughes were busy planning their next production, *The Conference of the Birds,* which would not take place until after the company returned from Africa. This would give the ensemble plenty of time to experiment and to work on the difficulties this ancient poem—which was written by the twelfth-century Persian poet Farid Attar—presented.

In the meantime, work at the Center was proceeding full force. All kinds of exercises and improvisations were going on. Some of the activity seemed puzzling to one not participating and only watching, for Brook always resisted explanations, believing the exercises were for the benefit of the participants. But in the following pages, Brook talks about the various exercises he chose for the group—however peculiar they may seem—and the rationale behind them.

——————————————— • ———————————————

Q: After you returned from Iran, how did you apply that experience, and what you had learned there, to your work in Paris?

PB: The work that we started after coming back from Iran was work with ordinary cardboard boxes. Why? In what we'd done our whole first year, the basic unit, or prop, had been the stick. Why again? The stick is as simple an object as one can find. Perhaps, the very first act of a man was breaking a branch on a tree, or making a pole, or a stick—all the purposes that a rod in a man's hand would have. With a stick, we found unending possibilities. The second year, we were doing pieces that directly involved the cardboard box.

Q: What were you going to do with a box? Why did you choose that for your work at the Center?

PB: The box is an object you can find almost anywhere, at every street corner. It's a very common, unpoetic, ordinary concrete object out of the everyday world, and it has got a million identities. Why not a glass? A glass is very specific; it's there for certain purposes.

The glass is actually an object made for one single purpose. And you can stretch it to a few different purposes and that's that. You can drink out of it. You can catch wasps with it. You can throw it at someone. It's a specific object.

Q: What is so special about a box?

PB: The idea that a box contains an enclosure—something that imposes space, whether to protect, or to hide, or to imprison—is endless in its variations. We found that between a man and a box, there's really no limit to the human situation that can unfold. The box becomes truly what confines somebody. Somebody goes into shrieks, wails, and disappears into a box. So that a box is the real instinct of imprisonment, the instinct of taking somebody, and something you want to steal, and hiding from everybody else, and boxing it away. It's like everything that is afraid of freedom and has to contain it. It's like everyone who is afraid of space and has to contain it. It is like everyone who shrinks from breath, and so the person climbs into the box and hides himself. And so you can extend out of the box a million negative meanings. But because it's real, it can't remain having negative meanings. And every one of those meanings has its opposite.

Q: Are you saying that you wanted to improvise using only the box? What kind of stories would you dream up if you used only a box?

PB: Well, yes, a box is what you can cherish, what you guard, what you protect, what you make a wall with, what you enclose. It's the nest, the secret—what you catch something with, what you preserve something in, what you hide in, what protects you. And one could go on in the first weeks of working just finding endless themes.

Q: But are these themes really interesting? A box is only just a box, after all.

PB: The theater is based on stories. Take Pandora. To tell the story of Pandora so that the audience is moved, you set up the known myth of Pandora. To tell this legend, you need a man playing one part and a woman playing another. Everything the actors do is an imitation of an intellectual idea, which is this legend. But if you don't know the legend, you don't know about Pandora; you don't know about Greek gods. If you are ignorant of all this, it can't really touch you directly; it can only touch you second-hand. But the moment that you see that the myth of Pandora is actually present without anybody even referring to it, the moment somebody looks at a box, any box, tears this box open, and something quite horrifying escapes out of it—that is something that touches you directly, whether you know what it's about or not.

Q: How do you know that this is someone's reaction? Aren't you just hoping this is so?

PB: We've discovered this so strongly that we put it in a text and made a children's show. It was direct theater. What happened was that we put the box in the middle of the carpet; an actor came in, saw this box, and went toward it with real apprehension about its contents. At that moment, we had a pure theatrical situation, because everyone was caught in the same game. The people watching genuinely wanted to know not what the story said last week, but at that moment. What was actually between him and that box? The tension was there directly between the actor's imagination, and the audience's imagination, and the box; there was no extraneous element. There was nothing alien to, or outside, the immediate set of references. What this means is that here you have something so direct that it will make the same sense wherever in the world you play it: People will have the human sense of enclosure.

Q: Perhaps they might have a different reaction? How can you be so sure? People have various reactions, don't they?

PB: A person sees two things at the same time. He or she sees a man in everyday clothes going toward a cardboard box . . . I will put this another way. There are two worlds: the everyday world and the world of the imagination—another level of reality. There are lots of words for it—*imaginative, poetic,* and so forth. No matter, we all know what we are talking about. When children play, they pass quite naturally and freely between the two worlds all the time. Children, at one and the same moment, hold a stick and pretend it's a sword, and yet it's a stick. And they don't get confused. Because if you say to them, "It's a sword," while you're playing the game, it's a sword. But if suddenly you come and say, "Drop that stick," it's a stick. There's no confusion. They can coexist. There is total freedom between the two worlds. And this is something that children have and then they lose.

Q: So are you applying what children are capable of to the work of actors? Would actors need to have the same kind of imagination? Would they need to be capable of living in the two worlds at the same time?

PB: In certain societies, most particularly in Africa, the poetic world—the supersensory world, the imaginary world—and the everyday world also intermingle all life long. What Western analytical minds call the "superstitious attitude" is nothing but a natural free passage between one sort of reality and another, which intermingle from birth to death, so that the two don't separate. The theater, always, in all its forms, has contained this double element. The theater is the meeting place between these two worlds.

Q: Do you think the commercial theater, for example, expresses the idea that theater is the meeting place between two worlds?

PB: In attacking the commercial theater—

Q: I'm not attacking the commercial theater . . .

PB: I would ask, What are the things that can only exist through the commercial theater? Why have I always worked in contradictory forms? Because I believe it's quite clear that certain things are incredibly corrupted. For actors to have to work within the three-week pattern of the Broadway theater is terrible. But the moment I say that, or write it, I qualify it by saying that because of this inhuman pressure, certain marvelous things can appear that don't happen if it isn't there. There are always two sides. In exactly the same way, the theater of illusion—the theater of curtains, of scenery and lights, which is rightly out of fashion— is not despicable. In its way, it is saying that theater speaks of a world different from the everyday world. Going into the theater, the curtain goes up, the world of the imagination; the curtain goes down, back into an everyday world. As though the everyday world has no imagination. And the imaginary world has no everyday. And this is, of course, both untrue and unhealthy. Because the healthy relationship is the co-existing one.

Q: How is that coexistence made possible?

PB: Coexisting is what the artistic form makes possible—the adult must find his way into what a child can find unaided. Which leads me right back to the simple example that if you put a cardboard box in front of an audience, and it is seen simultaneously as a cardboard box and as a poetic object, then real theater is beginning to take place. Perhaps the nearest we've got to it so far is something that lasted a few seconds. That happened when we did our performances, and demonstrated fragments from all the work we've done in the last year—work on *Orghast,* work on words, on sounds, and some of this work on boxes was included. To introduce this work in boxes, in the area where we were playing, an area surrounded by an audience, the small cardboard box-cube slowly moved from the side to the middle of the area as though by itself. It just slid. In fact, you couldn't tell what it was—whether there was a little note inside—but it was a box that slowly moved into the middle of the area. At once, everybody's attention is caught by something that defies the laws of nature—how does a cardboard box slide by itself into the middle of the area?

Q: Well, obviously there was someone inside the box, sliding it along. Why was this so remarkable?

PB: When the box stopped in the middle of the floor, there was a moment's pause, and then it started breathing. When five hundred people, seven hundred people, are looking at a cardboard box that's beginning to breathe, the very thing I'm talking about takes place without anyone knowing it. They are suddenly seeing this box in a double light. They're seeing it as a box. They're seeing it on an imaginative plane. Nothing at all tells them the way they're supposed to respond: They can both sense something strange and poetic and yet find it funny. The audience is surprised at the uproar of laughter. Yet both reactions are legitimate, because no reaction could be illegitimate. You react even if you look in silence. You find it rather horrifying. And that's legitimate. You look at it, and find it extremely comic to see a shape moving—that's also legitimate. Your response is totally freed, and yet there is nothing loose about the elements. The elements are absolutely precise.

Q: Aren't you assuming a great deal about the audience response? After all, you have not got a concrete and objective way of measuring the response, have you? Perhaps the response you attribute to the audience is your very own, and no one else's?

PB: I'm giving this straight, concentrated example to explain something.

Q: To get to another question: How does what you have described work with your upcoming project *The Conference of the Birds*?

PB: With *Orghast,* I said we were working in a very formalized area, and what was formalized gave it intensity but automatically limited its universality. It was restricted to those who were prepared to go along with it. People who refused it, refused it. It was in that way a very restricted area, as it should be. *Orghast* was designed for Persepolis. The next step in our work is designed probably for Africa. The reason I've chosen Africa is my conviction that one has to play before difficult audiences. And by "difficult," I don't mean pigheaded, or malicious, audiences—I mean "difficult" in the way an audience is demanding, and is highly responsive when the demand is fulfilled, and frighteningly indifferent when the demand is not fulfilled. While all audiences that haven't been to theaters before potentially have these characteristics—and, on the whole, popular audiences are more responsive than snob audiences—it isn't everywhere that you can find audiences that have not been conditioned by the current theater and yet are completely free to wander in and out of their imagination. For instance, the peasant audience in a number of parts of the world carries with it all the qualities of country people. But very often it doesn't carry any longer that free relationship with the world of imagination that was part of country life several centuries ago. I mean, in many parts of the world, that is gone. The peasantry still have the wisdom of the relationship with the earth and with the seasons. But there is also a part of it that is very bigoted, very narrow-minded, very closed.

Q: Does this apply to Africa, as well?

PB: What interests me in Africa is that certain traditional societies are still fully alive, and there you have people who have no conception at all of theater as we know it. They are unprejudiced but are very close to the movement from the everyday world to the imaginary world. For that reason, their background is full of legend, song, myth, religion, and ceremony. They are both open and yet not easily satisfied. A sophisticated or an intellectual audience in London or Paris or New York can very easily be bluffed. That's one of my main reasons for wanting to avoid, in experimental work, experimental audiences. I have seen how an audience is bad simply because it is too indulgent. It sits there and accepts anything. Or resists purely for haphazard reasons. On the whole, the biggest tragedy of the avant-garde is that the audience accepts it, good or bad. It has lost its capacity to hold a living bond with the audience. What you want is the lively response of the person who, if he is interested, is there a hundred percent. This is what we're going to Africa to meet. The material we're preparing is for what we consider to be the most difficult audience.

Q: Would this be more difficult than preparing for a Broadway opening night?

PB: Oh, yes. More difficult than the Broadway opening night, but in a healthy sense. A Broadway opening night is painfully difficult in an unhealthy way. It's a distractive obstacle to go past. This is more difficult than a Broadway opening night in real human terms, because if they don't like it, you have to ask yourself very clearly what is lacking in human terms for them not to have come along with us.

Q: Isn't that the same question you have to ask yourself if you do not succeed on Broadway?

PB: No, because all this work in going toward Africa is looking for the relationships between people, the elements of story, the characters, the concrete element.

Q: Since you're working on *The Conference of the Birds,* already a well-known published poem, what role does Ted Hughes play in this project?

PB: *The Conference of the Birds* is actually nontheatrical material.

Q: So then he is creating stories that will be, I assume, based on *Conference*?

PB: Yes. Last year, he worked very closely with us. Working closely with the actors, we tried, with Ted, to break past this bad separation between the author who loves to work with the group but who takes a very weak position and the author who just puts into order what the group wants. Both of these are unsatisfactory, because in one case, the author isn't doing his job, and in the other case, the author is doing an excessively personal job. Ted, in a miraculous and very unique way, bridges this gap. His work is intensely personal and authoritative, but his approach to it is completely open. He doesn't want to impose. He wants to mold. And this process was already there last year. This year, we go very, very much further, so that we approach form—the stories, the incidents— as a dialogue between Ted and the actors. What he brings to them, and what they bring back to him, gets them closer and closer.

Q: So you're working in the same way as you did in *Orghast*? He comes in with a story; the actors do improvisations; it goes back and forth in some way, and then eventually something evolves?

PB: No, this is quite different. In *Orghast,* Prometheus and the legends were closer to dramatic form. With *The Conference of the Birds*, we're working around tragic forms. We're doing a new version of a tragic language. *The Conference of the Birds* is a great poem in its richness and complexity. But there is nothing in it you could illustrate. You couldn't dramatize any of it literally, so that provokes Ted and the actors to find different forms.

Q: How does this actually work out?

PB: When we go in front of the audience, it is not to present finished material, but to present material that we can then evolve. For me, the analogy is this: In America, something bad is also something good. Nothing is more horrifying in the whole American theater than the system that plays on the road. Because everybody has their own version of the nasty experiences of hotel rooms on the road: sitting at four in the morning rewriting an act; everybody giving their opinions; people being thrown in and taken out. It's the sort of nightmare of American plays and American musicals, and it's a criminal, masochistic, destructive practice, one that could only exist in a country as completely corrupted by its money and power structures as the United States.

However, from one point of view, you do see how a corrupted, money-dominated theater produces the most crude, anti-artistic form there is. The authors' work, directors' work, actors' work are torn to shreds by a group of businessmen on the road, who must have a hit at all costs, or nothing. It couldn't be more base than that. From another point of view, it has great merit.

Q: Because of the necessary preparation before getting in front of the final audience? That, despite the duress, produces a good deal of energy, and often something worthwhile. Is this what you mean?

PB: I'll give you an example. We worked this year on Peter Handke's *Kaspar*. We wanted to give everyone, after all that work on inventive language, the possibility to make the link between that and an everyday language. So everybody plunged into a play. In fact, it was very interesting, because the group managed to do a play in French in a way that no French person could complain about. And if you know the French, you know it's quite extraordinary. I couldn't believe that the French could accept a play in which the whole group, the majority, were foreigners, who spoke their words and found them very natural. That was possible because the actors had an experience that enabled them to use a foreign language in a particular way.

Q: Through their experience in Iran?

PB: Well, yes.

Q: To get back to Africa: You were saying that the Africans you met couldn't speak a word of French or English.

PB: A few words. A few words.

Q: Okay. If there is a lack of a common language, how do you intend to play there?

PB: You know, it's very difficult to answer those sorts of questions accurately. Because if one could answer them accurately, then there would be no surprise, and no research possible. I can only tell you the direction we're going, but I can't predict what will be the end result. Out of what was a rigorously formalized work last year, we're going in a direction infinitely freer. The symbol of that will be the difference between the unmovable tomb at Persepolis, as a unique and necessary prop for *Orghast,* and the highly movable and dispensable cardboard box, which is all we need for this year's work. Which we can find and tear up and replace anywhere in the world. In Persepolis, we could not really be separated from that place. Certainly we're using the same basic elements of silence, sound, syllable, and word. And Ted is experimenting, and out of this will come a form that certainly will not be mime. It certainly won't be like any play all in one language, either. Exactly how that gets resolved is what this year's work is all about. When we go to America, we know that we're going to an area where everybody speaks English. And in Africa, we're going to an area where nobody speaks any universal language. So the whole circumstance is changed.

Q: Well, in a way, I can understand your aim for Africa. But what use would it be in America? If you come to a place where there's a sophisticated audience, everybody speaks English. What would be the point of working in syllable, sound, and sign?

PB: No, it doesn't follow that for America we would do the same. Because Americans . . . well, it's a different public.

Q: What you're saying is that *Orghast* had a certain context. And in a sense, would you say that that is finished now?

PB: Absolutely. We'll never do *Orghast* again.

Q: No, I know you won't do *Orghast* again. But I am talking about the principle behind *Orghast,* the way Ted worked it out. Apparently, you gave him some pieces of manuscript to look at.

PB: It depends which principle you mean. The deep principle is Ted's exploration of what syllables correspond with what, which is an exploration, not an achievement. In other words, Orghast is a lexicon, a dictionary. Of course, it's not as though *Orghast* is the first step toward what will become more and more theater Esperanto. Not a bit. *Orghast,* as an attempt to use nonidentifiable words in a certain way, is a very important first experiment, of which perhaps everything will be discarded. The words, the set of words, the grammar—all that may go—leaving only the discovery by the author himself of certain possibilities that can be further developed.

Q: Do you think that sound actually could ever surpass language?

PB: Well, I would put it the other way around. Do you think that the world's so-called language theater is satisfying?

Q: No, it's often poor. Maybe not always. But it is all we have, at any rate.

PB: You see, there's a funny double game that arises: "Look what they're doing to the theater! They're taking language away from it. They're taking away the only thing that makes our theater an expression of civilized man." But the basic point is, of course, that language is not an aberration. Language is an expression of a level of development. But that great principle doesn't alter the fact that the language as used, that words as used, in general—in the street, or in the theater—has precious little to do with language as an expression of man at his highest peak of evolution.

Q: Okay. The whole idea of what you're doing in place of ordinary language—well, of what use is it? No one is going to use Orghast, the language you're experimenting with.

PB: No, no. Orghast was a field of research. The research work is not the same as architectural work. An archi-

tect is not experimental. If an architect were genuinely experimental, his house might fall down. His
bridge might collapse. There isn't an architect in the
world who will take that risk. So the moment an architect starts his first lines on his drafting board, his
drawing board, the lines are a known basis from
which every next step can follow. We're not doing
that. We're not drawing first lines from which a building can arise like a skyscraper. We don't expect—
through a universal language, from which we make
that story—that eventually a great Seagram Building
will arise next year. No, that would be quite false.
You do that in a situation of total security, when
there is no problem with research, when the research
has all happened, and then you build with known elements. I do that when I do, for instance, a production
within the possibilities and limitations of legitimate
theater. When I did *A Midsummer Night's Dream,* it
was according to that principle. And you work suc-
cessively until the building emerges. But research is
quite different. Research is based on the possibility of
endless expendability, through which new forms appear. You do and discard. You do and discard.

Q: One wonders why you want to do any of this. Something less tiring and more fun, perhaps?

PB: It's perfectly true. What I'm doing is much less fun. It
is more fun to follow the pleasure principle.

Q: You're in the studio from ten o'clock in the morning
until seven o'clock at night in Paris—on sunny days?

PB: Yes, this is very hard work. The great advantage of
the artistic life—what leads any of us into the artistic
life—is a hatred of the bureaucratic life, the obvious
life of fixed hours and knowing where one is. The

great thing is that all my life I've thrown myself into something for never more than three months.

Q: Why is that so great?

PB: It is a marvelous feeling at the end of three months that it's all over, and you go away; things change. It is infinitely more fun for me now to do a series of shows and movies. That can be a much more fun way of living. On the other hand, behind everything, there has to be a purpose. Quite clearly.

Q: Well, what is your main purpose?

PB: That is what one has to discover. If your main purpose is fun, which makes some people spend their days and nights in casinos, for instance, searching for fun and excitement, then you have a very fulfilled life and your main purpose has been satisfied. Gauguin left his wife and family for the South Seas, fulfilling a certain purpose. I know in relation to my own work that, while I'm angry and puritanical, my main purpose is neither fun, nor prestige, nor success, nor any of the things that go with it. Although every one of those has its great qualities, its great attractions, they're all totally nonpuritanical. I'm delighted to play the game of the commercial theater. I like going into the office and seeing what the figures are, and knowing what the advance is, but they're all fringe. They're totally unimportant but are a highly enjoyable set of games. Fundamentally, all the work I've done, in all the different areas, has been like an airplane circling to land. It's been spiraling around one question—the only question that interests me: What is the nature of the theater experience? What am I doing it for? What is it about? For that, I have had to do farces, Western comedies, television, and so forth. I've worked in every area. I wanted to explore the field. Exploring the field is something you can't do unless you want to be locked in eternal adolescence; you can't just go on circling the field in exactly the same way. Circling the field, by its own momentum, narrows because the circling explores, shows, and eliminates. So all the circling in the theater that I've done has gradually narrowed, narrowed, narrowed, narrowed. I'm still doing it—it's no different movement—still circling around the point that I need to discover. I'm in Paris; I'm in Iran; I'm going to Africa—those are streaks in different directions. Actually, it's the exact opposite. It's absolutely necessary to go to Africa. Africa is not going off my way at all. To stay in Paris would be. To go to New York would be. Africa is directly in line with what needs to be explored.

Q: Have you come to any conclusions about what the theater experience means to you at this point in your life?

PB: All my life . . . I've earned my living. I have functioned. I've had my pleasure, my cash, my ability to live in a competitive world through a form, and my only interest is in knowing what this form is. I've lived it through not knowing any more than anyone else knows what that form actually is. And what it means. Particularly, the only way to know what it is today is to know what it could be.

Q: Some people have been saying that your connection, or friendship, with Jerzy Grotowski has brought about a decisive change in your life. Do you want to comment on that?

PB: These sorts of things are based on naïveté, on lack of information, or malice. They have read some articles about my work and perhaps seen one film. In New York, I was fascinated to read a piece by somebody who said that I was . . . a routine theater director until the day I met Grotowski. When was that? In 1964, I should think. At the time, I was working with LAMDA [London Academy of Music and Dramatic Art], and we were doing the basic things—work through exercises, nonverbal forms, words used in a different manner, and so on. It was during that work at that time that I was told that somebody in Poland was beginning to work in the same direction. Out of this work with LAMDA came the first production of *Marat/Sade*. When *Marat/Sade* went to New York, I first met Joseph Chaikin, artistic founder of the Open Theatre, and it was during that same period that I met Grotowski when he was in Paris. In each of these cases, there was the powerful meeting of people who, quite independently (and this happens all through history), have moved to a certain point and had begun to do research of their own. Out of that has come a deep bond between Grotowski and myself. And a very special relationship with Chaikin. And we all know that the direction we each take, the forms we produce, the different theater that we're going toward are exactly the same goal that we all share and understand—though we take different paths. And thank God for that. Many things touch and overlap; we also know many professionals who hate this sort of work and would try to find grounds for public dispute between any of us. But we're not so silly. We know first of all that there isn't one. And second, we would never allow the general differences of our paths to form an opposition. Because we really understand one another. There's an enormous confusion in the popular mind, because with the experimental work that I do, I take great care to avoid publicity. I don't think that experimental work needs to be explained.

Q: Speaking of experiments, at one point, you invited the Theater of the Deaf to work with you in your research. What was your aim? What kind of contribution did you think they could make?

PB: Our business at the moment is to explore channels of communication. The deaf, out of sheer necessity, have developed certain levels of communication way beyond what intellectual life is about. For instance, two of them gave a demonstration of how they communicated. Not through their fingers, not through their sign language, but through what they call "verbal vernacular," a sort of semi-spontaneous, comic-strip language that they use among themselves like slang. It is incredibly fast; it shows how technique is nothing but a means to an end. They learn this technique every minute of the day; they need to communicate, and they only have their arms to do it. So the result of using one's arms like this all the time means that there's a relaxation and a sensitivity in that appendage that goes far beyond the most trained technique of a ballet dancer or mime. Even a mime practices. One can't practice more than seven hours a day, while the deaf person practices from the second he awakens till the second he goes to sleep. The possibility of using his arms at incredible speed is coupled with the habit of using his eyes with incredible precision. When the deaf actors were asked to tell what a performance of *Swan Lake* looks like, they did something that was like the virtuosity of a pianist who hits notes at a high speed. Their fingers were doing the dancers, describing their costumes, their hairstyles, what they were looking at, and using their hands at an amazing tempo. The exchange between our actors and the deaf actors will produce a healthy result. I think that both groups will be really refreshed by this.

Q: Do you hope to find some kind of style as a result of working with these kinds of groups?

PB: Yes. Finding a nonstyle . . .

Q: But when you find a nonstyle, it does become a style.

PB: The French have tried to find what is the Shakespeare style, and they find nothing at all. Shakespeare is an example of the intermingling of . . . well, a thousand styles, so that it becomes not nonstyle, but superstyle. You want my answer on what kind of style it is, it's superstyle.

Q: If you find one style, or one group, fascinating one week, the next week, it may be already passé; the novelty is gone.

PB: That's why the theater never stops searching. That's why we don't stick to forms. The basis of our work has to be perpetual revolution. Perpetual revolution is a very great concept. And very much needed.

Paris, 1972

Five

Experiments in Africa

By 1972, Peter Brook had organized his group at the Center, and a number of actors, designers, musicians, and writers were firmly attached to the company. When he returned from Iran, he was convinced that working in foreign countries and playing to foreigners was vital to discovering something about theater and its relationship to audiences. So in December 1972, he and his staff organized what was to become one of the most daring and remarkable excursions that any theater company has ever made. He decided to go to Africa for three and a half months with his group, where they would play for Africans, study their rituals and their cultures and, hopefully, come away with yet another understanding of what theater is and could be. He was also interested in working on a new piece, *The Conference of the Birds,* which he and Ted Hughes had talked about in Iran. (Hughes, however, did not join the group in Africa.) Certainly this trip had to be the most intriguing and unique undertaking ever conceived by a theater director—as well as the most arduous.

The trip to Africa was no ordinary excursion. There would be no fancy hotels or fancy restaurants, no routes taken by tourists, no Western amenities. According to reports from those who went, living conditions were reminiscent of those at a giant campout, commune-fashion: cooking outdoors, eating around fires, sleeping under tents, and no toilets in sight.

According to the writer John Heilpern, who was part of the entourage and wrote a book about his experiences, *Conference of the Birds: The Story of Peter Brook in Africa*, the enterprise was enormous: "The equipment and food supplies weighed two and half tons," he wrote, "we were carrying reserves of 200 gallons of water and 700 gallons of fuel . . . 8,000 teabags . . . vegetable strainers, frying pans, rubber gloves, bleach, 12 packets of kitchen towels . . . four can openers, washing bowls, knives, forks, spoons, 40 mugs . . . all this and more . . ."—too numerous to list here.

There were eleven actors in the company, which also included a photographer (Mary Ellen Mark), a doctor, a cook, a stage manager, two observers, and numerous assistants. The cost of the trip, Heilpern said, was sixty thousand dollars, and the trip was to last three and a half months. The beginning experiments were to take place in the Sahara Desert.

Most people in the theater thought that the project was crazy, that Brook had indeed gone bonkers. Few understood Brook's rationale for this adventure. After all, explorers go to Africa for specific reasons—in the interest of science or anthropology, or to research certain things. No one knew what Brook wanted or what he was searching for. But apparently he knew.

When Brook returned from what was rumored to have been a most strenuous and painstaking trip for those who were part of it, I interviewed him in Paris. He had returned unscathed, so to speak, full of energy and ready to resume work. First, he staged *Timon of Athens* (1974) at the newly acquired Bouffes du Nord; and the following year, he directed *The Ik* in Paris and began improvisations on *The Conference of the Birds;* he also added Alfred Jarry's *Ubu Roi* to his heavy schedule. All three were later done at La Mama in New York in 1980. But what did the African trip mean to him? How did it influence his work? And, more important, why did he go to Africa in the first place?

——————————————— • ———————————————

Q: About Africa—I saw some pictures of the trip. I had no idea that it was going to be so rough, and that you were going to do all this camping. Did you plan it that way deliberately?

PB: Oh, yes . . . the conditions in Africa were supposed to be much rougher than in Iran. This was the way the work of the Center was going to develop. Each year, we will have a major task. And the first year, the major task that brought all the work together was Iran. We chose that to be in contact with a particular type of work, and with certain traditions and the effect of putting ourselves, our working group, in a particular environment. In going to Africa, we were taking this process much further, and living together became part of the general exercise.

Q: Why was that so important, the living together?

PB: Everybody has recognized that there are exercises that are necessary for developing a group of actors. But actors who go into a piece of work with nothing to prepare them as a group will not do this work as well as if they go through all the very well known processes for forming a group. I believe that exercises done within a room, or exercises just for the body or voice, or through improvisations, are inadequate; there are much more important exercises for the development of a group, which can take place only under certain conditions. And so, for a group playing and learning about the nature of theater, the exercise of going through difficult conditions together is part of its actual artistic development. The two are inseparable. And so I'd say that the direction we are taking at the moment—the experiences outside the rehearsal room—is toward more fundamental exercises.

Q: You mean all that communal life—setting up the camps and all the food preparation—is equally as important as the actual performance?

PB: Oh, yes, in the long run, particularly because it's so difficult. You see, there's nothing harder than to live together. And most communities break down because they start with a dream that they can all live together by wanting to do so. In fact, it's quite the other way around. It might take a whole lifetime for a group of people to learn how to live really together—even for a short while. And so we have approached living together step by step. This was the first time that this group spent a period as long as three months, day and night, in one another's company. Of course, this didn't at once lead to an ideal condition in which everything happened in a climate of brotherly love. Quite the reverse. The group had the greatest difficulty in living together; it was this difficulty that made it a good and important and revealing exercise. All good exercises are difficult, I have found.

Q: How did it reflect in the actual performance? Or did it?

PB: I think it will. There isn't an exercise in existence that gives you a reward straightaway, any more than exercises for playing the piano do. You have to do piano exercises over a long, long time before you suddenly develop a new facility with certain fingers. And in the same way, actors, and all of us, going through some very shaky experiences, will increase the possibility of an understanding based on shared references. The greatest difficulty for any group is quite simply to understand—at one and the same moment—what the references are. For an international group, when you have people coming from different corners of the world, with their own childhood and very, very distinctive backgrounds—all with their own different artistic and theatrical backgrounds—the life of the group, the working-together life, started the day when these people met and began working together. At that moment our history began.

Q: But can't the references be confused with people coming from all over the world?

PB: For the group to be able to have material to draw on, that the group as a whole can recognize, that material cannot be based on some individual's prior experience, but on the experience that everyone has been through together.

Q: Are you saying you think communal living is essential so that there can be a shared experience?

PB: There have been many experiences before, but this trip was the most complete. It touched on most aspects of living that we had not experienced up to then. So consequently, when we encounter a dramatic situation later on that involves, say, meanness and generosity, they relate quite directly to that day in the middle of Africa when such and such a thing happened. That's how a group develops its own personal history, and, eventually, its own material.

Q: Did you choose Africa for a special reason? Because it would be harder, let's say, than any other country?

PB: No, I chose Africa for quite different reasons. The work that we're doing is related to audiences. We believe that no theater work can exist except through its relation with the people who are watching it—that the spectator is a participant. And so, consequently, the relation with the spectator is something that has to be studied, felt, and learned. And for this, one needs to practice. And one needs to practice with good spectators. And it seemed to us that in Africa we had very special spectators. In Africa we thought we would find, and we did find in villages, people who had never seen theater at all, who had never actually seen people acting.

Q: How did that work out? Did they understand what you were doing?

PB: They didn't even know the language of make-believe. All this is starting from zero. They haven't seen anything of this sort in their natural experience, even with their ceremonies. So that we started with something

that's completely untouched, which was an interesting condition. However, you could find that in many
parts of the world. There are lots of places where
you could go into the country and find people who
have never seen theater.

Q: What, then, is so unique in Africa?

PB: The Africans live with very rich, highly evolved, and
complex traditions. The traditional African life is one
in which the imagination plays a vast and totally integrated role. As I have said, this passage between two
worlds—from the concrete world to the make-believe
and back again (which is what the whole of the theatrical form is based on)—this coexistence of a visible
and an invisible world has been nurtured, formed,
and developed in Africa. You play in front of an audience that is in no way influenced by a history of
theater forms but is a highly prepared theatrical audience. This form is, in fact, completely natural to them.

Q: But why choose foreign countries for your theater
experiments? First Iran, then Africa. Couldn't you find
the same thing in the West?

PB: The very nature of our Center experiments is connected with moving to different parts of the world.
In doing that, I wanted to have a piece of work—
something that we would develop, which would be
a witness to all our works, apart from a demonstration in which one can show a technique that's been
studied or an area that's been opened up. We wanted
a piece of theatrical work that reflected our experiences going to Persia, for example, our experiences
in Paris, experiences through Africa. We wanted all
of this to go into a certain piece.

And the piece that we've been developing slowly all the time is the Persian work, *The Conference of the Birds*. We come back to this material all the time and gradually build, and gradually change, and develop it so that, when it's finished, it will be the summing up of all we've been through. It took us three years to go through all these experiences, but it can then be told back again in two hours. And that's *The Conference of the Birds*. In Africa, we occasionally played a portion of it. But mainly our work there was entirely improvised.

Q: If you had had *The Conference of the Birds* in mind, why did you opt for improvisation, rather than work directly on the play?

PB: The force of the experience is in taking a total risk, which is to have nothing prepared at all. Sometimes we would plan during the day what we'd do, and sometimes, on the contrary, we would go into the village with no idea of what we were going to use, or where we were going to start, or whether we'd start with a song or with a movement or with an improvisation. Invariably, this terrifying total risk was the one that led to the best results, because it made the act of making theater really a dialogue—a conversation.

Q: How did this kind of experience eventually turn into a performance? What exactly did you do in the villages?

PB: It began with actors sitting in a circle on the carpet we used to carry everywhere, and with two hundred people gathering around them. There is in Africa no hurry, no need to get going and get something under way. And then gradually, somebody would start, one of the actors would start, just by walking across the carpet. And just that act of walking would lead to a second person walking. Which might lead to something that would get a reaction from the audience— maybe a laugh or some other response. After this first response, we would gradually develop all the other elements, which always took a new form. Even things that were done before would be done in a different way and in a different shape, and a different order would emerge. There was a great deal of invention, and a response all the time from the audience. Other performances were calm and gentle, and corresponded to the place we were in. And so each performance was made up and existed for that occasion, for the people who were there, and, as theater should be, when it was over, it vanished without a trace.

Q: How did the people treat you—foreigners coming into the village and just sitting down there and playing?

PB: The extraordinary thing is that here in Paris, or London, if I try to explain what we're doing to any intellectuals, it takes hours and hours, and they don't get it, and I have to explain it again, and then they quarrel with it and question in advance whether it should and whether it could happen. They find it highly complicated.

Q: Africans understand you better than English-speaking people?

PB: In Africa, the fact that for the very first time a strange group of foreigners from all over the world went into a village and wished to play was something that I would explain to the chief of the village through an interpreter in a very few words. I wouldn't say these were actors, because usually that word doesn't exist in translation. I'd say, "This is a group of dancers, and singers, and acrobats from many parts of the world, who are going through Africa, trying to discover what basis there is to understand one another directly." And that was all the explanation that was needed. They found that very clear, very satisfying, and we were very pleased. Then the work began.

Q: How was it accepted?

PB: The quality of attention that came from the audience moved the actors very deeply. There was interest and lightning intelligence, but not judgment, so that the actors found it possible to make a relationship with the audience. It was very different from the climate of battle where an audience has to be convinced, has to be caught. This is something rare and deeply satisfying.

It is this confidence that makes improvisation possible, because, on the whole, the best improvisations always happen when there's no audience. And that leads to something very unhealthy in our avant-garde theater, a conviction among groups of actors, who work sincerely on improvisation, that an audience spoils their work, and that when the audience is there, there's an element of compromise, and that you can't improvise in total freedom and total sincerity. You have to show something. You have to succeed. You have to make it good. They learn that it isn't as good when the audience is there as when the audience isn't there. With us, it is just the other way around. The presence of the audience was the factor of security, in which the actor felt that he could go much further because there were people around him. And so it made a very big change in our approach to improvisation in public.

Q: I heard some of the sound on tape, some excerpts from a couple of scenes from *The Conference of the Birds*. And there were really the most extraordinary sounds. Did you work directly with these bird sounds, or what language did you use? How did you communicate with the people who came to watch you?

PB: As you know, in the work we do, we refuse to be limited to any one style. The whole of our work is to deny the validity of a style. All styles serve certain purposes, and our job is to move freely among different styles, because one has different things to say, and different needs of communication. And so, in the work that we do, all forms of theater—whether it's through imitating, acting out, abstract movement, naturalistic sounds, bird sounds, other uses of the voice—these are all part of the available vocabulary. The only thing that we had to eliminate totally was language.

Q: Is that because you were playing for foreigners? Because they wouldn't have understood you in the first place?

PB: For much more practical reasons. In traveling through Africa, we traveled through many different language zones. In one area over twenty miles, there were four different languages. And if we used only one language, the work couldn't have been played, couldn't have been understood. In fact, it was quite surprising to discover how in English-speaking Africa, hardly anyone speaks a word of English, and in French-speaking Africa, hardly anyone speaks a word of French. Often in a village where not one word of English or French is spoken, the language of people a hundred miles to the north isn't even understood. So African companies are largely prevented, if they work mainly in language, from moving freely in their own territory. And so for what we wanted to do, it was necessary that we could go straight through all of these barriers, because the work didn't depend on words.

Q: When I talked to a director about your work some time ago, he said he agreed that you were a genius, but he wondered what experiments in Africa had to do with him in the West. Do you want to comment on that?

PB: I've heard some generalizations, but that is the vaguest statement that I've ever heard.

Q: I think he meant, well, it's okay to go out and experiment in Africa, but what is its relevance to our contemporary theater?

PB: The world, at the moment, is, perhaps, divided into two very distinct categories. In parts of the world, people can rediscover meaning in what they are doing through a return to their roots. In the West, a particular global culture is shifting and is made up of elements from hundreds and hundreds of sources.

Q: Well, what about it? What significance are you giving this?

PB: For instance, you and I are sitting here talking, and if the question is put, are we of the same culture or aren't we? This becomes a much harder question for us to face than if, for instance, we were both Cubans. Then we'd have an absolutely clear, very compact racial, musical, artistic heritage, because we'd come from the same island, with a strong political set of events shaping and involving us. I know nothing about your background, origin, or parents, or what they are doing in America. You know nothing about me—what I'm doing in America, coming from England, or what my antecedents are. What is very typical today is a very complex mass of elements coming into this floating urban culture. If only we had the simple authenticity of a person born in one place who is all of a piece with his neighbors.

Q: But this mixture of people is typical of the West today. And very soon, it will be typical of the rest of the world.

PB: We have to discover where the roots are for our culture.

Q: Why? Why not accept this fragmentation, and possible assimilation?

PB: I'm interested in trying to find the authentic roots of our culture, and one finds that it's found more in the *body* than in the background. For instance, you and I may not share political or ethnic references at all. We might find, if we really got down to it, that you and I share a tremendous organic world—that is, in relation to our both having eyes [we both have blue eyes, as it happens], the capacity to smile, to breathe, to stand upright, to make gestures, and so forth. And once one goes into that, one finds that we have roots, and that our world is very much rooted in discovering what is common between us. In our Paris group, there is an enormous amount that is common to a Japanese, an African, a French, and an American actor, and that is not tied to cultures in the way that Africans are. The most moving thing we discovered was that the closest relationship we ever made in Africa was through certain sounds—or certain movements that would be called abstract—but a certain type of specially produced vocal sounds. This represented the end of a long search for a relationship between breathing and making a sound that corresponded exactly with a sound made by a certain African tribe.

Q: So do you consider this a remarkable discovery?

PB: Well, we discovered—sitting for a long, long evening, working together—that the sound that they were making completely corresponds to ours. There was a tremendous understanding; something lit up in their eyes, and something lit up in ours, because we knew that we'd reached exactly the same conclusions, and that the sound touches one in a certain way. It is an emotional sound, charged with meaning. But you can't put it into words. It isn't a sound that speaks. It is an actual sound produced by the body in a certain way that corresponds to a certain emotion. And there was instant communication. And the same happened often with certain gestures that one can call abstract, in the sense that you can't say, by looking at them, "Oh, that means this," but which communicated instantly. And so if one talks of countercultures, there is still a great area of culture that has nothing to do with words, pictures, references to our backgrounds, references to our everyday problems.

Q: With all these exotic trips you've taken, some people have come to think of you as an English romantic, or, worse, a colonialist trying to contact the natives, or even a Sufi mystic.

PB: *Sufi* is a very dangerous word. There's a man who wrote a book about Sufism to prove that every man is a Sufi, and he ended up by giving a list of world Sufis, including General de Gaulle. If anything could lump General de Gaulle with Sufism, I think that anybody can fall into that category.

Q: Well, how do you see yourself?

PB: I don't.

Q: What do you think of these categories that people have put you in?

PB: The moment something's in a category, it's wrong—the pinning down kills the life, exactly like the butterfly. The moment the pin is through the butterfly, it's not any longer a butterfly. It's a dead butterfly. To produce a play of Shakespeare, one knows that the trap is difficult to avoid: It is imposing a mental scheme, an idea. For instance, an actor who's going to play Hamlet and who starts with an idea—"I think Hamlet was the sort of man who . . ."—you may be sure he's already destroyed Hamlet, because you always have to approach everything just the other way around, reaching toward a definition from the inside through exploring and discovering. And the moment you reach the definition, you know that the work's gone dead, and so you have to smash the definition and start again.

Q: You once said that Shakespeare is your model. But the Shakespearean theater is based on language, and you seem to be—

PB: It isn't. Shakespeare's theater is based on life.

Q: Which involves the word.

PB: Which involves everything.

Q: Yes. But your theater, right now, seems *not* to be involved with language.

PB: I know. But then, this was for very practical reasons. This study we're doing—the countries we're visiting, the bringing together of people who have a lot to give to one another but who haven't got a common language—depends on our temporarily eliminating a whole vast world, which is the world of language.

Q: Why is that necessary?

PB: By doing that, one sees more clearly what is there that isn't language. When we started the first experimental group, the Theater of Cruelty, with actors from the Royal Shakespeare Company, we began with a company totally committed to the spoken word, for the sake of discovering something beyond the spoken word. Words are the ultimate expression, but for the word to mean anything, life has to be there underneath. A good actor must develop meaning that supports his word. If not, he's just a TelePrompTer.

Q: Can you describe your typical theatrical experience in Africa?

PB: We just stopped, even in the middle of a forest, and played. Naturally, we played for everybody who turned up. There were the tiny babies on their mothers' backs. There were always hundreds of children of all ages. There were the young people, the middle-aged people, and the old, old people. That was an audience. And in Shakespeare's day, in his playhouse, there was something similar. All levels of society were there at one and the same moment. And at one and the same moment, each aspect of his plays had the capacity to appeal simultaneously to these different people, not always in the same way. You could have one section of the audience that was following the crude level, and one level of the audience that was following a sophisticated level. And yet they were satisfied, and were responding at the same time. And this is an ideal. The fact that what is being presented is understandable in a way that takes people who would not normally be rubbing shoulders and makes them rub shoulders because they're all linked in a common event—that, to me, is a great theater model. And one which, on a very, very simple scale, we found when we played in an African village.

Q: Do you think you could find those answers elsewhere—for example, in other places in the West where you might find untutored audiences?

PB: One of the things that is very striking about our going to Africa and playing in this manner is that other people aren't doing it. One of the first conclusions we all had was that if every drama school in the world were to substitute a journey of this sort in place of their usual curriculum—so that a handful of actors, a young director, a writer, and a designer were to go out into these sorts of conditions for six months—you can be certain that they would connect more directly with the basic problems of what theater's about than any other form of educational method that I know. This seems to be a great possibility that is too little developed.

   If you want to be a designer today, or you want to become a director, or you want to become a writer, or an actor, there are three basic questions: What am I doing theater for? What's theater? What is it about?

Q: Don't you think many artists ask themselves those questions all the time?

PB: You can't answer this intellectually. You can't settle down and have an inner debate and emerge with a conclusion. The only way that those theater questions can live is by putting yourself in front of an audience you respect, and realizing that if you don't reach them, it is your loss and your mistake. You need to ask what is the common ground and what are the means by which you can enter into a relationship with them. And then all the questions begin to emerge in a very, very immediate form.

Q: Does going to Africa, or playing for foreigners and experiencing their cultures, really solve the problem of how you deal with the audiences right here, or in whatever country you happen to be playing?

PB: It does, because you can't separate things in this way. It's not as though all Africans are African, and therefore nothing like all Americans, who are American, and all English, who are English. The elements that you find everywhere are the same, but the mixtures are different. For instance, in Africa you find something you will find in the Bronx, and in Stratford-on-Avon, but you find it in a more intense form, so that, for a certain time, this is invaluable for your study. It's as though in theater work there may be acrobatics or singing. At a certain time in your work, you may concentrate enormously on singing. To work among people who can sing and make music is obviously enormously valuable, even though the following year you are working on acrobatics, because neither of those is what you are after. You're after an all-around development that relates to every-body everywhere. For instance, it's very clear that the musical values in Africa are not incomprehensible to the rest of the world. On the contrary, they're highly comprehensible. What is very interesting is your question, and that makes me want to ask you one back.

Q: Okay. Ask.

PB: We do a piece of work, in unusual circumstances like the one we've just done, and it is particularly interesting for all of us, but one of the things that's fascinating is how many people ask questions designed to persuade us that we really shouldn't have gone. Now, why should you want us not to have gone?

Q: No, no, it is not that I don't want you to go. I don't have a real opinion on that. I'm a journalist, and it is my role to go into things. Readers want to know what is not obvious. They want to know things, and I have to be the devil's advocate.

PB: It is very funny how many people will say, "Are you sure that you're getting something out of it?" There's a sort of suspicion that if something strange is going on, there must be something bad about it somehow. The puritanism of our culture is unshakable.

Q: I'm not searching for something "bad" about your quest. I am simply trying to clarify and understand what obviously has been a unique experience for you and your group. I don't see this as either good or bad. I see this as something unique and sometimes mysterious. To get back—a question that comes up is about form. You've been searching for new forms—and I understand all that—but sometimes, when one gets into this kind of search, the content is left behind.

PB: It's an old, old argument, that of form and content,
but they're inseparable. What is separable is where
your interest lies. If you let your interest be entirely
on form, then, of course, you can easily get trapped
in becoming interested in form for its own sake, and
aesthetics for their own sake. But if, on the other
hand, you recognize that without form no content
can ever be carried, and that a frozen form is a barrier through which no content can pass . . .

A couple of years ago, a man came to see me
with a play. He was a novelist—he had never written
a play before, and it was a play about a situation involving Jews in Russia. And he felt passionately
about this, and wanted to try to tell the world something about it. He said, "This is urgent. I need people
to help me. This play must go on, and it must go on
fast, because this message will tell what is really happening." He was a very sensitive and imaginative
novelist. But his play was no good because he hadn't
come to grips with what the theater form is. So he
wrote what one would call a journalistic play—one
in which the texture is so thin that the burning issues
don't burn in theatrical terms. I remember our discussion, sitting in the Chelsea Hotel, talking about
what an actual theater scene is made of, and he got
very impatient and said that he didn't have the time
to go through all of that. But it was absolutely clear
that his urgency, his journalistic need to propagate
information, could not be done through the theater,
because his lack of theater form turned his strong
message into a weak message.

Q: Is that what you're looking for—passion and the
proper form?

PB: Yes, of course . . . When a whole town is suddenly concerned and responding to a show, it is very, very thrilling. But the interesting thing is that people often seize on whatever has been last in the air. For example, after I do a play of Shakespeare, and then do some nonverbal experiment, I meet someone who says, "I see you hate the word." But the two things can't be separated if you are a popularist. If, through some sort of naïve love of the masses, you believe that everything you do must be for four thousand people at a time, then you need a big heart to appeal to a big range of people, as some entertainers do. Eventually, that doesn't get properly fed, because the feeding can only go through something inward that only a small number of other people can be interested in.

Q: Some people believe that they cannot afford to go off to experiment, and that you are one of the lucky ones. You are in the position to do whatever you like, where you like, and when you like, while others have to remain in their own town, as it were, and do the work there, and earn their living. Some people have thought of you as an elitist.

PB: It's really curious, because I actually spent most of my life working, always in different forms, in trying not to get caught in any one, but very largely in popular forms, from musicals, to movies, or to shows I very much liked. The sense of a big show on Broadway is thrilling. In fact, I've always alternated that experience with experiments that cannot be done on that scale. And the two have had to go hand in hand. In fact, I think that the two things can't be separated. One mustn't stop. One has to go right on, and perhaps discover a seed that enables you to make something large enough for the largest audience, and one needs to do something for the tiniest audience; the truth isn't with either. We haven't developed any-thing far enough to take something fragile and ex-perimental and put it on in a city like New York. And yet we must not lose sight of the fact that the most satisfying events in the theater are when there is this big vibration of lots of people throbbing together—a part of what theater is about.

Obviously, the Greek theater was carried to its greatest glory when fifty thousand people were all there throbbing together—at the same moment. But one can't switch on material for fifty thousand people just like that. It's a swing of the pendulum.

Q: In New York, in any case, the theater remains, by and large, second to film and television. How can the the-ater compete with all that technology?

PB: Nobody's going to reform the theater. The theater, as it exists in New York, is neither going to be reformed, nor is it going to collapse totally, because, after all, all theater is a reflection of its society, and we are liv-ing at a time when the big social organisms are to-tally divorced from reality. As society is an enormous entity, there are always crosscurrents going through it, and even in the most corrupt society, there is al-ways the opposite face—seeds of something quite different. One can't say that the whole of Broadway is going to be totally influenced by television and lead to a total collapse, nor that Broadway will be in-fluenced by one play or one person's work and take off in a new direction. One can say that nine-tenths of theater will carry on in the direction it's always been going, which is apparently toward a tremendous crash, a tremendous explosion, like the whole of American society is going. We would think that American society is heading for the greatest material and spiritual disaster in the history of the world.

Q: Well, that's an extreme statement, and a pessimistic one, as well.

PB: Yes, but, at the same time, nobody can predict the future and know by what extraordinary survival tricks a society can temporarily catch itself. But as long as society is in its violent, paranoiac, and sterile condition, the bulk of its cultural products will be violent, paranoiac, and sterile—not all, but most. It can't be otherwise. The forces unleashed are so tremendous that no handful of people, or handful of works, will make any difference with the mainstream.

Q: But right now, do you think that theater can have any social value at all?

PB: It depends where. I think that you can't talk about theater in general. In certain places, it can have an enormous social function, and that is what it should be going after. In other places, none. And what happens, alas, is that in the places where the theater can have the most social and political function, the conditions are too dangerous. The police are too active. The censorship is too ruthless. And if it really could do something, it is repressed out of existence.

In liberal societies, where it can change nothing at all, theater can flourish, and often does, but uselessly. In liberal areas, the polemical event in the theater is doomed to get nowhere, other than give a few people a useless good conscience.

June 3, 1973

Six

Meetings with Remarkable Men

In 1978, the unpredictable Peter Brook, already famous for his groundbreaking productions as well as his experiments with his international group in France, Africa, and Asia, now turned to filmmaking on an epic scale. Brook had worked in film before—*Lord of the Flies, Marat/Sade,* and *King Lear,* for example—but never on as grand or as unconventional an undertaking as this effort, which recounts nothing less than a philosophical quest for meaning in life.

The film, *Meetings with Remarkable Men* (1979), depicts the youthful odyssey of an early twentieth-century philosopher and spiritual master, the Greek-Armenian G. I. Gurdjieff, whose ideas about reaching a higher consciousness, ideas largely unknown except to a few devotees, were attracting wider attention at a time when such movements as transcendental meditation and such religions as Tibetan Buddhism and Zen Buddhism were appealing to people from all walks of life. Long before variations of these Eastern-based movements became popular in the West, Gurdjieff combined Eastern philosophy and practices with Western ways to create his own spiritual discipline.

Based on Gurdjieff's autobiography, Brook's film tells the story of a young boy who grows up in a provincial town in the Caucasus at the end of the nineteenth century, wonders about the significance of life, and, unsatisfied by the traditional beliefs of his elders, sets out on a journey through the Middle East and Central Asia in search of better answers. On the way, he meets and befriends other "searchers," all of whom are remarkable men—hence the film's title—with whom he undergoes various adventures, each bringing him closer to his goal, as well as teaching him a practical and spiritual way of life.

The film was shot mainly on location in the plains, mountains, and deserts of Afghanistan, with an international cast and crew of sixty. Yugoslav actor Dragan Maksimovic played the young Gurdjieff; Athol Fugard, the South African playwright; and the actor Terence Stamp also had important roles. And codirector with Brook was one of the few living students of Gurdjieff, Mme. Jeanne de Salzmann, with whom Mr. Brook adapted the scenario from Gurdjieff's book of the same title. A Frenchwoman, Madame de Salzmann, together with her late husband and others, had helped Gurdjieff settle in France and establish an institute there in the 1920s. She was a key figure among the artists, intellectuals, and scholars for whom Gurdjieff became a spiritual teacher during the following two decades. Since his death in 1949, she has been instrumental in perpetuating his ideas.

Gurdjieff believed that, psychologically speaking, the average person lives and dies in "sleep," without questioning the meaning of life; that one's "energy centers"— intellectual, emotional, and instinctual—are disconnected from one another. But he believed in the possibility of one achieving harmony of mind, body, and feeling by working with various disciplines to become "awake." To this end, he developed a complex system of thought, including a comprehensive cosmology and metaphysics, and a theory about the process of evolution in individual man.

Gurdjieff believed that Western man as he was could not change his own consciousness, despite being armed with precise scientific knowledge and the latest methods of investigation. "Everything is just the same as it was thousands of years ago," he told P. D. Ouspensky, his first disciple, who related it in his book *In Search of the Miraculous.* "The outward form changes. The essence does not change. Man remains the same. Modern civilization is based on violence and slavery and fine words. But all these words about 'progress' and 'civilization' are merely words."

As people are "asleep"—living a routine, habit-filled existence—they cannot find their true essence, the real and permanent "I" (or soul). We are machines, Gurdjieff said, victims of the many divided, illusionary "I's" that distract and enslave us (the "I" that feels one way and the "I" that acts another). But once awake, in Gurdjieff's view, we learn to develop the real and permanent "I" that reorders and unifies the psychic functions.

Gurdjieff's central aim was self-transformation through mindfulness, self-awareness, and self-observation—the primary steps in awakening. According to Ouspensky, Gurdjieff stressed method, process, and the practical side of transformation—known as the Fourth Way, and distinguished from the three others: the way of the fakir, which concentrates on the body alone; the way of the monk, on feeling; and the way of the yogi, on the mind. Unlike other traditions, the Fourth Way requires no commitment to a guru, saint, or idol, or adherence to ritual, and can be practiced in a temple, an ashram, or a commune. Practitioners need not give up home, job, or family, or eat certain foods and abstain from others.

The "awakening process," the "Work"—the name given to the Gurdjieff teaching—is actual work on oneself every day in one's own environment or in a group with other Gurdjieff followers. Most important are the "movements," or sacred dances—a set of rhythmic dances or physical stances designed to liberate the energies of the body. They involve hundreds of complicated postures and asymmetrical movements, each of which aims to elicit a certain state or awareness of one's own body rhythms—which contribute to a subtle change of consciousness. The language of the body—which Gurdjieff developed long before it became a popular concept—was one of the means toward the harmonious development of the whole person.

Brook saw in the Gurdjieff story and in the man's quest the kind of hero and heroics of which good drama is made. In no way did he want the film to be esoteric, and he concentrated on the theatrical elements of Gurdjieff's life, rather than on his philosophy. Nevertheless, the film does give one an inkling of Gurdjieff the searcher, and shows, however subtly, what Gurdjieff was looking for—clearly expressed in the filming of the "movements," which were seen by a large public for the first time in the Peter Brook film.

Q: You said in an interview that you wanted to film a man and his search and also explore his story as heroic. Many people might fit that picture. Why have you chosen G. I. Gurdjieff, a man whom very few people have heard of?

PB: It's no different from saying to me, "Why did you want to do *King Lear*? You could have done *Othello*." Any artist has to try to be as little subjective as he can, knowing that he's totally subjective. You can be more self-indulgent with your subjectivity, or less self-indulgent; there is a certain margin between the two. Just to give oneself wantonly to all one's own hunches, fantasies, dreams, and fears doesn't interest me greatly. The opposite road is accepting everything one does as personal, prejudiced, biased, and subjective, but, at the same time, finding some objective value that can be shared with other people. So why did I prefer at a certain moment of my life to commit to *King Lear* rather than to *Othello*? It is subjective fact. Yes, I preferred it. I liked it. I was drawn to it. If a Hollywood producer brought me twenty books and twenty scripts and told me that I had a choice of doing films about various searchers, I would go toward Gurdjieff for reasons that are personal and not personal. The two come together. I believe that among them all, he is the most interesting, the most immediate, the most valid, the most totally representative, the most particular.

Q: Well, what makes him more representative than doing a film, say, about a Zen master? What about Gurdjieff interests you more than Zen?

PB: Ah. There I think you touch on something enormously interesting. Perhaps more than anyone, Gurdjieff built the bridges between something out of everyday life and something right in everyday life. Although Gurdjieff was half European—Greek—and half Armenian, and spent a lot of time in the East, he had nothing of the exotic Eastern mystic about him. If he had this at all, it was because of false, uninformed legend. Gurdjieff was constantly searching within himself (and for the people with whom he worked) for links between levels of inaccessible experience and the levels of experience that were one's own—the way one lived. He brought something—found only in monasteries—into what we call life. For him, that life was life in the West. Gurdjieff made the link between something that was developed and preserved only in the East and something that today is possible only in the West.

Q: Didn't Zen Buddhism try to make the same link between East and West?

PB: To me, there are two Zens: the real Zen and the joke Zen. Real Zen is the Zen monastery, and its master and pupils in Japan, which, again with rare exceptions, are all Japanese and encompass the Japanese psyche, the Japanese organism within the Japanese culture, and the Japanese way of life. There is always the exception that crosses the barrier, but it's always the Japanese. And then there's the joke Zen, which has nothing to do with this superb and rigorous and extraordinary monastic life in Japan. The joke Zen comes from picking pieces of Zen out of paperback books in New York drugstores, popularly known in the West as Zen, and has all sorts of diluted and eventually ridiculous forms: It is not Zen in its pure form, but a hybridized, watered-down Zen.

Q: What is different about Gurdjieff's way?

PB: Gurdjieff was bringing something essential from the East; he was not dismissing or despising the New York drugstore. Here was a master who had found something in the East, who wrote about it, sitting in Child's restaurant, and found it congenial soil. He was not sitting on a mountain peak writing, but writing his book in the restaurant.

Q: What is significant about that?

PB: He did not ask people to deny any of those levels of reality. He urged them to find how those levels of reality, which they can't deny, which they needn't deny, and which they shouldn't deny, can be transformed by a set of different relationships that can be discovered—relationships that normally they are not in touch with.

Q: What about you? Do you have a personal relationship with the Gurdjieff Work?

PB: My relationship is that all my life I've been interested in the whole range of thinkers, teachers, and philosophers of many different cultures in many different parts of the world; I've read a great number of them, and encountered a great number. In the twentieth century, the most remarkably interesting and significant figure is this man, Gurdjieff, whose works I've known for a long time, and followed with great, great results.

Q: What do you mean by "great, great results"? Are you intimately acquainted with his work? Have you followed his work?

PB: One can't be seriously interested [in him] . . . and not be interested in knowledge of his work. Just as you can't be interested in the theater and not be interested in Grotowski. It sticks right out. That, I think, is one level. The other is that the question put—"Do you follow this? Do you practice this?"—is something that isn't a serious question, because it shows a complete misunderstanding about what anybody's involvement with a search can be. On a very naïve level, there are followers and disciples and adherents of different religions, of different schools, and of different ways, but that doesn't go very far, and isn't really serious. You don't get committed to somebody's methods and somebody's teaching because of some hero worship or because you think they have a panacea. It's something very different. You have your own personal search, and that becomes illuminated at certain times by certain things that you receive. I don't think that the moment you reach a deep level, you can say there is such a thing as a disciple or a follower. That's very external. In other words, it's not the way one has to look at it at all. Do you see what I mean?

Q: No, it's a simple question. Do you actually participate in the Gurdjieff Work? Do you belong to the movement, if that is what it is, or do you just respect Gurdjieff's ideas from afar? If so, how do the ideas actually affect you, or influence your personal life?

PB: Belonging to a movement always carries with it a great element of passivity. Because all one's problems are resolved once one joins the movement, religious or political. I remember meeting, to my horror and amazement, when we were in Africa, a very committed French boy of about nineteen, who was there to do political education. He told me that two years ago, he had made up his mind: "I now know what's right and what's wrong, and there's nothing for me evermore to put into question," he said. I wondered if there was something deep in him to put into question. And he said, very accurately, "I am not putting anything into question, because if I admit that, then I haven't a commitment." A commitment means, I know where I stand for the rest of my life.

Q: What's wrong with that?

PB: What he thought was great activity on his part was [actually] the last word in passivity. He now had found somewhere to hang his hat, and that was it. Hanging your hat, hanging your coat on a peg, turning it from one language to another, is total passivity. From then on, however ardently you struggle for it, you've made up your mind.

Q: Well, isn't that better than being ambivalent about one's choices? I have always thought that most disciplines demand decisive commitments. How else can it be?

PB: On the crudest and most misunderstood level, people hitch themselves to popular religious leaders and mystics; it is a way of dropping out of the lonely active search. Someone of great aura, of great influence, a charismatic personality, is there to carry you along, maybe for the rest of your life. Whether it's a guru, or whether it's an entire tradition. You can be carried by a guru. You can be carried by a culture. You can be carried by an ideology. It's always about being carried. And within that being carried, you expend energies that are never really independent or active.

Q: Well, what about Gurdjieff? He had all the makings of a guru, from what I read about him. How does he differ from those you have just mentioned? Didn't he start a movement like the rest? And haven't there been people completely committed to him?

PB: It's false to talk of Gurdjieff as somebody starting a movement, because he was constantly going in the other direction. He was demanding of other people what he demanded of himself: to find an understanding that would come from one's deepest efforts and deepest loneliness. Only through one's deepest loneliness could one eventually reach deepest independence, and the greatest, truest freedom. In that way, to call Gurdjieff a guru, and to talk about people being his disciples, is a total misconception about his relation with the people around him. He was trying, in a very clear way, in all his written works, to arouse thought and provoke independent activity in other people. I think what's interesting about him as a young man in the film is to show how he went through events without being subjugated by them or influenced by them; on the contrary, he was stimulated by them—so as to increase his capacity for free, independent, open searching.

Q: Is that what the film really is about? His youthful adventures?

PB: No, the film is about more than that. The film is about what it takes to be a searcher. The film is one thing and the description is another. The description must be less than the thing itself. So saying what it is about, of course, is much less than the thing itself.

Q: About being a searcher—how does the Gurdjieff movement help people who are, as you say, searchers? What about the Gurdjieff exercises? People have published them.

PB: Yes, but he himself didn't ever publish exercises.

Q: No, but his students wrote about it. They wrote about the classes.

PB: Yes, but you see how dangerous that is. Because if you look at the accounts of the man, if you look at the way he lived, you see that he was constantly moving from one point to another. He was changing the way he was doing things. He was going through totally different phases of his work. He was always changing, always adapting to different circumstances, always evolving. He did perhaps give an exercise to a group which corresponded to those people at a certain moment in history. He asked them only one thing, which was not to write it down or try to reproduce it or repeat it. But someone did write it down; some people got the false idea that it was a secret, not realizing that the real secrets, once you take them out of their context, are worthless anyway. Then, by the time it got through a few hands, it got to be slightly wrong. And all the life had gone out of it.

Q: But what about the so-called exercises—or "movements," as they are called?

PB: There are exercises that somebody, not Gurdjieff, wrote down, which somebody else picks up and says, "Ah, that may be the panacea to help me become a better man." And they start doing it. But you can't hold Gurdjieff responsible for that. There is no written guarantee coming back from heaven saying, "If you do this, you'll become a new man." I have never claimed that at all.

Q: That brings up another question. There is a Gurdjieff Foundation and Center. Everybody knows that. How are the teachings of Gurdjieff to be continued when you don't have Gurdjieff himself? When you have all of these people who, you say, may be secondhand. It reminds me of Grotowski in a way. You have a Grotowski. And you have his students, who claim to teach or work in his way. That, too, may be second-hand. Isn't this always the case? The disciples are never as good or as genuine as the master.

PB: I've seen this continually. Unfortunately, there are people working with me where the same thing happens. That somebody works with you doesn't mean that it's possible, however much you deeply wish it, for you to transmit the very thing they wish to get from you.

Q: To get back to Gurdjieff; I have heard he was a great charismatic figure and that he had a special kind of knowledge. But what about those who came after him? How effective are those people?

PB: This is absolutely true. He gave a very good answer to that when he said that everybody who wants to search wishes to be taught by Jesus Christ and no-body else. If they can't get Jesus Christ, then it's not worth bothering. The truth is that a teacher has to have something of a fantastic intensity. In electrical terms, each circuit that it goes through, the energy diminishes and diminishes and diminishes. But even if you get a hundred circuits down the line, what is left is of immense value to anybody who comes toward it, in the right spirit. If they come toward it thinking that here's a panacea, like taking a drug, and it's going to keep them going, then they are putting themselves in the hands of an unqualified person. A person, a hundred times removed from the source, is standing there with a book in his hand, saying he represents this teaching. If you naïvely put yourself into his hands, thinking you now have found a guru and all your worries are over, then you're really stupid.

Q: Well, that's a pretty gloomy outlook. What would you tell the innocent searcher who is truly looking?

PB: Well, if you come with a totally nonaggressive or detached but totally risk-taking spirit, determined to search everywhere in the hope of finding something, you may be a good searcher. That's what the film is about: The searcher is not naïve, not feeble, not passive, but searching with his mind open. Gurdjieff, in his search, was not taken for a ride on a mystical level or for a ride on the bizarre level. This is a big lesson: he talks a lot about the shrewd man in his books. And his way—the way of the sly man.

Q: What does that mean? It sounds very negative and very cunning—"the way of the sly man."

PB: When he says the way of the sly man, he means that if a man (and this is in relation to the hard school of the Middle East) is going to go into a bazaar, and can't fend for himself, and can't cope with life on the level of the bazaar, he's going to be led by the nose; he is going to be gullible. He can't do the practical things. He has to eat; he has to make money. There's no time to question the social right or wrong. To make money, he has to earn it. Having eaten, he needs, if he's a searcher, to buy certain books. To buy those books, he can't wait for society to be transformed and for lending libraries to be available. He needs it today, and he's in a very unjust feudal society. Today is now. So he has to find a way to get that book without hurting other people; he has to use his wits; his wits have to be sharpened to the nth degree.

Q: This may all apply to some young people in that part of the world. But is this applicable for others?

PB: Gurdjieff's father teaches him rectitude and a belief in the sense of justice, of decency, of morality, and of courage. That's the very first level. But he doesn't just become the righteous man. Gurdjieff then encounters, in the bazaars, a certain person who's presented as a remarkable man and yet is the opposite of his father's teaching. The man is righteous in the sense that he is a deeply passionate mystic, searching for truth. He is a member of a community that is extremely shrewd, more than the other ethnic groups. This man knows by his own observation, and by his family tradition, how to sell everything at the best price, how to differentiate between the man who will buy and the man who won't buy.

Q: But again you are talking about a specific geographical place at a certain time.

PB: It is about human nature—and Gurdjieff knows all about human nature, and therefore understands people, and understands something about himself. Through his meeting with this man, Gurdjieff learns about another face of his "inner god"; another aspect of his inner possibilities is developed. Going from the rectitude of his father, he needs the ingenuity of the everyday life of the trickster. One sees that his father is portrayed as a noble man but also a very naïve man, constantly losing all his money because he trusted people too much.

Q: Is this father figure diminished because he is naïve

and not a trickster? That doesn't sound too noble. And the image of a sly man isn't very noble, either.

PB: He is a magnificent father. But then, like in any fairy story, there comes a time when the young man goes out into the world, and the next thing that he has to learn is how to be a sly man, how to be a trickster.

Q: I don't see that as a necessary thing for a young man to learn. As I have said, if you are living in a certain society, it is needed for survival. But in general terms, I see nothing rewarding in being a "trickster."

PB: Our crude popular morality says, Well, if he's a trickster, he can't be a good man; if he's a good man . . .

Q: Are you saying that being a trickster does not exclude one from being good or righteous, that the two can go together?

PB: There could be something that rightly marries the two. And again, it only takes place in the thick of life. Here you see this figure developing himself, and developing his proper understanding by knowing how to be resourceful within the bazaar.

Q: Is there any other way to deal with society than being a trickster? Why choose a way that by its very nature is negative?

PB: I am saying that bit by bit all these steps build up to a picture of a seeker who is not easily gulled by the first mystic he meets. On the contrary, when he reaches this monastery, the opposite of a Shangri-la, he finds something not found all the way along the line, something that he can confirm by his inner experience—and this is constantly where the accent lies. What is interesting both in the book and the film is the picture it gives of the searcher. It is diametrically against the popular idea of guru and pupil.

Other people may have created a movement, and inside that movement something is already frozen. But his is a living spirit. A living spirit that, at the same time, is not accessible. At the same time, to say that one therefore only needs a book of Gurdjieff is also ridiculous. You cannot meet the living spirit just by reading books. Seekers may look at books, but they don't find what they want through books. Everybody goes through that phase, and books don't do it.

Q: Well, how does one go about searching, or, rather, making a film about searching, or a film about authentic experiences?

PB: I would in no circumstances whatsoever, for any inducement under the sun, have attempted to make a film about Gurdjieff if I hadn't had the extraordinary fortune to do something completely authentic. And that is to make a film through the person who is alive today who was closest to Gurdjieff.

Q: You mean Mme. Jeanne de Salzmann?

PB: Yes. That is the entire basis of this relationship. That without her active work on this film, I wouldn't have—

Q: You never met Gurdjieff?

PB: No.

Q: So without Madame de Salzmann, you—

PB: In no circumstances could I see myself being involved with trying to make a statement about something I know nothing about. I couldn't make a film about a man who is recognized as a great man in his maturity, because no actor can play a great teacher in his maturity. You can make a film about a young man on the way to becoming something—a condition shared by many young men. But when it is a very particular one, I couldn't do it just out of literary fantasy. But a totally different possibility did exist. Today somebody is alive who actually is the nearest thing to Gurdjieff himself. And who is the link in the chain.

Q: Are you saying that Madame de Salzmann is the link?

PB: Yes. Madame de Salzmann is also someone with an extraordinarily precise interest in the cinema as such, and in what the film *Meetings* is all about. The possibility of making a film about a subject that almost always falls apart in the making because it's vague and mushy and loose and is the result of generalized fantasy and imagination [is a problem]. On the contrary, making a film with the help of a real source is the whole secret of this collaboration. This film is a total collaboration between Madame de Salzmann and myself, and my associates.

Q: Granted, she's a link with Mr. Gurdjieff and all that, but how does that work itself out in the practical form? How do you trust her judgment? She's not an experienced filmmaker.

PB: She has an extraordinary sense of cinema. She's made, over the years, a number of documentary films of her own about the Gurdjieff movement. And [she] has a very precise awareness of all the elements of making images and putting them together. This she approaches in her own way. But it's something that has made it a highly professional collaboration. And so we work very simply together. We worked together on the script; we worked together on all the different aspects of filmmaking.

Q: Yes, I've noticed the way you work on the scenes. You confer all the time. Is she going to have a credit on the screen in that way?

PB: Yes.

Q: So, actually, this is a new thing for you?

PB: What?

Q: Well, you've never worked so directly with anybody. It's a Peter Brook film, so to speak. Shared credit is a new thing, isn't it?

PB: Only for people who worry about those things. It comes right back to what I was saying earlier. That each artist's responsibility today is not to turn toward his subjectivity as though that was the most interesting thing in the world, without questioning—like Fellini, say—but to go toward the opposite. There is a subjective reality, and then there is a reality outside the apparent faculties of perception. And the linking of those two is a theme I've always been a part of. Linking the rough and the holy.

Q: If that's the way you put it, do you think that you are linking all these realities in this film?

PB: I don't like pretentious claims like that.

Q: Is all this related to your own personal experiences with your own search?

PB: No, the hell with my personal experience. Every minute of life is a personal experience. That's unimportant. You can't work without becoming aware that there is a responsibility in the work you're doing, and that responsibility is what makes the work interesting. So there can never be a real conflict between what's responsible and what's interesting. The two end up going hand in hand. The responsibility is to look for work that has some meaning, rather than to look for work that has no meaning. That is a constant, developing search, which turns you to more and more specific fields. To me, there's no choice. It's not as though at this moment I might be doing something else. There's no conflict. This is the most interesting task. To do something that comes out of my own fantasy and all by myself is obviously much less interesting than to do something with a person whose experience is totally different from my own, and with whom I can make certain links through this work. I have made this choice. That's all.

Q: Let's talk about the actual filming of *Meetings with Remarkable Men*. What did you gain by going to Afghanistan to do this film?

PB: It's a very interesting thing, because one always wants a film to be real. It's just like this double thing of acting. You know that acting is unreal and you want it to be real. And that's fine. It should be both at once. You know that a film is a fiction; it isn't really taking place; it's done with microphones, cameras, lights; and you want it to be real. But the artifices of filmmaking for the most part are not real.

Let me take the simplest example: the art of makeup. In a way, makeup artists are very limited people. They can't really give to a face lines that come from a deep inner humanity. They can paint lines on that face. They can do it cunningly, so that you don't quite realize the lines are painted. But they cannot turn that face into one that comes from real human experience—from a living human being.

Q: How does this all apply to your going to Afghanistan?

PB: Okay. The first reason for going to Afghanistan, a beautiful country, was not for its landscapes, but for its faces. In Afghanistan, more than in many Eastern countries, there is still a deep, ancient way of life, not completely destroyed, which has a harmony, integrity, a quality that no makeup artist can touch, but which every camera can see, which is the look in the eyes. No technique can give a look to people's eyes except something that comes from deep sources that very few people know. In Afghanistan, any day of the week in the bazaar, you see more people with depth in their look.

Q: Couldn't that look be found anywhere else in the West?

PB: In the same way, in the West there are places you can go, in the subway, for example, and see more people with vacant looks, tragically vacant looks. If you wanted to take photographs, as Cartier-Bresson has done, of empty faces, you go into the subway and you can get hundreds of them; it's tragic and a comment on a whole way of living. If you want to get people in difficult circumstances, in acute poverty, which can't be sentimentalized, but who nonetheless have a fiber in their being, if you want to show that, you go to Afghanistan, and go to the bazaar.

Q: Did you choose Afghanistan because Gurdjieff went there, as well?

PB: Well, the first reason was for this strength and spirituality genuinely reflected in the Afghan people. True, it is among the places that Gurdjieff did visit in his travels and talked about. We had to find one country that brought together, more than any other, all the elements of his search. I felt that more in Afghanistan than anywhere else. So Afghanistan is not about Afghanistan. The film is about many different countries at a time when there was a quality across the Middle East that is still there in Afghanistan today.

Q: I'm sorry I missed the opportunity to watch you film there.

PB: Well, it's your own fault. You were genuinely alarmed and worried about the conditions of the place. I pooh-poohed that and said it was nonsense to be worried, because I knew we were building a great camp in the best European conditions. But when we got there we not only saw the heat and the amount of walking involved, but, on top of that, we were in a panic discovering that there was this great snake-infested area by the camp, which then had to be abandoned. Then I thought you were right; we were not going to bring you into that situation. I have, as you know, a taste for this kind of thing—in Africa, and in this film. It wasn't nearly as tough as Africa, but it was for our unit. Everybody was ill; they were all suffering. The heat, the snakes. After what we went through in Africa, I didn't think anything else seemed particularly difficult anymore. But sandstorms, earthquakes—

Q: Sandstorms, earthquakes? It was worse than I thought it would be.

PB: Yes, we had an earthquake. A minor one. The heat. The extremes of heat. When I would go around and say good morning to the unit, it was like making rounds in a hospital, because "Hello, how are you?" was not a routine question.

Q: Well, I'm glad I missed it. I wouldn't have survived that.

PB: We had about a third of the unit ill every single day. From that point of view, we took an incredible risk, particularly because we didn't want—for reasons that I've talked about—to make this film in the Western way. We did not want to go, in a completely insulated way, into a foreign country and impose filmmaking on that country, and then go away again. We wanted to do it our way, which was to be in as close relation as possible with the country itself, in order to capture something of its quality. We undertook a long preparation, went back to the country, talked to people, and established relations. In the end, the help we got from the Afghans was absolutely staggering. Nobody can believe this, but we did not experience the popular Western filmmaking myth that everybody is inefficient in foreign countries. In fact, not only did we get out of Afghanistan ahead of schedule with very, very difficult things to do but there was not one single holdup during the entire production due to local conditions. It's unbelievable. People go to Egypt, to Turkey [and come back] with all their stories of "mañana." They say that all over the world, it is "mañana" except at home. Cars don't turn up and trucks don't turn up and people forget. Not a bit of this in Afghanistan. It did not happen one single time. Everything the Afghans promised came through.

Q: How did you manage with everybody being sick? How did you get production going with people having diarrhea all day long?

PB: Because we had a very capable and devoted English unit. They came, and they stayed away, and came back again.

Q: They stayed in bed for the day and came back the next day?

PB: And some didn't stay in bed. They just tottered away in the bushes and came back again.

Q: But you didn't become ill?

PB: No, not once.

Q: You're fantastically strong. You didn't become ill in Africa, either?

PB: No. In Africa, it was very amusing. As long as everybody was eating the European food that we brought with us, almost everybody got ill. Then there came the time when a few of us started eating in markets, and then gradually others followed. When we really started eating in the markets—meatballs and things like that, straight off of street corners—nobody was ill from then on.

Q: Perhaps by that time you had developed a certain kind of bacteria in your body that was able to help.

PB: The worst time is the beginning. Heat will get you, too.

Q: Was the most difficult problem in Afghanistan the illness of the actors and the crew?

PB: The subject of the film. Just making the film.

Q: Do you want to elaborate on that?

PB: I think it was difficult all the time.

Q: What was the specific difficulty? Did the film have a special problem? In reading the book, I would assume it would have.

PB: The problem is that Gurdjieff spoke a great deal about quality—how ordinary things exist on different levels of qualities. The whole film is about qualities of experience. Which you can only capture by a certain quality of work; filmmaking is collective; everyone concerned has to produce work of a certain quality. This is always difficult; the harder the conditions, the harder it becomes. Something the unit was very aware of and something we talked about on the very first day. The specific thing about this film is that we were trying to reach a certain quality. To reach that, it must be a true reflection of the quality that everyone brings to it.

Q: I would assume a lot depended on the actors' understanding of the subject—the Gurdjieff personality and his work. How did the actors get involved with this subject matter?

PB: We rehearsed a lot.

Q: But did you work with them in any particular way because the film was a bit different? What did they know about Gurdjieff?

PB: We found that it was absolutely impossible for any actor to work on the film blindly. We started to rehearse every actor before we started filming. The rehearsal process was absolutely a mystery. You don't rehearse a film like you do a play, of course. So it's wrong to talk about rehearsals being solely preparation. Rehearsals for films are a different sort of thing. It's a form of preparation that involves everything, from exercises to discussions, to working on the specific scenes. But without that work, it would be impossible for any one of the actors to function, because they need some things to lean on that are useful, something of their own experience. Which can only be awakened by preparation and work. Otherwise, they are just going from the top of their head.

Q: So the actor playing Gurdjieff has to know something about Gurdjieff? How did you cope with that? You pick an actor for a certain quality as an actor, not for what he knows. It must have been quite a problem.

PB: But then he has to work. It goes for any actor studying any part.

Q: You mean he has to study Gurdjieff, the man and his work?

PB: He has to know a lot about it, as much as he can.

Q: Well, how did that work out?

PB: That's sort of basic. An actor can't just play Churchill; he has to know the background. It's a big role; he knows the background. This is a richer role, so he has to know more. He had to get interested.

Q: Was that possible—to know something of Gurdjieff's experience? Churchill is a different thing. It is easy to find out about Churchill.

PB: It's a difference of degree. No actor can play a character if there's no sympathy. Sympathy means you've already got some seed of experience. If you've got some seed, it can grow. If you haven't got a seed, it can't grow. That's why you often find ridiculous, absurd casting. People who try to impersonate without having the seed. That's just bad casting. Good casting means that the person isn't the thing itself. He has the seed of it. Ryszard Cieslak (the brilliant Polish actor) isn't the sort of village idiot fool, the lead he played in Grotowski's *Apocalypsis cum Figuris*. But he has the seed.

Q: And a certain kind of madness, yes.

PB: Which he blows up for the occasion.

Q: People say that the Gurdjieff groups and the Gurdjieff Work have always been secretive. Was this a deliberate choice by the Gurdjieff people to make this film, and to come out in the open? Or did you just want to give people a taste of his life?

PB: Those aren't questions that should be put to me. I'm not a spokesman for the Gurdjieff Work, or the Gurdjieff Foundation.

Q: Okay. How does this film fit into the pattern of your work in the theater? Is this a continuation of the *Orghast* production? Is this part of your research?

PB: I don't think I'm self-conscious in that way. Heaven forbid, I don't have a theory of what my work is and then put things in or outside it. I think it's the other way around. You understand the relation of things. You understand the events in your life only backward, afterward, looking back. And then you say, of course, one thing leads to another. Because if you do anything other than that, you come to the most horrendously puritanical position of following intellectual lines, of thinking what your life's work ought to be, and you end up taking yourself—your life and work—too seriously.

Q: I still wonder how everything fits together. And how you make certain choices.

PB: Everything is part of the whole.

Q: But your choice in making this film certainly presented difficulties that you would not have had with ordinary filmmaking?

PB: What we have been doing here from the start is making a film whose content is very special and has nothing to do with the ordinary run of moviemaking—but whose images dictate all the normal elements of big-feature production, or any great big epic film. There's no shortcut. Whatever the inner meaning of the film, it is still on a big scale. At the same time, it has to be made on a budget of a quarter of what any self-respecting person making a big epic film would have. There is no shortcut to doing a scene. It wouldn't cost us any more, or less, money than if it had Charlton Heston in it. It's all the same thing. What's very attractive about the subject is that it has all those different things in it, but when all linked together, something quite different than an adventure story comes through. It is a spectacular film.

Q: What are your plans after the film?

PB: The preparation of this film has gone on with other things, as well. There was a time when I could do nothing full-time but this. But now, I long to get a holiday. But come what may, I have to pick up all the responsibilities—Paris and that group of actors, and, somewhere along the line, London and the Royal Shakespeare Company. And yet I continue with this enormous editing job.

Q: I understand that you are scheduled to do a production, as well. How do you expect to do that?

PB: Well, I have to do at least two at the Bouffes du Nord. We're doing *Ubu* because I hope that it's the one play I can do, after all this, with a different sort of energy.

Q: By the way, *Meetings with Remarkable Men* is considered by some to be esoteric. Do you want to comment on that?

PB: This is in no way an esoteric film. I believe that you need not make any concessions to reach a large public. To the best of my knowledge, I, never never made—in any form, whether in films or plays I've done—anything with a double-think. One "think" of what I want to do, and the other "think," of how to make this attractive to the public—that's something that I've never gone into at any point. I have always done something aimed at a large public or aimed at a small public. And to me, there's a great difference between making something destined for a large public and making concessions to a public. Those are quite different things. For instance, with *Dream* or *Marat/Sade,* we hit an enormously big public. That came from doing those plays to the limit of their own possibilities, and not by changing things, and soft-pedaling something, and distorting something else so that it would please. When we do something with the Center for a small public, it's for a small public. In both cases, we aimed to develop the work to its strongest state, knowing that certain types of experience, when they are authentic, cannot fail to interest a large number of people. My whole interest in Shakespeare is related to that—that something that touches such broad experience immediately produces a broad response. This is very much easier to achieve in the theater than in the cinema.

Q: Why is that so?

PB: In the theater, it is still relatively easy to find the means to go in any direction you want—the physical means. Because nothing in the theater costs so much that it's out of one's reach. Perhaps in New York, but nowhere else. In the cinema, you are immediately up against the contradiction that few possibilities exist for making something entirely true to its own elements—if those elements are serious ones—and, at the same time, making it for a large public. There is this strict division in the cinema between the esoteric and the popular. And that division is based on subject matter.

Q: It seems that making a film like *Meetings* would hardly appeal to a mass audience. If this is the case, how can you make such a film without compromising?

PB: I think it's completely possible with this theme to make something without concessions of any description. The material is tremendously serious in one way, and touches on so many aspects of people today that it can be immediately recognized and related to by a wide public.

Q: I don't see that the story of Gurdjieff, who was a spiritual teacher and largely unknown, can be of genuine interest to the main moviegoing public. How would you be able to overcome that?

PB: This project is in many ways unprecedented and totally unusual, but not in any way esoteric. Quite the opposite. The reason for this is that we're actually telling the story of a particular hero and his adventures. Up to now, I think Gurdjieff has begun to have a rather well-known name. But the actual man is so totally unknown: what the man was, what he represents. What images there are, are all based on very sketchy and usually completely distorted things from much later in his life. This figure, I think, is dramatic because he is actually a man of our time—whether he existed or not. That's what makes the book interesting. The hero of the book, called Gurdjieff, could be a work of the imagination, and could have a quite different name—and would still be a hero.

Q: Why is he a hero of our time?

PB: In each age and in each culture, certain figures come out of literature who crystallize a whole period. From Hamlet to the Russian heroes of the nineteenth century who spent all their days in bed and couldn't get up, or spent all their days sighing of boredom, or having duels with one another—these figures crystallize a time. Today, the image of a searcher is an idea that touches many people in many, many different ways. If there's one thing people—of different ages, of different backgrounds—have in common, it is searching. I think you could really divide the whole population into those who have given up searching and those who continue to search. That's the broadest division there is.

Q: Isn't this a bit abstract and arbitrary—this business of searchers? How does one differentiate between people who are searchers and those who are not? Why, in any case, make that a division? Are you about to divide the public into those who are educated or not, those who are open or not—or a million other divisions—and draw conclusions from that?

PB: Nobody really trusts, in any field, people who are other than searchers. Those who have the book, nobody trusts. Those who know it, nobody trusts. And those who have given up, those who don't know and don't care, nobody trusts, either. There are always different levels of the same idea. And you can say that the rebel is one step in this spectrum of searchers. The revolutionary, the rebel, the militant, the dropout, the punk rocker—all these are different steps on the ladder of something. The more powerful and richer form the searching takes, the less it's an act of dropping out and the more active the searching becomes. Perhaps there have been times where the warrior has been the epitome of the searcher . . .

Q: The warrior as searcher?

PB: There have been other societies, simple societies even, where the warrior is the epitome.

Q: How does all this relate to Gurdjieff and your making a film about him?

PB: I believe that, in this particular sense, Gurdjieff is seen, and is becoming more and more to be seen, as a dramatic figure. What's fascinating about Gurdjieff's book *Meetings with Remarkable Men* is that you cannot say what in it is biography and what is storytelling or imagination. He uses his own life as only a great, highly imaginative Oriental, Eastern storyteller could do. He uses all his own life, background, and material as a story to dramatize, and to make his points. It no longer matters whether it really happened, or what was dramatically invented through his imagination. The figure of himself in that book is a dramatic figure. He takes this generalization of the searcher, of the young student, the young rebel, the young man looking for God, and turns it into something unmistakably specific—something that bears a name, a place, an identity—all crystallized. My interest in turning the material into a film is precisely because it is dramatic. It makes a significant and real figure of today, who is there on the page, come to life in the strongest form there is. And the strongest form is the cinema.

London, 1978

Seven

Antony and Cleopatra

In between his filming of *Meetings with Remarkable Men,* his productions of *The Ik* and *Ubu* in Paris, and his preparation for his Indian project, *The Mahabharata,* which he was constantly working on, Peter Brook managed to direct what was to be his last production for the Royal Shakespeare Company: *Antony and Cleopatra,* starring Glenda Jackson and Alan Howard. It opened first in Stratford in October 1978 and then moved to London in June 1979. He had first worked with Ms. Jackson in his famous *Marat/Sade,* and Mr. Howard was his leading man in *A Midsummer Night's Dream.* Besides the two stars, the production also featured several well-known actors: Jonathan Pryce (Octavius Caesar), Patrick Stewart (Enobarbus), and David Suchet (Pompey), as well as some riveting music by Richard Peaslee, who had worked with Brook previously on *A Midsummer Night's Dream.*

Antony and Cleopatra ran for three and a quarter hours, which flew by swiftly, each scene rapidly melding into the next, as if it were a film. Brook had actually trimmed the play down—the work is enormous, with forty speaking roles and forty-two scenes, and takes place in numerous locations, both on land and at sea. But Brook managed to indicate through clever staging and some scenic maneuvering the scope of the drama, without any ceremonial pomp or lavish displays. Somehow in a miracle of staging, we were in Cleopatra's room one moment and then on the battlefield the next. Early in the production, Brook had managed to indicate the playing areas without actually doing an additional setup.

Sally Jacobs's setting was, as usual, pristine, sparse, minimalist—nothing superfluous, nothing spectacular or elaborate. There was a semicircle of opaque glass panels, which were rearranged as the play unfolded; a neutral-colored cloth served as the backdrop. One could see against the panels the battle, the stormy blue-green sea, the bloodstained corpses, and, silhouetted in black, some of the main characters, who stood in stony silence, witnesses to the ongoing tragedy. Colorful pillows, benches, stools, and cloths were the only visible decorations used to evoke the ambience of Rome and Egypt.

Glenda Jackson's performance was notable for its strength and force, if not for its sexuality, and Alan Howard was admired for being able to convey a sense of tragedy as well as the suggestion of a glorious past gone to hell. Some people faulted the stars for failing to create any heat between them, and some did not believe that Alan Howard's Antony would give up a kingdom for Ms. Jackson's Cleopatra.

Ms. Jackson was an unusually straightforward Cleopa-

Sally Jacobs's production design for the Royal Shakespeare Company's
production of *A Midsummer Night's Dream,* directed by Peter Brook.
(*Photograph by Sally Jacobs*)

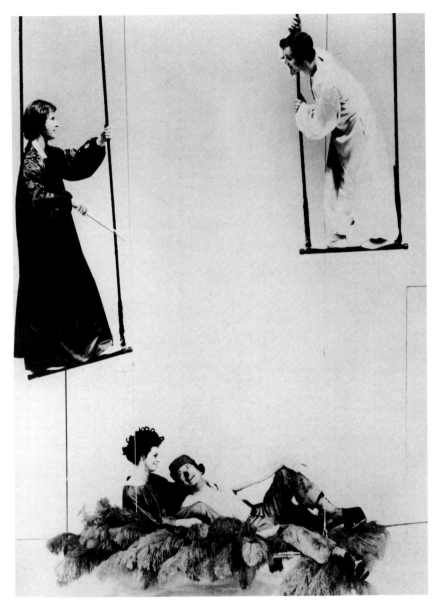

Alan Howard as Oberon, Sarah Kestelman as Titania, John Kane as Puck, and David Waller as Bottom in Peter Brook's Royal Shakespeare Company production of *A Midsummer Night's Dream,* New York, 1971. (*Photograph by David Farrell, London*)

Margaret Croyden and Peter Brook in conversation, New York, 1970.

The company in *Orghast* in Persepolis, Iran, during the Shiraz International Theater Festival. *Orghast*—written by Ted Hughes—was presented by Peter Brook's International Center for Theater Research, August 1971. (*Photograph by Nicholas Tikhomiroff*)

The British poet Ted Hughes (left) and Peter Brook during rehearsals of *Orghast*, August 1971. (*Photograph by D. Kinnane/UNESCO*)

Peter Brook at his studio doing the famous "stick" exercises with his international company and members of the Theater of the Deaf, who were visiting at the time; Paris, 1972. (*Photograph by David Hays*)

Peter Brook with his company in Africa. (*Photograph by Mary Ellen Mark*)

Helen Mirren, a member of
the company, acting for
young people.
(*Photograph by Mary Ellen Mark*)

Dragan Maksimovic as G. I. Gurdjieff in the Peter Brook film *Meetings with Remarkable Men,* which was filmed in Afghanistan in 1978. (*Photograph by Remar Productions*)

Peter Brook directs Mikica Dimitijevic as the young G. I. Gurdjieff in a scene from *Meetings with Remarkable Men,* Afghanistan, 1978. (*Photograph by Remar Productions*)

The company in the Peter Brook production of *The Conference of the Birds* at Ellen Stewart's La Mama Theater in New York, 1980. (*Photograph by Enguerand*)

The company in a scene from *The Ik,* presented at the La Mama Theater in New York, 1980. (*Photograph by Enguerand*)

Carmen (Patricia Schuman) and Escamillo (Carl John Falkman) at the tavern near Seville in one of the famous scenes in Peter Brook's production of *La Tragédie de Carmen,* presented by Alexander Cohen at the Vivian Beaumont Theater at Lincoln Center for the Performing Arts in New York, 1983. (*Photograph by Martha Swope*)

The Mahabharata: the young warriors taking instruction for the battle. The company in New York, 1987. (*Photograph by Gilles Abegg*)

The Mahabharata: the final battle. The company in New York, 1987. (*Photograph by Gilles Abegg*)

Bakary Sangaré as Ariel and Sotigui Kouyaté as Prospero in Peter Brook's production of *The Tempest* at Les Bouffes du Nord, Paris, 1990. (*Photograph by Gilles Abegg*)

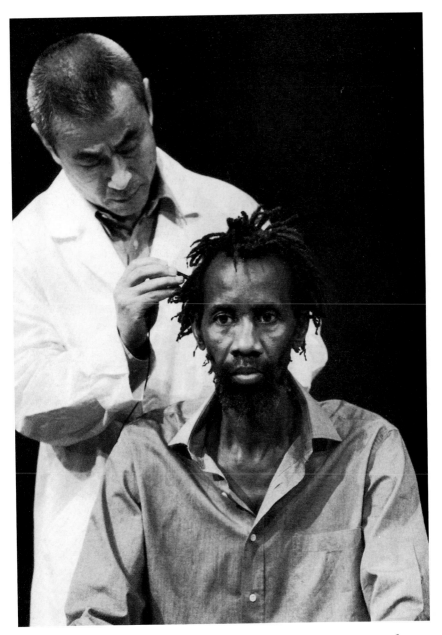

Yoshi Oda as a doctor and Sotigui Kouyaté as a patient in a scene from Peter Brook's *The Man Who* at Les Bouffes du Nord, Paris, 1993.
(*Photograph by Gilles Abegg*)

The Tragedy of Hamlet at Les Bouffes du Nord, Paris, 2000.
(*Photograph by Pascal Victor/MAXPPP*)

tra, a mature woman with a strong character, a powerful voice, and a determined and commanding presence on-stage (not a sex kitten, which some reviewers might have hoped for). She startled some people when she appeared with her own short-cropped hair (not the wig usually worn for this kind of role), adding a sense of modernity to the play, which, one presumed, was part of Brook's conception. Dressed in plain-looking caftans and flowing skirts, she wore no elaborate jewelry or accessories, except for thick bracelets on both her wrists and, in one scene, an African headdress made of cloth. Clearly, her wardrobe suggested Egypt without actually denoting it.

Most of the critics appreciated the cleverness and originality of the production and Brook's ability to stage this massive play by concentrating heavily on the central issue between the lovers. But some felt that because of this, the production almost bordered on a domestic drama, rather than conveying a power struggle between two giant states. But Richard Eder, writing from London for the *New York Times,* said, "It is a production of great intelligence and some startling moments of discovery. At no point does Mr. Brook's artistic energy obscure or distract from the dramatic and poetic lines of the play. Almost invariably it is used to clarify them, to preserve them, to nudge things back in balance whenever the force of a particular performer with a particular line provides a momentary blinding distraction. *Antony and Cleopatra* is full of such dazzlement; the director curbs it without dimming it."

——————————— • ———————————

Q: Why did you return to Shakespeare after so many years?

PB: Because I had never left it. I've always said, and proved by my actions, that Shakespeare is always the source. Because Shakespeare has shown something which, if he hadn't existed, everyone would have argued was not possible. Outside Shakespearean theater, there's been a division between popular and esoteric theater, and the belief that all the fragments of the theater exist simply as fragments because they can't be combined. People who make avant-garde, intellectual plays don't believe that they can combine that with popular theater. In my book *The Empty Space,* I make this division between the "rough" and the "holy" theater. In the chapter about the "rough" theater, I talk about Brecht; and in the chapter about the "holy" theater, I talk about Beckett. And then the last chapter brings them both together. These are arbitrary divisions, much like the masks that come from Greek theater. A smiling, a frowning, and a scowling mask are arbitrary masks, like the mask of comedy and the mask of tragedy. And, in fact, in real life, tragedy and comedy intertwine all the time; so does the spiritual and the gross. If the theater is a reflection of real life, then in the theater there is a place for everything. The only author who has totally captured this combination is Shakespeare—he was the only one who did this completely, although theoreticians try to prove that it's impossible; you can always prove that something's impossible. Only a creative person can demonstrate directly that it is possible. And Shakespeare demonstrated this possibility.

Q: How do you use Shakespeare as your model when you're not directing Shakespeare?

PB: Our research work is Shakespearean and Elizabethan in the sense that we're trying to find a new form that can carry this same spectrum. The reason that we started work in Paris on *The Mahabharata*—and we really only started a year ago—is that this great Indian classic could be called Shakespearean. It's Shakespearean in the sense that it makes a link between the gods and clowns in everyday life in the most extraordinarily rich and comprehensive way.

For a long, long time, we've believed that to make Shakespeare come alive today, the people who work in Shakespeare must go away from Shakespeare, toward work that relates to their own times, and then come back to it. Because Shakespeare is perpetually contemporary. But you lose that sense if you treat Shakespeare the way the Grand Opéra treats grand opera—a closed crystal ball of its own.

Ever since I did my first production, when I was twenty, I've always done a bit of Shakespeare, and gone away. And have come back and gone away. Three years, five years. That's always been the rhythm, because I dread the idea of being a Shakespearean director who does nothing but Shakespeare plays. It would be completely false to all the work I do to completely lose contact with it, because it is always a source. And yet, anybody living in his or her time has another need, a responsibility to find other forms for that time.

Q: But you haven't explained why you chose *Antony and Cleopatra*. Why that play?

PB: Why that? Since I first started directing Shakespeare plays, they've always been the ones that I've felt closest to. *King Lear, A Midsummer Night's Dream, Antony and Cleopatra,* these are plays that I've always, always felt that, one day, I wanted to do. There are other plays that I'm delighted to see other people do: *Pericles, Cymbeline, Henry V.* I'm very interested to see a production of *Othello* but have no interest in doing it. No urge whatsoever . . . none of those touch any particular thing in my heart.

Q: Well, what is it that *Antony and Cleopatra* touches?

PB: First of all, I think that it's like *Lear,* a play that has been, up to now, an obstacle trap. It's been something that has tripped up people for a long time—perhaps a century—for quite precise reasons. As a result, the play has never been seen. So it's a new play. It's a new play by Shakespeare. I've seen it a few times and I've never seen performances of it, never seen the play. That's one reason.

Q: Well, how was it tripped up, as you say?

PB: Very rarely has it been done by adequate actors. First of all, there is a misunderstanding about Cleopatra, as well as a misunderstanding about Antony. The misunderstanding about Antony is a Victorian one. Everything wrong with Shakespeare anywhere can be traced back to the Victorian conception of Shakespeare, which was the other side of the moon; the exact opposite. If anything is true in relation to Shakespeare, the Victorian is the exact opposite. Because the Victorian climate, and the Victorian era, and the Victorian worldview are at the other end of the pole from the Elizabethan. And the Victorian influence spread right into our century, based on the grand actor-manager tradition.

Q: How did that tradition play a negative role in producing Shakespeare?

PB: In that tradition, it was not playing Shakespeare for
what the plays were, but for the opportunities that
they gave actors. Antony was considered an inferior
part to Cleopatra. As Antony, actors—male actors—
were always selfish monsters; few selfish monsters
could be found who would adequately support the
lady, the bigger part. Add to this the machismo of the
period. A man toiled for four acts—Antony dies at
the end of the fourth act—and there's a whole fifth
act, where Cleopatra steals all the glory. So no out-
standing tragedian would play the part of Antony.
Much as in *Boris Godunov.* When I staged it, I had a
tremendous fight with the opera singers about wanting to do Mussorgsky's original version, where after
the death of Boris, there's the greatest scene in the
opera, the scene of the revolution. And every time
there's been a production of that, a leading singer
would use his influence, and the scenes would be re-
versed, so that the last scene of the opera is not the
great revolutionary scene, but the death of the leading character.

It's exactly that same ridiculous operatic set of
values that plagues *Antony.* Because of this, the part
of Antony has got a bad reputation. Like the part of
the Duke in *Measure for Measure,* one of the greatest
parts in Shakespeare, has been discarded as a great
role because Angelo is considered the more showy
part.

Q: It is hard to see how these considerations actually influenced a Shakespeare production.

PB: Well, over the last twenty years, all these things have changed. The minor plays have suddenly been seen for all their great virtues. Plays like *Timon of Athens* and *Titus Andronicus* have been seen for being remarkable plays. The part of Antony is still waiting, we discovered. Occasionally when major actors have played it, they based it on a misunderstanding: that because Antony is a middle-aged general, he is a tired man. And so, theatrically, they are consequently very uninteresting. In fact, if you look at the actual play, you can see that not only is the action very close to us today but the characters all have their contemporary equivalents.

Q: Contemporary equivalents? Such as?

PB: The contemporary equivalent, for instance, is no less than the Israeli general Moshe Dayan, who, like Antony, is dealing with Egypt and who, at the age of sixty or sixty-five, is certainly not diminished in his force and vitality and his flamboyance, any more than any great general. If Antony isn't played from the premise of a man in full vigor, and is played as a man who is, at the start of the play, in decay, then we have exactly the same thing that happens if Lear is played as a gaga old man. Lear has to be played by a youngish actor. Paul Scofield played Lear when he was in his forties, for instance, but he was acting a man of eighty. But it's not at the age of eighty, or eighty-five or ninety, that you can play King Lear. Because you have to bring all the passion, vigor, and vitality of a man in his prime to illuminate King Lear.

Q: So your idea was to cast an actor, preferably someone who could bring all the passion and vitality of someone in his prime, to play the greatest general of Rome?

PB: Yes, of course. Antony realizes that because he is in love with Cleopatra and he's living in Egypt doesn't mean that Rome is no longer of interest to him. I'd say that it is exactly the other way around. You ask me why I've gone to Africa, or Iran, to do all those experiments? Because being English and working all these years in Stratford-on-Avon, and touching the greatest theatrical material with the very best means, how could I possibly throw all that away? Everything has to come in its right rhythm. And certainly I've got a very intense need to return from time to time to Shakespeare—in relation to particular Shakespearean subjects that touch me greatly.

Q: What is there about *Antony and Cleopatra* that you think is relevant for today? Is it the two worlds? Is it the whole idea of the union of the East and West through Egypt?

PB: I find that you can never talk about Shakespearean themes without belittling them and trying to pinpoint them. And I feel, as I did about *Lear* when we did it, that *Antony* is highly relevant. But then the moment you say it's relevant, that it's like this and like that, it disappears. I felt *A Midsummer Night's Dream* was relevant. And it was. But not for reasons that could be pinpointed as easily as in *Marat/Sade,* and yet the people who saw it found it as close to them. So I can only state the fact that I feel very strongly about *Antony,* and the work we're doing to express that. He is a man who, having lived one life totally, begins to lead two lives totally—in two hemispheres. In two hemispheres, which you can say are two worlds, even spiritually two worlds, where he leads a total life. But each world could be a hundred percent world. Like a brilliantly successful general, like Patton or Rommel, Antony is a general who becomes a president, so he is like Patton, Kennedy, and Dayan combined. His world of action is a totally demanding world. And yet, having reached this point of total success and total command, he feels that there is another world, and finds that other world through a combination of a woman and a place—Cleopatra and the East. In leading a double life—many of us lead a double life—he leads it a double hundred percent. And a double hundred percent is something rare. And rationally impossible. And the tragedy, because it's a tragic story, the tragedy of Antony comes from a man attempting the impossible, which is to bring together a double hundred percent world.

Q: What does that mean, a "double hundred percent"?

PB: Well, both existences, both worlds, demand not fifty percent of his devotion and his commitment, but a hundred percent. So there you have the double hundred percent.

Q: Is that what appeals to you most about *Antony and Cleopatra*—the double life?

PB: Well, you know quite well that's the sort of question I don't answer. But it is one of the things that appeals to me. Equally the part of Cleopatra, which has led to a great misunderstanding. Shakespeare uses, somewhere in the play, the word *gypsy* metaphorically, [spoken] by a man who dislikes Cleopatra and wishes to abuse her. This has set up a tradition in Europe in which the middle-aged, sexy woman in a national theater anywhere in Europe, who has curves and flashing eyes and is considered sexy, is told to play Cleopatra.

Q: So Cleopatra has been reserved for the sexy, voluptuous woman, or someone's conception of gypsies?

PB: Yes. In fact, Cleopatra is a very curiously complex part. From the moment that I started working with Glenda Jackson a long, long time ago, I felt that she could play it. And before we did *Marat/Sade,* I used to say two things to Glenda when we started working on our first season: "You're one of the great actresses of the world" and "It is quite clear that one day you're going to play Cleopatra."

I don't say that she's the only person who can play it. Because there are great actresses who have played it and who can play it. But she is the one to whom I'm closest, because of all our work together, and I thought right away that she should play it, but she was too young at that time. So, this is a project with Glenda begun over fifteen years. I've just been waiting quietly for her to be old enough. And now she's the right age.

Q: Well, I understand your feeling about Antony, but I don't get your feeling about Cleopatra. Do you consider her not really very sexy?

PB: No, I'm not saying that she isn't sexy. She isn't a sexy lady in the obvious sense. I said that that has caused another misunderstanding. The word *gypsy* has influenced much too much of the play, and at the expense of the fact that Antony and Cleopatra are inseparable. You have to have a pair of actors, a pair you can work with in exactly the same way as you would in *Romeo and Juliet.* If you do *A Midsummer Night's Dream,* you have to have a team of actors. In *King Lear,* you have to have not only Lear but the daughters and the Fool. To do *Measure for Measure,* you have to have a Duke and an Angelo and an Isabella, or it's not really worth attempting. In *Antony and Cleopatra,* just to have Cleopatra as a sexy lady in a vacuum means nothing. It has to be Antony and Cleopatra simultaneously.

Q: So was it your idea that Glenda Jackson and Alan Howard were the perfect couple for this play?

PB: Alan Howard, as an actor, is in full vitality, and Glenda is in full vitality at the right age, and together they bring forth a play bursting and flowing and exploding with power. And it isn't a history. It is a play about life in the most brilliantly kaleidoscopic way. It has got more scenes than any other play of Shakespeare's—about forty scenes, [although] some are only four or five lines long. The effect is like a Jackson Pollock: You actually can see the action, and the actual vitality of the movement of the interrelating fragments in this kaleidoscope. That's why all the people involved in it, all the leading actors, have to bring into a middle-age story a tremendously powerful, youthful energy.

Q: You were talking about the youthful energy despite the fact that they're middle-aged, but Alan Howard, your Antony, is comparatively young. He is still playing romantic leads.

PB: Well, you know this has become quite a good fashion in Shakespeare, which is to downscale all the ages in all the plays relatively. And if you look at the sort of actors playing twenty years ago, you'll find now that all the ages have come down about fifteen or twenty years. All through Shakespeare.

Q: That's true with *Romeo and Juliet,* yes. But there it is appropriate.

PB: Oh, in everything. When we did *Timon of Athens* in Paris, Timon was considered an elderly man, but our actor played him as a man of thirty. I think it is good that today the theater is less naturalistic. The imagination comes into play in Shakespeare in the way the imagination is supposed to. And the actor is there to tell a story, and to conjure up the story. And so now today, one can see that a young actor can suggest, and conjure up, what's needed by his vitality, by the truth of what he's saying, and that maybe the young actor today has a flexibility and a freedom that enables him to conjure up a more compelling picture than an older actor. Anyway, Alan Howard is not a young actor in acting terms. He has done his apprenticeship and reached maturity in playing Shakespeare. And so he is now an actor for the mature roles.

Q: You always say you search for something special in these plays. Did you find something particular that you were searching for in *Antony and Cleopatra*?

PB: Yes, I did.

Q: What was that?

PB: I'll tell you after this interview.

Q: Oh, come on Peter . . .

PB: No, I can't speak about the real, central things that can only be expressed through the production. Because the reason one does a production is because one can't say what one has to say by words. You can say just so much in words, and then you do a production. That's why there is a complete gap that can never be filled by the academic and the practical theater person in relation to Shakespeare. Because the language with which you can talk about Shake-

speare, the legitimate language, is not discussion, description, analysis. It is making the plays reveal their
secrets in performance. Once that has happened, you
can, along with everyone else, talk about what you
think is there.

Q: I presume you have a certain objective in mind, a
certain aim when you work on a play. Do you communicate that to the actors? Do you ever discuss your
conception with them?

PB: If you are looking for a mystery, looking for an
enigma, you can't tell people what you're looking
for, because it would cease to be a mystery or an
enigma. It's very simple. What you can do is to make
actors aware through the way that you work that any
great play by Shakespeare exists at least on two levels. There is the apparent play. And then there is
something more hidden behind the apparent play—
common to all the great plays by Shakespeare. The
balance between the apparent play and the hidden
play is clearer in some plays and less clear in others.
In *The Tempest,* it's quite clear that there is an external play, and then a hidden play. As in *The Magic
Flute*. There is a pantomime for children, and then
something infinitely bigger hidden away behind it.
The two go together. It's through that attractive and
naïve form that something more comes into life.

In all fairy stories, one knows that there are three
things. There is the naïve story, told as a bedtime
story to children, and then something infinitely darker,
and then, much more powerful, real background material. In *A Midsummer Night's Dream,* we worked
on two plays: the apparent play and the play lurking
behind it. In performance, it was the play that was

lurking behind it that penetrated and touched audiences. Often without them knowing it. And in some plays, it's very difficult to see that the two exist.

Q: What is the hidden play in *Antony*? What is "lurking" behind the text?

PB: *Antony* is less a chronicle and a history than a play that carries inside it an equally hidden play. The hidden play can't be described. I can't give you a lecture about it. It can only be revealed by acting, and the techniques that make actors reveal it are, in a way, very simple.

Q: Now that you're talking about it, what are these techniques? Is it possible to be more concrete, or give an example?

PB: They are techniques that encourage the actor to search for the hidden play. In archaeology, for example, for trained archaeologists to find a hidden and as-yet-unknown Egyptian tomb, the first step is for someone to take them to a place and produce good reason for the archaeologist to believe that there is a tomb buried in what otherwise looks like an ordinary strip of ground. The moment he has been convinced that that exists, he uses his special gifts to start researching, digging, and eventually finding it. It's the same way with actors. It's not a question of telling them what they're going to find hidden away, but of getting them to believe that there is something worth digging for.

Q: How do you get them to believe?

PB: That's what the business of rehearsal is about. It's creating a certain climate and exercising certain faculties until the climate and the exercise faculties come together.

Q: When you work with stars like Glenda Jackson and Alan Howard, how does this compare to your work with your group?

PB: There's no difference whatsoever. All my life, I've worked with known and unknown actors, with stars like Laurence Olivier and Alec Guinness, one of the first big stars I worked with, as well as with unknowns. Unlike the general public, I've never experienced any difference—

Q: Wait a minute . . .

PB: Except in the opera. And that's why I've given up the opera, because the opera is a ridiculous world. You have to waste too much time on ridiculous things. I've had the fortunate experience that I've never worked with famous actors. I've only worked with good actors. I mean, I'm sure that this monstrous thing called a star exists. And from what one hears, it exists in movies. But I've never worked with those people. I've only worked with very good actors who also happen to have a high reputation. But when one comes down to work, work is work, and a part is a part, and an actor is an actor. And one works in exactly the same way. And if it weren't so, I couldn't go on working with them.

Q: Do you do improvisations with them?

PB: If I were to find myself working with somebody who could just as easily be a young actor whose ego prevents him opening himself, we would part company within a matter of hours, so that question doesn't arise. But here, in the case of Glenda and Alan, one is dealing not with two stars, but with two artists. And a good artist is a good artist.

Q: Why did you go back to the Royal Shakespeare Company for this production?

PB: Because I never left it. You could look at the stationery. I've been one of the directors of the RSC right from the start. I'm in constant touch. I'd hate to perpetuate this myth that suddenly, one day, I gave up the legitimate theater, because it's totally untrue. As far back as I can remember, I have worked in many spheres at once. The work of research and the work of big-scale theater have always been necessarily interconnected. Over the years, the work has taken different forms. My first experimental group goes back fifteen years, within the Royal Shakespeare Company—before groups of this sort existed anywhere else in the world. It was group work, exercises, improvisations, work on sound; it was fifteen or sixteen years ago. It was the Royal Shakespeare Company that made that happen, and paid the actors a small sum of money, and provided the rehearsal hall. That research work led eventually to *Marat/Sade,* and it was with the Royal Shakespeare Company. Glenda Jackson was part of that. That research work led to the first international season in Paris with a number of people from the Royal Shakespeare Company. *The Tempest,* the work we did in '68 in the Roundhouse, was financed in London. All that work led straight into *A Midsummer Night's Dream.* And *Dream* was connected in many ways to the work that we continued to do with the Paris group, when the Paris group came to London. With *The Ik,* it was the Royal Shakespeare Company that presented it. All this time Trevor Nunn [then director of the RSC] and I were in constant touch. I mean, my being physically in Paris, and all over the world, did prevent my attendance at all meetings of the governing bodies, which I had been able to attend some years back. But I've never broken my relationship to the Royal Shakespeare Company, which fundamentally is an essential organism to which I've been connected here at Stratford for thirty years. So I have no reason to lose that connection. It is a strand of my work. The possibilities of my doing Shakespeare through this organization are very special ones.

Q: Now, about your Paris production of *Measure for Measure*. You have done it a couple of times.

PB: I've only done *Measure for Measure* once, at Stratford. It's one of the few plays I've done a second time.

Q: With Gielgud, you mean?

PB: Yes, it was over twenty-five years ago.

Q: But why are you doing it in French?

PB: Because we've got a theater in Paris that we're running in a very special way. We don't play nearly as often as other theaters, so that the theater is also our Center. To make the research we want to do possible, we have to produce things that are very bold and strong for a big public. I want to fulfill that need in a way that carries no compromise. There's a need and an interest to see Shakespeare in France—to see Shakespeare done by an Englishman. And to see Shakespeare done through translations that have been done by somebody who understands the background and the language. This need corresponds to something that, for me, is no compromise, because I can do a play of Shakespeare's anytime with the

same devotion and interest. If I were to do a commercial comedy to pay our way in the theater, that
would be a very strong compromise. I can do Shakespeare there, knowing that this is what everyone
wants more than anything else from an Englishman
living in France.

Q: But if you are doing it in translation, doesn't that
make it difficult for you?

PB: For me, it is interesting precisely because of the
problem of translating Shakespeare into French, and
of finding actors from a totally different tradition who
can interpret it—and that the result may take on a
different quality. The *Timon of Athens* that we did in
Paris is different from the *Timon* done in English, different because in translation, the play has become
more direct and more immediate. So that there is
something that is lost and something that is gained.
All of this, plus the fact that one can then appeal to a
wide audience, which is what we want to do, makes
it very interesting to do Shakespeare with our group
in France.

But there is another overriding reason, which is
the most powerful. And that is that everything that
this international group has been doing since we
started is a step toward our big Indian project—*The
Mahabharata*. For the group to be prepared for *The
Mahabharata,* it had to have experience in many different forms of theater. *The Ik,* the African journey,
and its improvisations were one necessity. *Orghast*
was another necessity; *Ubu* was another necessity;
the Shakespeare plays were another. So that the actors are all totally qualified through their own direct
experience to work as a team, because that's what

we're doing to make a vast play out of this Indian material. And for that, the group has had to learn— we've all had to learn together—how to live together, how to make a journey together, how to draw the essence out of a journey together. How to work freely in forms belonging to foreign cultures. How to bridge cultures. These are all things that very good actors experience. For instance, in the Royal Shakespeare Company, it's obviously a quite different world because of our different aims. But having a direct model of a theater devoted to Shakespeare is vital.

Q: I see that. But I don't see how your doing the English *Antony and Cleopatra* now, with no one from your group—it's just a star production—fits in with your work in Paris. How does all this relate to *The Mahabharata,* since no actor from your group is involved with *Antony*?

PB: Because I want to do it. It's as simple as that.

Q: Yes, I understand that you wanted to do it; otherwise, you wouldn't. It's just that it's a strange sidestepping, this *Antony and Cleopatra*. One wonders why you have to do this when you have your work cut out for you with your group in Paris. Perhaps you need this as a commercial venture?

PB: This isn't a sidestepping at all. I'll put it completely the other way around. It is possible to live many lives at once. It's as simple as that. I've made seven films. If I had done nothing but make seven films, this would be very clear, and, from a journalistic point of view, highly satisfying. Because there're lots of film directors who have made only seven films. I can think of quite a few eminent directors who spend several years surviving on that sort of rhythm—making a film and then digesting it, and then making another. Nobody would think that one is wasting one's time if one's made only seven films. To have directed a chain of Shakespeare's plays is also considerably honorable. Only to have worked with an experimental group would be, as well. But one feeds the other. The only thing is that it prevents me from having a holiday.

Q: Do you have your own personal reasons for doing this play?

PB: It's quite simple. Somebody says to you, "You're a journalist, so how can you write a book?" You can see that that is a totally absurd question. You can answer, "Because I wanted to write a book." But that isn't it. It's a different interrelated thing, and the action week after week doesn't prevent you from writing a book. In exactly the same way, I have relationships, like the relationship with my children, that don't prevent me from having other relationships. I have a relationship with Shakespeare—a relationship that goes back to the first production, which I did when I was twenty. And out of that, there is a line of developing and evolving work. It's a line of research, if you like, which makes me get deeper into certain plays. Because each one of the plays deepens one's possibilities. The more one understands the play in making a valid presentation of it, the more one understands something very considerable about a certain aspect of life. I mean, the play is an investigation; it's a creative investigation of life. If you happen to be connected with something of such power as the territory opened by being in a living link with Shakespeare—this is inexhaustible. And so one is fortunate to have that link, as I have. So I purely appreciate what I've got, and I am not being cavalier about it, either.

Q: Let's get back to the production. What about the design of the play? Can you tell me anything about that—the colors, or the sets, or anything that could give some picture of what it might look like?

PB: No. Because Sally Jacobs, the designer, and I work in a very, very close way. And we have now a working system that's gone on for a number of productions over a number of years. Which is meeting in New York and designing in the Chelsea Hotel. And this was no exception.

Q: You met in the Chelsea Hotel and designed it there?

PB: Yes. It's a secret between us and the cockroaches. So that what people know most about are the different stages of the cockroaches at the Chelsea.

Q: But has it stayed the same since the Chelsea Hotel?

PB: No, because we never work that way. We evolve it, and then every few months we change and develop it. Her work is always inseparable from the play, and the understanding of the play that happens as one rehearses it. And she was with us in Africa.

Q: You're keeping this a secret?

PB: It's a secret now. Later, we can talk about it. I make the set that's going to seem right for the play. Neither Sally nor I impose an outside idea on the play. One makes the conditions in which the play can come to life. So for that reason, you can't talk about it. When I was much younger, I used to do productions—in a certain style—that I couldn't do anymore today. So I did *Love's Labour's Lost* in the style of Watteau. And I did the first *Measure for Measure* in the style of

Brueghel. And these came from a thinking that is quite different from what I think today. All the work I've been doing is so much harder . . .

Okay. The difficulty over *Antony and Cleopatra* is that, basically, I'm not talking to anybody because I just don't before something opens. I don't like making claims. I don't like showing what something's going to be. Because that's either pretentious or misleading. So what can I say? I mean . . . I don't like verbalizing about something which . . . after the event, turns out very differently. It's a very crude analogy, but it is like painting a picture. Once it's finished, you can talk about it. But while you're halfway there, and you're about to take up a tube of red, and then you look at it and decide to go to green instead . . . this is not something you can make a commentary on as you go along. And if you try to, it's not meaningful.

Q: How do you feel about the reception *Antony* may receive? You've got this great reputation with *Dream*. Does this make you nervous that people might be waiting for another *Dream*?

PB: Not a bit. I work for the sake of the work. I mean, this has happened before. *Dream* came after *Marat/Sade*. But in between these things, I do all sorts of things. And sometimes they catch people's attention, and sometimes they don't, but I go on working in the theater. Of course, it is always infinitely more satisfactory for something to be a success than for something to be a failure, for simple reasons. It's destructive and depressing to play to empty houses and to unconvinced people. But, in fact, with all the work we're doing with our Paris group—when we go to an

Algerian workers' hostel, or to a home for disabled
and handicapped people—every single time that one
does that with an improvisation, one has exactly the
same tensions as one has on a great Broadway opening night.

Q: How do you mean?

PB: If it goes well, everyone is totally elated in our group.
And we all know this, and talk about it among ourselves. If the improvisation goes badly, then everybody can be as destroyed, as they would be if they
were in *Sade* and getting bad notices after a great
opening. Because it is the work that counts. So here
it's exactly the same. I'm totally engaged in trying to
make *Antony* as good as possible. If it doesn't work
out, it would be less painful, in a sense, than if an
improvisation for a group of expectant Algerians in
a hostel goes badly. Because there something even
more intense is spoiled. If you've come among a
group of people full of expectations, and that's the
only thing that they've been promised for a long
time, and if it goes wrong, it's a disappointment. It is
not like big-scale theater, where if you don't like
what you see one night, you go elsewhere another
night. It's a question of the work and nothing else.

Q: You work in a variety of ways, and one wonders why
you go through all these different experiences. There
is the Gurdjieff film, *Meetings with Remarkable Men*.
And then you're running back to Paris to do *Ubu*,
and then preparing for the French production of
Measure for Measure. Then off to Venezuela. And
then rushing back to London to do this *Antony and
Cleopatra*. Then going on to finish the film. Then
maybe you take a short holiday. And then you have

this Indian project—*The Mahabharata*. What does all this running around mean?

PB: Living.

Q: Living?

PB: You said I look well.

Q: You do. You look very well.

PB: So there's your answer.

Q: But within this terrific activity, something else must be going on. It's not just work?

PB: The whole problem of success has to be seen much more simply. As I said, a success is more satisfying than a failure. Because everybody works for things to work well, rather than to work badly. Like an engine driver. But the aim is never the production as a separate goal. It isn't making it work that is a goal in itself. The goal is that one has a certain field, which actually has become one's own field, and the development of one's inner life and one's outer life are inseparable. In exactly the same way as the developing of something very personal and private and the developing of one's responsibility to the social scene that one's part of are also inseparable. And they all come from cultivating one's field. Now, if one happens to have one single field, one cultivates it as best one can. And that's why, if you happen to have a farm with a number of different fields—this goes right back to your question about Shakespeare—if you happen to be a farmer with a lot of fields, with a lot of different crops, and you have vegetables and fruit, you let some fields lie fallow for a certain time. And you cultivate, as best you can, the other fields. And you look after the animals, and you make your whole farm active. And a farmer goes from the bulls to the vegetables and to the orchards as a natural movement. And yet what he is doing is making his farm turn over. And in making his farm turn over, he is also living at the same time. Living the life that corresponds to him, and that makes him grow old as a better farmer. So that in that way, the richness and variety of one's own work and the development of one's own most intimate life can't be separated.

Q: Intimate life? You mean your inner life?

PB: Yes. I try to avoid that cliché. Because I think that this is one of the big myths about the East that has begun to be exploded now. It isn't by sitting and waiting cross-legged, or otherwise, that the inner life develops. The inner life develops through its interaction with the outer life. But they are all part of one life. It's easy in words to talk about inner and outer, but when you come down to it, you can't separate the two in such an easy way.

Stratford-on-Avon, 1979

Eight

The Ik, Ubu,

The Conference of the Birds

Peter Brook had been absent from the New York theatrical scene since his *Midsummer Night's Dream* in 1971, but in 1980 he returned to New York with his experimental troupe, organized by his International Center of Theater Research. For six weeks at Ellen Stewart's La Mama, a now-legendary Off-Broadway theater, Brook and his company offered in repertory four productions that represented a significant part of the exploratory work he and his group had been conducting in Paris, Iran, and Africa during the past decade. On the program was Alfred Jarry's *Ubu Roi*, preceded by a curtain-raiser, an African fable called *L'Os* (*The Bone*); *The Ik*, based on the book *The Mountain People*, by anthropologist Colin Turnbull; and a new version of *The Conference of the Birds*, by the twelfth-century Persian poet Farid Attar.*

*These four pieces had opened as individual productions beginning in 1975.

In a mood completely different from that of his *Dream,* with its white walls, flying disks, and airborne actors, Brook's work that year suggested a new path. Leaving theatrical artifice behind, he was concerned with what he called "the essentials"—the stripping away of unnecessary accoutrements in an effort to reach a new simplicity, a simplicity directed toward achieving a "unity" among actors, audience, and material. Nothing reflected this more than his production of *The Ik.*

Adapted from the Turnbull book and dramatized for the stage by Denis Cannan and Colin Higgins, *The Ik* is a true story about an African tribe in northern Uganda. When the Ik lost their traditional hunting territory and were unable to adjust to farming, they began to starve, losing, in the process, their culture and social structure. With a cast of six adults and two children, the actors themselves built the set to tell the story of their plight: a house made of sticks, a fire made of stones, and a floor strewn with dirt.

Devoid of sophisticated symbolism, and with no coup de théâtre, such as one would be accustomed to seeing in a Peter Brook production, the piece relied on the basics: the people and their story. And it is a harrowing story. One saw the once-proud Ik fighting over food, a child eating stones, an aged parent turned out of house and home for lack of food. All this was played without sentimentality or flourish. Brook had deliberately distanced the audience, mitigating the possibility of bathos associated with such material. There was a "here and now" quality to the acting; the cast sought to achieve perfect naturalism through highly integrated ensemble playing; their moments of stillness, ritual singing, and evocation of the Ik's language were stunning.

Ubu was quite different. The play is an exercise in

clowning, a chance for the actors to express their comedic expertise. The famous Alfred Jarry play—considered scandalous when it was first performed in 1896—is full of grotesque humor, scatological allusions, and mocking caricature, depicting the stupidity and rapaciousness of men and monarchs. A ridiculous flunky and his wife decide that they, too, can be monarchs, and they become embroiled in the power game of murder, usurpation, and flight. In the end, they are defeated—but not before leaving a trail of carnage all over Europe.

As a curtain-raiser to *Ubu,* Brook chose *L'Os (The Bone),* based on a story by the African writer Birago Diop and adapted for the stage by Malick Bowens, one of the actors in the company, and Jean-Claude Carrière, the screenwriter. *L'Os* is a farce about a man in a poor African village who, in order not to share a morsel of food—a bone—with his neighbor, pretends to be dead, only to be buried alive, bone and all, in the end.

Adapted into English by Brook, *The Conference of the Birds* combined the various modes in which the company had been working through the years. Essentially, *Conference* is mystical, but under Brook's direction, it was not without its farcical elements and lighthearted gaiety. In the six years since fragments of it had first been shown publicly, it was thoroughly reworked into a production replete with costumes and scenic elements by Sally Jacobs. *Conference* is an allegorical fable: A group of birds, seeing the world in a state of chaos, set out to find their king. In the course of the quest, some birds lose heart and die; those that survive discover that they are themselves the embodiment of their king, or the divine. Along the way, there is a bird leader, who encourages the others on their journey by telling stories that dramatize their weaknesses and foibles.

Implicit in the subtext, however, is a more sophisticated theme: the struggle to achieve greater knowledge and greater consciousness.

Conference was played on a bare stage, except for Oriental carpets hanging at the rear. The actors took on various roles: Sometimes they were the birds—a proud falcon, a wistful dove, an arrogant peacock—while at other times they were various characters in the story within the story told by the leader. They also employed handheld bird puppets and Balinese masks, as well as gestures that suggested tiny characteristics of the birds—a hand movement, a turn of the head, a crooked finger—with the rest left to the audience's imagination. Added to this was an assortment of esoteric Oriental and Occidental music: gongs, drums, birdcalls. Dialogue, as in a child's fairy tale, had been pared down to the essentials.

The production expressed the simplicity and esprit de corps that was the hallmark of Brook's work at the time and may well have been the direct—or indirect—result of Brook's journey in Africa, where the company had, from time to time, worked on this piece. With the engagement at La Mama, *The Conference of the Birds* had reached its final stage. Indeed, the performances were flawless—an example of the harmony of the ensemble and its ability to involve the audience in an unforgettable experience.

——————————————— • ———————————————

Q: The simplicity of *The Ik* seems like a Zen piece at times. Is that so?

PB: That's for you to say, not me.

Q: All right. Well, I mean, that's how it affected me. Did you actually use any elements of Zen? Or is that too much of a label to put on things?

PB: I'm very respectful of Zen as being a very great spiritual tradition. And I have a horror of exploiting ill-digested bits and pieces. And for that reason, I would never claim anything more than a sort of distant admiration of Zen.

Q: But it had this quality of happening in the here and now. In some ways, *The Ik* seemed also like a Noh play. It appeared so simple that some people asked, "Where are all the trimmings?"

PB: I think it's very important to say that we're bringing work that is unspectacular.

Q: Some wondered where the trapezes were. It's a complete departure from *A Midsummer Night's Dream*.

PB: At the time when everybody was talking about *Dream* as being inseparable from its trapezes and everything else, we did this big experiment, of playing *Dream,* without any of that, and found that what mattered most of all were the human relationships.

Q: And was this successful?

PB: Yes.

Q: I wonder if *The Ik* is an example of getting away from your past style—stripping away all the obvious theatricality that you used in your other productions, like *Dream*?

PB: I'm more interested in what I'm going toward, not in what I'm getting away from. And I'm going toward the essential elements. Not the essential experience, but the essential elements. That's really like in writing when you go back and cut out all unnecessary adjectives. You're not really so much against the ad-

jectives themselves, but you look at what you're trying to say, and you see that the adjectives are fogging
the meaning. That's why you take them out. You don't
take them out because it's better style. But in a purely
functional way, you are trying to find the most appropriate form for reflecting something, and you see
that certain things stand in the way, so you take them
out. For instance, when I did *Antony and Cleopatra,* it
was quite clear to me that the real focus of interest in
the play is the intricate human relations. And not even
remotely interesting is the spectacular aspect of old
Rome and old Egypt. The *Aida* side doesn't exist, so
that it slipped away by itself. I didn't even have to eliminate it. I did know that it's always been given great
importance. But, to me, it slipped away by virtue of
the fact that it didn't seem of any interest.

About *The Ik*—I'll take it a different way. I think
that over these years, we've really done every sort of
experiment. And, as you know, we've performed at
every hour of the day. In *Orghast,* in Persepolis, we
started in the evening and went through to the next
dawn. We've done enormously long things. We did
get several hundred people to come across to Brooklyn for our last performance at five in the morning.
And they came. And we've done performances at
Bouffes, our theater in Paris, at midnight. We've done
improvisations in every social setting. We've done
them in odd places like a business school, and with
sessions of doctors and psychiatrists, and with handicapped people in asylums, and with children, indoors and outdoors. And we've been in big spaces,
spaces with impossible acoustics, tiny spaces, spaces
with people crammed together, and in cellars. We've

been on the same level as the audience, above the audience, and below the audience. We have tried all these different structural things. And out of that, we found that the most exciting form of theater and the most dangerous one are the improvisations we've done, with nothing prepared whatsoever. But the moment you go into different conditions, which is every single time you perform, certain things are clear. The first thing one sees is that concentration is highly important. So if a place hasn't got good acoustics and good visibility, there's no theater experience. And on the other hand, if the place you perform in is abstract, if it's divorced from life, as most theaters are, though they've got good acoustics and good visibility, something already is lost: The humanity of the surroundings, the sense that it is part of your everyday world, must be a precious part of the experience. When I go into a new theater, however beautifully it's laid out, however logically the seats have been placed, however cleverly the architect has placed his lights, I don't find the same degree of humanity and life as in the streets.

We found another basic thing: Storytelling of some sort is the most powerful lifeline there is. One can make up shows in a million ways, and one can have all sorts of themes, but we made a real lifeline between several hundred people and ourselves with certain universal rhythms and certain sounds, certain ways of standing and behaving and dancing that we found in Africa. To achieve a shared concern on every level, nothing is more powerful than the story, and that is why we often say about our work that we are storytellers.

Q: How does *The Ik* fit into the storytelling mode?

PB: *The Ik* is like what you do every night when you tell a child a bedtime story. You start very simply with certain elements that can't fail to win the attention— through something shared. But once one has done that, the story is not everything. The story is the life-line and the support. And if that story is touching and of real interest to the people watching, it enables something else to take place: a sense of the here and now. And that's why with *The Ik,* we have put all the emphasis in making the story realistically convincing. Well then, you would say, if it's about Africa, why not have black actors? If you have black actors, why not starving black actors? Until you end up by making an image of what you're talking about.

What interested us about *The Ik* is that in telling a story about the Ik, people realized that we were talking about themselves. In the theater, there's this double vision. Everything to do with the theater is double.

Q: What do you mean by "double vision"? Has this to do with Artaud's idea of theater?

PB: Yes, Artaud did use that word . . . Let's put it this way. The very best, truest, and most natural theater takes place when the actors and the audience all the time are in the same world. In other words, when we're sitting in a marketplace in Africa, like a story-teller who's also sitting in the marketplace, then he and his audience are all in the same world. Maybe there is a famine nearby and the storyteller is talk-ing about a great banquet. But hungry people are sit-ting together. They do not forget their hunger; at the same time, they're living a second image, which is a story about foods and richness. And that's a double image.

Q: How does this apply to theater?

PB: In any form of theater where the audience and the actors are sharing the same space, the possibility of the double image comes up. The double image is the one thing that always arises through play. All children's play is based on this idea. Children don't forget that they're running about in a playground, and yet they have the double image that they're pirates on a ship, or gangsters on a street corner. It's evoked with a stick. It's evoked with a twig. It's evoked by a way of standing or of shouting. And this double image is the force, the power, and the meaning of everything to do with the theater.

Q: How much of this idea is relevant to the actor when he is actually working?

PB: The reality of the actors' world is, in fact, the audience. All the work we've done has constant reference to the audience—seeing the audience, hearing the audience, feeling the audience. The audience is the witness of today's world, much more than the walls or the chairs. Walls and chairs can go just so far. But the real witness at any given moment of any given performance today is the audience.

Q: You have spoken about the double image as one of the most important factors in theater and that it is experienced by both actors and audience. But how can you be sure of that? You may be having that experience and the actors may be having it. But how can you tell about the audience?

PB: One of the biggest themes of all our work was to put all our emphasis on feeling and on understanding the audience. I mean, that's why we went to so many different places.

Q: But that still does not prove the point. This may be part of your research, as you say, but what proof do you have that your goal in relation to the audience has been successful?

PB: Our research was oriented to the actor-audience dialogue. The one thing our actors can't forget is the reality of the audience. They can forget other things. But that they can't forget because of the tremendous danger the moment you go into theater with a higher ambition. There you are in danger of becoming pretentious or exclusive and of thinking that what is happening to you is most important. The terrible danger of the avant-garde movement is taking itself more seriously than its audience. There has to be a balance, which at times is precarious; there has to be a lifeline. I've found that few lifelines are as compelling, actually, as a simple line of narrative. You may want to suggest to the audience all the pictures and images that feed that narrative, but also, at the same time, let the audience remain within its own world.

Q: How would you know if the audience watching *The Ik* was actually in its own world, or in the world that the actors created, the world of hunger-ridden Africa? Or, in fact, in both worlds?

PB: In *The Ik,* our aim was not necessarily to construct an illusion of Africa, nor to deny it. Because we realized if we denied it and said, "Look, we're not going to tell you a story about Africa; we're just going to talk about ourselves," we realized a story about ourselves most likely wouldn't capture the poetry and imagination of the audience, which needs to be caught up in that way. But we say, "We're going to tell you a story about Africa," and at the same time, we're really telling you a story about New York, or if we're playing in Paris, it's about Paris. If we can maintain those two, you get the illusion that people, when they see *The Ik*, see an American, an Englishman, a German, a Japanese, and an African playing in it, because there's no pretense about that, and then they—the audience—get the double image. When the story unfolds, you'll know the story is about Africans; everybody's trying to preserve the African nature of the story, to a degree. And yet, to another degree, we do try to keep in touch with you, so that we're not going away from here toward Africa. We're turning Africa into a reality. Africa is us here and now. Because we're here and now, we're going to be here and now together. It's through the constant interplay, the tension, the conflict, the harmony between here and now, and the double image, coming together or not coming together, that you produce something that is essentially a theatrical impression.

Q: Now, what about *The Conference of the Birds:* Why are you doing *Conference* again when you've already done parts of it at BAM?

PB: Because there are very few masterpieces in the world's literature that touch on something that involves a real witness of man's essential experience.

Q: You think *Conference of the Birds* is a depiction of man's essential experience?

PB: Yes, an aspect of man's essential experience.

Q: An aspect?

PB: Yes, an aspect of it. And it's going to be beyond any of our capacities to penetrate completely. Nobody can take hold completely of *The Conference of the Birds*. It's way beyond that. As something to work on, it's inexhaustible. Somebody could just make it their life's work—like monks used to sit painting to illustrate something. In our early period, we used fragments of this work, and just fragments, as the basis for improvisations. And so we never touched the whole piece. We took corners or crumbs from that loaf, which were quite sufficient to keep one going for years. Then we put it aside.

Q: I understand you did a strange experiment of *Conference* at a workshop in Brooklyn. What was that about?

PB: Yes. At the Brooklyn Academy, we did a different version of *The Conference of the Birds*. We did three completely different shows with three different groups of people leading them. Yoshi Oida and Michelle Collison did a show at six and at eight in the evening, which I called "rough theater"; it had giant rough energy. Later, that same energy in performance was turned into *Ubu*. Natasha Parry and Bruce Myers did the midnight *Conference of the Birds* by candlelight, which was exquisitely sensitive. And it was "holy" theater. Liz Swados did the dawn show, which was entirely ritualistic and musical. And then we all sat together and said good-bye at the end. We first talked, as we always do, of the shows that we'd just done.

Q: What did you talk about?

PB: I told them that one day, perhaps, the work that we'd done there would enable us to incorporate these three small pieces into one work. We left it until this year. All through the last years, we've been do-ing formal pieces, two Shakespeare works, using Shakespeare as a real challenge and exercise for everybody. And then we did *The Ik*. And went on to do the "rough" piece *Ubu*—a real marriage between what we want to get out of the soil of the present-day world and something invisible.

Q: What was the larger significance of *The Ik*?

PB: *The Ik* is really not a document of the Ik. It's about the decay of tradition in society, which, through its need to survive, destroys tradition. *The Ik* is about the quality of life as seen through the negative. It is like a photographic negative of the quality of existence. What it's really talking about is what it isn't.

Q: And *The Conference of the Birds*?

PB: *The Conference* has many themes. After I worked with the writer Jean-Claude Carrière on *Conference,* we developed a first script and then brought it back to the actors. And then we left it for several years. Now we have come back to it in a completely new way, so there's no relationship in form between what we're now calling *The Conference of the Birds* and anything we did in the past.

Q: You told me that *The Conference of the Birds* re-flected all the techniques you've used with the group. I found it very theatrical, almost elaborate, and very different from *The Ik*. You said that *Confer-ence* represented a kind of sum total. Can you ex-plain?

PB: Well, by elimination, we have come down to minimal techniques. But those are very precise ones. For in-stance, all the work we've done on language and sound, our work on bird sounds, our work on syllables as opposed to articulate language, our work on pure language, on the French or English language as such, in comparison with others. I would say that work reflected not techniques but, it might be clearer to say, modes. One expresses oneself in different modes, and slips from one to the other as necessity demands. What you can say with a word, you say with a word. When, in the next sentence, the word is not enough and the word needs support by being distorted or turned into a half cry and then that half cry isn't sufficient, it needs to take on a rhythm. And when the rhythm isn't sufficient, it needs to be extended into a melody. The work we've been doing has been on the passages from one mode, one technique, to another, so that, in exactly the same way, for us, all styles are useful, and all styles are repellent. In *The Conference of the Birds,* because it is neither about realism nor about something that is completely abstract, and because it is always about human beings and human possibilities, it is about a group of actors telling a story to people of their own world. Which is what the start and the end is. And within that, the actors become as individuals more prominent, or less prominent; their faces are close to you, or less close to you; or faces disappear entirely; their faces are replaced by masks; or your eye is taken entirely off them and goes to a finger, or to a bird. All are elements of storytelling, and we know that we couldn't take away any one of these elements without the story being less well told.

Q: What you're saying is that all these various modes were necessary for this particular piece?

PB: Exactly. There are two basic images: a bird and a valley. Now those are very concrete, and yet they speak more and more of hidden significance and levels of meaning. Poetic meaning, if you like. Spiritual meaning. If the bird isn't there at all, the evocative power of that symbol doesn't reach you. If the bird becomes too much like a bird of this world, the other level—the spiritual meaning—is lost. At another moment, something more is needed. At another moment, the bird is a head. Another moment, it is in flight and suggests the actual energy and feeling of flight. In that way, the actors have been most particularly trained to slip from one mode to another. What I have said was that a theater event is something that takes place always here and now, for us, in our world. And yet what makes it an event is that, at the same time, it is conjuring up the here and now of another world, an invisible world, so that there is always this double level. Us, here and now, and us connected with an invisible world.

Q: You have spoken often of an invisible world. What is this world, and if it does exist, when does it become visible, if ever?

PB: To be connected, the invisible world can only become real through some sort of imagery. In other words, something like communion, which has nothing to do with the theater, where the experience is entirely through contacting something invisible inside yourself and which remains invisible even while you're in contact with it. That's the religious experience.

Theatrical experience is reached through a rich and sensitive image that has some overtones, and some vibrations that the here and now isn't furnishing—so that the here and now meets its double, meets the image, and you have the two. It is vital to keep the two in balance: There is the here and now all the time, and all the time the other image. If one gets overpowering, the other vanishes. The two have to be kept balanced.

Q: How do you keep the two in balance?

PB: The theater uses suggestion rather than illustration. Suggestion means conjuring up, evoking in the lightest possible way, so that the impression is strong but the evoking is light. Illustration, on the contrary, shows us something with all its details and all its spots. There's a great difference between suggestion and illustration: In suggestion, you half-show. And by doing this, one wants to know more. The imagination fills in the rest. The real act of participation— which everybody yearns for—is always present in good theater, whether people participate with their bodies or not.

Q: How do you evoke people's participation? And do you know that they are, in fact, participating?

PB: Participation depends on whether the imagination wishes it, and is stirred to the point of wishing to fill that void. The more completely it goes toward filling the void, the more complete the act of imagination. Imagination can be just a little imagination (which isn't the imagination of the whole person) or the totality of the imagination, which can rise up and fill the void. In which case, you have a great act of participation. Going toward the imagination is an activity, like any going toward, where the person is made active. And there is where you have great participation.

Q: *Conference* is obviously a mystical piece. Or it can be interpreted as such. You said that it's a very rich piece.

What specifically interests you? Does the philosophy behind the work attract you?

PB: In the end, there's only one theme that interests all of us. And this theme comes dressed up in different clothes and different images. The theme is how to live. And how to live means knowing more about the world one is in, and knowing more about what one is. In the theater, the emphasis can go more on one, and/or more on the other.

The imagery in *The Conference of the Birds* is all parabolic imagery—I don't call it philosophical, in the sense of philosophy being something abstract—because in *The Conference of the Birds,* you go between the everyday world, the world as we are, all the time, and the world of what can happen to us if we mobilize, if we galvanize ourselves in a certain way.

Q: What "certain way" are you referring to?

PB: The journey of the birds is very precise. They go through very specific adventures, all of which make clear something that would otherwise remain very vague and hazy to us. For me, going through the adventures of the birds is actually going through a journey that makes one clearer about the world one is living in.

Q: Are you referring to one's own journey? Is this what you mean by "galvanize" and "mobilize"?

PB: Yes. One's own journey, yes.

Q: Putting on *Ubu, Ik,* and *The Conference of the Birds—* such different pieces all in one program—how do you tie it all together? Is there a relationship between them?

PB: *Ubu* is about powerful energies, the rough energies. It is a celebration of how many things can be overcome through energy, including destroying Ubu by mockery, by laughter, and by something even more anarchic than Ubu himself—the Ubu energy.

In a way, it's a celebration. It's about the lowest forms of crude imagery, which really isn't imagery, because it is quite a true image of the world in terms of the most brutal forces that rule it. And these brutal forces are opposed by ridicule. So it's a picture of the brutal forces that cross our world. And it celebrates our capacity to answer them with ridicule.

We want to do these three pieces as a cycle. It's a real progression of meaning. First, you go through the low, the world of the stomach, which is really the world of *Ubu*. Living with the stomach and yet living with another world the whole time is *The Ik*. Which is a picture of our world. Which is a picture of London when we play it in London. Which is a picture of Paris when we play it in Paris. And a picture of New York. The picture is of a tragic modern world that is betraying its possibilities. And then *The Conference of the Birds* is a conference because the birds are living in a world of chaos and the question is implied: Is it true that there's something else? There it is . . . complete. A three-part play.

New York, 1980

Nine

La Tragédie de Carmen

After Brook's experience with opera at Covent Garden in his twenties and his naughty version of Strauss's *Salome,* which was followed by a dispute with the management, he swore off opera. But to everyone's surprise, Brook, in 1981, directed his own version of Bizet's *Carmen*. Again, he managed to create controversy. This was not Bizet's *Carmen,* some music critics screamed, but an eighty-minute stripped-down version performed without a full orchestra, with no chorus, no children, no crowd scenes, no gypsies, with just a company of five alternating the principal roles.* But most scandalous of all, they said, Brook and his conductor, Marius Constant, had reordered the Bizet score and, at one point, included recorded tape. Only

---

*Although some music critics disdained the production, many theater critics hailed it.

fourteen musicians played—one from each section of the orchestra—not in the pit but on the stage, and Mr. Constant, unseen by the audience, conducted the ensemble from an unobtrusive place in the wings. As for the Halévy-Meilhac libretto, it underwent a radical deconstruction, as it was stripped to its essentials and rearranged by writer Jean-Claude Carrière and Peter Brook himself.

Brook maintained that his production of *La Tragédie de Carmen* was not a dismissal of Bizet at all, but a pure enhancement of the original story written by Prosper Mérimée in 1845, which had inspired Bizet in the first place. In fact, Bizet had changed many of the characters from the original story and had even added a few new ones. That the original Mérimée story was more lean and clean than Bizet's justified the adaptation by Brook and Carrière; they claimed they were following Mérimée's original intention and, in fact, that their *Carmen* was a considerable improvement over the earlier version.

In the Brook production, Carmen is not an unrestricted seductress, but a humanized, contradictory woman. Sometimes she seems to love Don José; at other times, she is willful, unrestrained, manipulative, and childish. Wanting freedom yet believing in fate, she is plainly conflicted. But as Brook was later to say, Carmen, though unconventional in many ways and liberated from the mores of her time, was, nevertheless, attached to her gypsy culture. Which accounted for her dilemma and her ambivalence about her fate.

Critics and controversies aside, *La Tragédie de Carmen* proved to be one of Brook's greatest popular achievements; it played to thousands of enthusiastic audiences, toured Europe and Japan, and in 1982 opened in New York at Lincoln Center's Vivian Beaumont Theater (which for a long period had remained dark and was then refurbished especially for Brook). The New York theater critics acclaimed the production and people flocked to see this version, though some music critics and classicists still thought Brook had done an injustice to Bizet. But audiences had their own ideas: They loved the production.

To be sure, the mise-en-scène was stunning. The heat of southern Spain and the barrenness of the land was rendered in muted colors. Persian rugs and throw pillows were used for the tavern scene and for changes in scenery, while the flickering little fires surrounding the mountain hideaway of the lovers, who were lying in each other's arms in total silence, captured for a moment the idyllic possibilities of their affair—a truly mystical and transporting effect. In the background, Bizet's famous interlude was heard.

In contrast to those for Don José, most of the props and symbols for Escamillo's scenes were phallic; in one instance, he cut a piece of fruit and let the juice drip into Carmen's mouth. Rope, used several times, was the ultimate symbol for binding the lovers together.

A sense of magic—the gypsy world—permeated the production. In the beginning, an old beggar woman drew an ocher circle around the playing area, the shape of a bullring covered with red sand. A fortune-teller sat hidden underneath a shawl. Maybe it was Carmen, maybe not. She extended her hand and offered a card to Don José. He glanced at the card and casually rejected it. Suddenly, the woman threw off the shawl, and one saw that it was indeed Carmen. At that moment, one heard the foreboding chords of the destiny motif, signaling the beginning of the familiar tale of fate and murder.

The singers were accomplished actors, as well; they sang sitting up, lying down, walking, running, jumping, executing tricky movements in the fight scenes, and doing whatever was necessary to tell the story without missing a single note. But the most impressive aspect of the production was its enormous energy, driven by an incredibly swift telling of the story, which gripped the audience immediately and never let go of it, so that the tragedy at the end was a remarkable coup de théâtre, even though one knew what Carmen's fate would be. Without a doubt, this was opera as pure theater—apparently what Peter Brook meant it to be.

——————————— • ———————————

Q: After all these theater productions, why have you chosen to do opera now?

PB: I first started working in opera when I was twenty. I got a permanent job at Covent Garden. I gave it up not because I was disillusioned by opera itself, but by appraising the situation realistically. The cold-blooded fact was that every opera house I knew was so bound by restrictions that it seemed totally impossible to do good work. And so it became a waste of time banging my head against a brick wall. I just stopped doing opera. I don't believe in going into a situation where most of your energy is squandered by the stupidities of world opera houses. I was appointed director of productions at Covent Garden, a title that never existed in opera and is now commonly used. The first day, I was asked to do a rehearsal of *Carmen* to try to shake it up; they had a disgracefully bad production of it. After that, I did a number of productions, and had enormous fights and quarrels, and ended up with Salvador Dalí's sets of *Salome,* which was a total scandal. I was given to understand that the opera house would be relieved if it wouldn't see me anymore, and it hasn't.

Q: Why choose *Carmen* and not *La Traviata,* for example?

PB: First of all, within the last couple of years, *Carmen* has been in the public domain. There are very, very few operas that are really popular. Out of the ten most popular operas, there is one that is the most popular—*Carmen*. And it's not only an opera; it's a phenomenon. The ingredients have all come together. It's like saying, Why is Coca-Cola so popular that you find it all over the world? It's a question of ingredients. If you sit waiting for a plane somewhere in Lapland and you turn on the Muzak system, you are more likely to hear *Carmen* than *Traviata,* because of the combination of the story and the music—the ingredients. First of all, I like it. Second, all our experimental and research work is directed to the widest audience, to which a theater event must be totally available and accessible. That's why we have always taken our research into popular surroundings to make work that is transparent and clear so that it reaches anyone. In a sense, if I were blindfolded and asked what opera is nearest that, I would say *Carmen*.

Q: What is there about *Carmen* that makes it so?

PB: Bizet has a fantastic quality. He wrote many works but only one masterpiece, a masterpiece in the sense that the music has extraordinary truth. *Carmen* is not a noisy, showy, brash work, and it's not popular because it's noisy and brash. *Carmen* is popular because of its extraordinary purity and the truth of its music.

Q: I understand that your *Carmen* is more connected to the story by Mérimée. Is that true?

PB: Yes, one of the elements of truth that inspired Bizet is the Mérimée story. Mérimée wrote a very simple, coolly written short story; there are no literary flourishes. There is no local color; there are no sexual scenes; there is none of the lush writings of other writers of his period—just a cool piece of journalism, a little incident. But that incident was sharp. It touched off many archetypal images of the two main characters. And that, in turn, touched off something deep down in Bizet. Having read this, Bizet decided at once to make an opera of it.

Q: How do you respond to the criticism that you, in effect, rewrote Bizet?

PB: In his day, in the socioeconomic conditions of his time, Bizet could not do the opera in a short space of time, as the Mérimée story indicates. Bizet had to do what they did in those days. In our terms, what one would do if Hollywood were making a big musical: One would have to turn to the top screenwriters of the day. Similarly, here we have two guys, Meilhac and Halévy, and they were two smart kids, who sat down with Bizet and said, "Now look, Georges, you've got a great idea; this is a great subject, but one's got to make it work for a big middle-class audience. We have to soften down Carmen; we've got to bring in some choruses; we have to bring in a lot of local color; we have to have fun; we have to have three intervals; it must be four hours long; it has to be a big show." It's exactly like when I was working with Sam Spiegel on *Lord of the Flies:* We were always disputing. I wanted to make a small film, but he said, "It has to be a big film." In the same way, the Opéra Comique and the smart "screenwriters" of the day were saying, "Look, we'll go along with you, Bizet, but we've got to make something more of it than what it is." We know that Bizet was shocked by a lot of things in the production. He thought the way it was staged was corny—the way the choruses just came out of the wings, sang, and went back again. But he went along with it. The result is that the finished opera is like an enormous elaboration on something very pure and simple.

Q: Did this idea of the "pure and simple" attract you the most? Is that the justification for your *Carmen*?

PB: Marius Constant, the musical director, Jean-Claude Carrière, and I decided on a very interesting experiment. We were going to find a way to make *Carmen* live in our conditions at the Bouffes du Nord theater. In examining it, we found there were two operas: A very intense opera concealed in the spinal cord runs through the big opera. What we did was pick out the very austere opera—going back to the fact that Mérimée was a great stylist. Mérimée had a horror of any unnecessary words. He was a writer like Graham Greene, who eliminates, eliminates, like Harold Pinter in the theater, and leaves just the most necessary words on the page. If there was one adjective too many, Mérimée was appalled.

We tried not to go back entirely to the Mérimée story, but to go back to the nature of Mérimée's style. His style was something very simple—not a word wasted. And we found that the most sensitive, pure music is connected with the pure, central line of the story. Which is, in fact, the music of the protagonists— their story.

Q: What about the children's chorus and the bandits, and the other trappings? Why were these included in the original opera?

PB: These were all the trappings of the Opéra Comique of the time. What is interesting is that once it was done at the Opéra Comique, it was a failure at first, and then it became a success. The tendency of the nineteenth century was to make it even bigger. So it moved upward from the Opéra Comique to the Grand Opéra, and was put on a grander scale. What was spoken was rewritten by another composer and was blown up even further. They took the spoken dialogue and made it into recitatives by another French composer. After that, *Carmen* was in the big tradition: a noisy opera to be done in arenas, to be done as a big spectacle with a cast of thousands. It became the big show. And this is what often happens in the theater. *The Boy Friend* started with this tiny little show in a little London theater and then gradually got to the point where the author said it wasn't his show anymore. It was so blown up, reorchestrated, restaged, and that old tendency of things being blown up happened with *Carmen*. We are going exactly in the opposite direction.

Q: But people have loved the opera the way it is. Why change it at all?

PB: Of course Bizet is a marvelous composer, even this blown-up version is a marvelous work, but not something you can recognize as being true to life, only true to the conventions of the nineteenth century in a big theater. When we recognized that there was this skeleton inside, we decided that we would take the opera out of grand artifice and bring it back for a twentieth-century audience, and make it a natural, simple human story with real human emotions. To do this, we decided right away that we would call it *La Tragédie de Carmen*.

Q: Why tragedy?

PB: Like a Greek tragedy, it is an austere play with a small number of characters. Like a Greek tragedy, it is a story of destiny and fate. And we wanted to make it clear that we were not duping anybody and we were not attacking anybody. We were not saying that we were throwing out the *Carmen* everyone loves but that we were now giving you a new way of seeing *Carmen*. The *Carmen* done at the Met or anywhere else is what it is and always will be.

Q: What about the fate motif? You begin with those bars of music that announce her fate. That comes in much later in Bizet. How do you justify changing that?

PB: Marius Constant felt very deeply that the core of the music comes out of the card aria and the destiny theme. The fundamental clash of characters, which is what deep down appeals to everyone, is that, on the one hand, José and Carmen are just lovers, but at the same time the two of them represent two enormous worlds that cannot coexist without conflict. As I worked on it, I thought I was back to *Antony and Cleopatra*. *A and C* is just an enormous legend because the love story between a man and a woman carries with it two halves of the world, the East and the West. Antony is everything that the Western man is, and Cleopatra is everything the Eastern woman is. This can't fail to be an attraction. It is fundamentally a tragedy because it is unresolvable and produces conflict.

Q: Do you consider Carmen a heroine like Cleopatra? What, in your view, does she represent? A whore? Or a free spirit?

PB: Well, she talks about freedom. Everyone does nowadays, what with woman's lib and so forth. But her sense of freedom is not really in those terms. Her sense of freedom is truly related to the gypsy—not in the superficial idea of what a gypsy is, but in something that is little known, little studied, because it is a race that has been on the move at least as long as the Jewish people. They have never stopped moving and their way of life is a necessity because gypsies need to live marginally. The gypsies have always been hounded and blamed for everything. But their lives have to be one with nature, and with spirits, and with the spiritual forces around them—that's why the gypsies have always been related to fortune-telling, talismans, with good and bad luck. The gypsy doesn't live in any way in the rational, material, bourgeois world. The values of the gypsy are absolute.

Q: What are gypsy values?

PB: Those values are totally different from the very best values of the ordered world. Don José and Micaëla and the mother represent different values. There is the army, the sense of military discipline, army discipline, and the laws behind that. There is the sense of religion—as a Spaniard, José is a Catholic, and behind that is the concept of law and order, and the idea of people living together decently. Don José and Micaëla represent the whole conception of living in a decent, honorable way in a Christian society. On the one hand, there is the question of order in the brutal sense; on the other, the nice sense of the mother, who is concerned that her son live honestly and that he doesn't become a junkie or something like that.

Q: How does all this fit into your conception of *Carmen*? Or into the world of Carmen?

PB: The world of Carmen is opposed to all this. The whole of constructed society meets the gypsy world and it's quite obvious that this is a fatal opposition. Neither of them is prepared to take the third path, which always exists: the way of going beyond an opposition—the transformation of an opposition.

Q: What if there is no possibility of transforming an opposition? Does that mean that inevitably a clash is turned into tragedy?

PB: The theater has been based on ignoring that possibility because it is always theatrically more rewarding to carry an action to the bitter conclusion than to transcend it.

Q: Do you mean rewarding as a piece of theater? Do some plays, albeit tragic, manage to transcend the bitter conclusion?

PB: One can say that the transcending of the tragedy is always with the audience. The audience emerges unscathed. And that is always the appeal. That's what catharsis is all about. You are sitting there and watching this tragedy, pretending to yourself, This is what I would do. But the mere fact that you have witnessed it, and emerged unscathed, proves to you that there is always a way out of tragedy, and you have actually gone through it. There they are, lying dead in pools of blood, and you get up and leave the theater. And as Aristotle says, you're uplifted. In fact, you have confirmed to yourself that there is a way out. You are taking it. You are living beyond the tragedy. But theater shows you this without a way out.

Q: I don't get the impression from Mérimée's *Carmen* that Carmen is any kind of heroine. In his version, Carmen is a liar and a thief and totally unscrupulous.

In Bizet's *Carmen,* she's a femme fatale. In your production, she seems to have a tender side; she seems more human.

PB: I think all that makes her an interesting character. If you try to limit her, you destroy the character. She is all things. She can't be shown as a liberated woman in itself; she is all things to all men. And because of this, she is full of apparent contradictions. She has an extraordinary capacity for living for the moment and therefore living each moment totally. She can be willful, wicked, innocent, pure, full of hatred, ruthless, kind—all those things rotate inside her. Which is of course what makes her so high-powered. In the music, you find what's in Mérimée. In the libretto of Meilhac and Halévy everything is soft-pedaled, and that was even considered shocking and caused a tremendous outcry. What we have done is try to bring back the many-sided woman who can be dirty and violent and dramatic—all these sides that exist together in one person.

Q: You rearranged not only some of the music but some of the scenes. The flower song is later, and Escamillo enters sooner than in the original. Why?

PB: This was an experiment within the line of our research at the Center. The special factor in our Center is that Micheline Rozan, our manager and producer, has developed conditions in which we can actually control audiences. In other words, we were doing an opera for the first time, and we had our theater, so we could start from zero. That means we could experiment simultaneously with a million different things, as though we were starting from scratch.

Q: How did working in your own theater change things
in terms of this production?

PB: When I gave up doing opera, I gave it up for the simple reason that it seemed impossible to do good
work when one was quarreling all the time. I saw
that a stage director's possibility in an opera house
was limited, because basically he is hemmed in by so
many elements, elements that he can't change: inadequate rehearsal time, a bad spacial relation between
the stage and the audience because of an enormous
orchestra pit; a difficult relationship among the cast
members, who are frightened because they haven't
had enough time to prepare; difficult relationships
among the singers because they are glued to the conductor. Also, there has to be enormous scenery because the stage is enormous, and they have to have
long intervals to change it and so on.

Q: And your approach, your working method? What was
different from working in the regular opera houses?

PB: When Micheline Rozan and I agreed to do an opera,
we reassessed everything. We had to have a group of
singers who would commit themselves for a long period of rehearsal and a long period of performance,
because even if you have had enough rehearsals,
you don't have enough for something really to grow.
In our first season, we wanted two hundred performances, where we could really settle down with
several casts so that they would not need to sing
every night. We started with twelve weeks of rehearsal and with three groups of singers, and conducted a series of exercises for actors to break them
of their habits and get them into the habit of working

all together by sharing the same kind of experiences and therefore becoming responsible.

Q: What you do mean "becoming responsible"?

PB: Becoming responsible means that they get so intimately into their score that they don't need to watch the conductor. Marius Constant, the conductor, gave them exercises, which taught them the orchestra score so that they knew it as well as he did. All of this learning was unheard of in a normal opera. We offered low prices so that we could play for different kinds of audiences and establish different relations. We charged six or seven dollars, instead of opera-house prices. We experimented with putting the orchestra in a place that would balance the orchestra with the singers. We didn't want to have a gap created by an orchestra pit, which would put singers in a different contact with the audience.

Q: How did you work with the conductor, who usually ends up with complete control of the production?

PB: When I worked with the conductor in *Salome,* there was immediate conflict. Here our conductor, Marius Constant, is also a composer, and highly esteemed in France; he is also one of the adapters. From the start, we worked together harmoniously. When I worked in opera before, the conductor was the enemy. Now, as I looked radically at the construction of the work, Marius Constant also looked radically at the musical construction. He rescored the music for the needs of a small theater. He scaled a whole orchestra down to fourteen musicians. In the process, we discovered that by compressing things and changing the musical order, the story was told better.

Q: But this is an opera; the music is what is important. Sometimes the story is forgotten, but not the music.

PB: You must understand—we were doing a twentieth-century transposition, as people do in adapting a film from a novel. However deeply you feel about the novel, you recognize that a film is a transposition, and you try for the same effect, but in another form. Therefore, what we were attempting was a radical act of transposition, which forced us to put everything into question: the music, the rehearsal method, the contractual method, the seat-selling method, the disposition of the theater. In other words, for us, experimentation and research were not one thing or another, but an attempt to look at everything at the same time.

Q: I know you had reasons for all the changes you made, but one in particular seems strange. Why is Garcia, Carmen's husband, introduced? Does he have some function?

PB: If you look at the novel, he is there. This is another shock to this well-brought-up young man, José. Carmen may be deeply in love with Don José, but she can, within a second, go to bed with another soldier—really a great shock for Don José. Don José's way of looking at things is that if you are in love with someone, you don't go to bed with someone else. According to José's set of laws, Carmen belongs to him, but according to another set of laws, the gypsy way of life acknowledges the claims of a former husband. What to José is wrong is freedom to her. From his point of view, he discovers that she is a liar. From her point of view, it's related to the moment, to her sense of freedom, to her sense of not being bound;

she is in another dimension. She has a conception of living totally differently from the ordinary bourgeois life. She's a gypsy; she's E.T.; she's from another planet.

Q: Actually, she can be viewed as a bad number—one without scruples or any sense of fidelity. Not a very appealing character, would you say?

PB: She is like Genet. On every level, Genet was Carmen, and Sartre made a saint of him. And this is the fascination of Carmen. Carmen carried to the limit becomes Genet. And Genet carried to the limit becomes Saint Genet. And then suddenly Saint Genet is up against the Catholics—in this case, José's mother and a whole list of Catholic saints.

Q: What is José's obsession with Carmen? He sees her for what she is, and yet he goes on.

PB: Inside every respectable José, there is a Carmen. Her character is inside of him, and that's why she is irresistible. You can only appeal to what's latent in somebody, and a latent Carmen is awakened by the real Carmen. A femme fatale is a revealing agent who wakes up the dark forces buried inside the man— forces that he can neither repress nor beat down with moralities, nor can he live with them, so he cracks, or he possesses them in some way.

Q: You seem to like Carmen?

PB: Sure. I like all the characters.

Q: Someone said that when you directed this, there was a part of you in every character.

PB: I think this is absolutely true. You can't work on anything in any other way. You do just what an actor does, the same as the author. The director can't just sit outside. He has to feel all the contradictions of the drama. It's not a question of being outside or inside.

It's both at once. On the one hand, you're looking at things at a distance; on the other, you are implicated. I usually choose things where I am implicated.

Q: About the ending: It is quite different from the Bizet opera. Is that in line with the fate motif?

PB: I thought that the ending in Mérimée was more powerful than the ending in Bizet. In nineteenth-century playwrighting terms, they very skillfully built their last-act climax, where she is onstage. In the book, they set off on a long journey into the mountains, until they find the spot where she knows that this is the spot where she must die. And he kills her there. We made Escamillo die because her matador in the book, who is only a picador, is actually killed. And this is what releases her to accept her death. She realizes, in a tragic way, she must die, whereas in the Bizet opera, the scene is melodramatic. The point has come where they can go no further; they are beyond passion. She is moving from man to man and has completely lost her love for José and is deeply in love with the bullfighter. When that love is over, she feels doomed. There is no future with any man.

Q: Do you think that she really loved José? In the "Habanera" she sings of love that can't be captured.

PB: Yes, she does love him, but it's love in a different way of understanding love. When she's inside this passion, she lives it to the last degree, and then she's out of it. In the scene in the mountains, I wanted to suggest that there is a period of time that elapses, and she and José have a sort of honeymoon; they have their moment together. They live in complete harmony, perhaps a period of three months. And time stops. But she knows that this cannot take a bourgeois form.

Her nature doesn't allow it. Her destiny is something else. It cannot be what is called "settling down." It has to be lived fully within the moment. Perhaps José believes that it will go on forever, but she knows that it will end and that makes her live it all the more.

Q: She lives a male life, as it were. Not too many women live that way.

PB: *Carmen* was conceived by men, don't forget.

Q: How did you get Escamillo and José to fight and sing at the same time? You don't see that too often in opera.

PB: Western opera is bound by a dreadful state of tradition, which has become destructive and wrong. The opera world is riddled with false beliefs, which are all based on something, but something untrue. One of the great beliefs is that singers are stupid and incapable. And to sing well, you need an enormously fat stomach. None of this is true. Singers develop fat stomachs through laziness and overeating—and being spoiled. This came out of nineteenth-century Germany and Italy, where people ate a lot. Singers were terrified to go out for walks, in case they caught cold. They would sit at home eating chocolates. Of course they got monstrously fat. They explained their weight by claiming they couldn't sing without that fat stomach. But it is a total lie.

Q: What kind of singers did you look for?

PB: We had a wonderful group of young singers who were desperately interested in doing theater work. They wanted to be real onstage. So we worked on specific exercises. For example, a singer took one note and would try to sustain the best sound quality of that one note and combine it with different movements. First, we did just simple arm and leg movements, and then we worked on the judo mat and did rolling exercises while singing. The singers got very excited and saw for themselves what they could, in fact, do. We did all the work together; it was group research, not my research given to them. They discovered that they could do all the things they were told no singer could ever do. And what amazed them is that we didn't work the hours the musicians worked—opera houses everywhere work these rigid hours; every rehearsal is a three-hour session, with a break in the middle. This wasn't our way of working. We would often go on for hours and hours, with no break at all, because no one wanted it; sometimes we would work for nine, ten hours.

Q: How did you get away with that? I guess you have no unions. No union would allow that in New York.

PB: It was interesting; people were involved. They didn't want to stop. The singers discovered that they had been singing every day for ten hours, and their voices weren't tired. In normal conditions, if you have sung for two hours, your voice is exhausted; you have to go home and rest, and you won't have any voice for the next day. We did this for twelve weeks. So it wasn't as though a director came in for a few weeks to an opera house and worked with a lot of singers who were frightened by a bullying conductor. And that then the singers had to get into awkward costumes that they hadn't been consulted about, and then a director came to them and asked them to roll on the floor (as do Escamillo and Don José). Of course they would absolutely refuse, obviously, because they would be too frightened, and not sure of doing it. But the moment you make it all possible for them, then of course they can do it.

Q: Did you have special voice teachers at hand?

PB: No, all the singers shared their own vocal experiences. We thought of having some coaches, but we felt that a voice teacher would be on the side of tradition. We did have some coaches for the musical style with the notes and words.

Q: What about the orchestra? Did you think the right place for them was on the stage?

PB: To me, in the twentieth century, there is something politically unacceptable in the idea of musicians being stuck underground, musicians who are the co-producers of a certain performance, who are equal artists, and yet apart from the conductor; nothing is a more rigid totalitarian approach to theater than the conductor stuck up on a podium. He can see the stage and see the orchestra, and then there are ninety people who cannot ever see, or feel, what is happening onstage. Compare this with the Oriental plays, where it is inconceivable that the musicians should be anywhere other than in the same space, watching the performance. The musician is part of the action. We put musicians on the stage because we wanted them to be part of the piece.

Q: But it's obviously not practical to put an entire orchestra onstage. You had only fourteen musicians.

PB: For me, the opera-house construction is a rigid image of the nineteenth-century way of seeing the social system—the servants belowstairs. And one pays a price for such abominable rehearsals and exaggerated performances.

Paris, 1983

Ten

The Mahabharata

Imagine staging a nine-hour production based on an ancient Hindu poem that weaves elements of the Wars of the Roses and strains of *Die Götterdämmerung* into the cosmic grandeur of an Indian epic. Stir in a clash of two great dynasties in the hands of the gods, opposing armies locked in battle, and the moral struggle of ideal heroes representing divine forces that are arrayed against demonic ones. All this—set against a background of primordial forests and sumptuous palaces—is encompassed in the monumental saga *The Mahabharata*, a theatrical challenge that would intimidate most directors.

However, the difficulties inherent to this awesome project did not deter Peter Brook, who for ten years had persisted in putting together the complex and diverse elements contained in *The Mahabharata*, until he finally mounted the production in August 1985 at the Avignon

Theater Festival in France, to overwhelming critical acclaim. No stranger to challenges, Brook sought to represent in his production of the Indian epic a culmination of a lifelong search for theatrical expression of mankind's greatest dramas and deepest dilemmas.

In his colossal French-language adaptation of *The Mahabharata*, Brook, synthesizing all his previous theatrical inventions, did nothing less than attempt to transform Hindu myth into universal art, accessible to any culture. This vast enterprise was undertaken by Brook with a team of colleagues, including the noted screenwriter Jean-Claude Carrière, who had collaborated with Brook on *La Tragédie de Carmen* and many of his other productions; the set and costume designer Chloé Obolensky; the lighting designer Jean Kalman; Marie-Hêlenè Estienne, assistant to Brook; and a company of twenty-one actors from sixteen countries, as well as five musicians, under Toshi Tsuchitori's direction, who played dozens of Oriental and African instruments. They had all visited India several times—and closely studied Hindu scripture, costume, art, and music. But the total concept—artistic and philosophical—was that of Peter Brook.

An immense work, fifteen times the length of the Bible, believed to have been written in Sanskrit between 200 B.C. and A.D. 200, *The Mahabharata* is the longest single poem in world literature. Consisting of eighteen volumes and ninety thousand couplets, it is a compilation of the myths, legends, wars, folklore, ethics, history, and theology of ancient India, including the Hindu sacred book, the Bhagavad-Gita. Revered in India but relatively little known in the West, *The Mahabharata* is to South Asians what the Bible, along with the *Iliad* and the *Odyssey*, are to Westerners. In translating this great work for the stage, Brook and his company had to make it meaningful to us through the creation of real characters and highly dramatic action rooted in Hindu culture and religion but at the same time archetypical and symbolic. There are, for instance, the blind king, the ideal warrior, the devoted wife, and many other mythic yet human figures.

Presented as a cycle of three plays (*The Game of Dice, The Exile in the Forest,* and *The War*) over three days, or in one all-night nine-hour production, Brook's *Mahabharata* first unfolded in an environment that, in the outdoor Avignon setting, combined nature with artifice. Later, in 1987, there would be productions with a similar stage set—one indoors—in Paris and in other cities, including an English-language version coproduced by the Brooklyn Academy of Music's Harvey Lichtenstein and Los Angeles Festival director Robert Fitzpatrick.

In Avignon, Brook's "theater" was an open limestone quarry outside the city. Here, spectators sat on scaffolding facing massive boulders, rose-tinted cliffs one hundred feet high, and a vast playing space filled with tons of luminous yellow sand. A canal of real water flowed across the back of the space; a small pond reflecting the action was down front. At one side was an altarlike arrangement of low-burning flames and Indian garlands; at the other were the percussion, string, and wind instruments for the musicians who each night became an integral part of the action. When it grew dark, the lighting transformed the colors of the rocks, water, sand, and cliffs to gold-yellow, deep beige, and slate blue, so that the terrain seemed to become a unifying image in a dream, expressing the enigmatic, primitive beauty of the elements.

At the start, after the musicians took their places, a character in a beige Indian cotton robe—his red hair and shaggy beard standing out against the stones—entered, accompanied by a young boy, also in beige cotton. The character Vyasa, symbolic poet of *The Mahabharata*, told the boy that he has been writing a story about the history of his ancestors, their vast wars, and, by extension, the story of mankind. The tale, said Vyasa, was the great poem of the world. Then the great god Krishna appeared, wearing an elephant's head—traditionally used at the beginning of a stage performance in India—and offered his services as a scribe. Krishna then wrote in a large book, and thus *The Mahabharata*, the awesome story of the great Bharata clan meeting their tragic destiny, began.

Part I introduced the main characters—their mythic origins, their characteristics and aims, the role of the gods (especially Krishna), and the growing discord between the Pandavas and the Kauravas, two branches of the Bharata clan. In a game of dice, which the Pandava leader lost to his cousins, the Pandavas forfeited all their property and worldly possessions and were exiled to a forest. In part II, they lived there in a primordial existence while procuring arms for the inevitable battle to come. In part III, the devastating war, foreordained and controlled by the god Krishna, was unleashed, threatening the entire universe. After a gruesome massacre, the Pandaras regained their rights and were later reconciled with their enemies in heaven. Vyasa, the storyteller, warned ambiguously that *this*—meaning heaven, or earth, or the entire play—was "the last illusion." According to Hinduism, life is the dream of the gods and, as rendered by them, is but an illusion. The characters, dressed in pure white, dropped their personae, ate delicacies, and exited. The game of the gods was over.

Embedded in the text are eternal philosophical questions examining the paradox of the human condition: Why do men lust for power? What are the causes of jealousy and hate, of the destructive forces of mankind? What is the mystery behind man's motivations and his relationship to destiny and choice? Will mankind survive? Does man have a choice? What is the game of the gods?

Brook attempted to convey the essence of *The Mahabharata* through the strength of his aesthetic vision, rather than through philosophy. Eschewing minimalism, he treated *The Mahabharata* with unabashed grandeur and daring theatrics. He utilized every theatrical mode at his command and used all the aspects of his years of travel and research in Asia and Africa: ritual theater, Oriental storytelling, Indian classical theater, magic, and clowning; the broad scope of epic staging; the tone and timbre of Shakespearean tragedy; and the savagery of the Theater of Cruelty. A unique feature was the classical acting by a cast of international actors, whose expressive faces and varied styles and physiques gave the production a generic quality.

Struggling to find a dramatic form, Brook aimed for a pristine simplicity in some scenes, an economical ordering of the elements, and a fluidity of action, so that the nine hours seemed to fly by. A montage of distilled images and architectural patterns, moving with rhythmic grace into the space, one after the other, like film frames, suggested both the timelessness of the universal and the presence of India.

The ruling images in the production were fire, water, and earth. Fires of all sizes and shapes were ablaze. Some were used for religious or ceremonial scenes; some burned throughout the night to evoke the divine forces; in one dazzling scene, a trail of fire ignited the water, calling forth the hated enemies. The water, a constant factor, was used by the characters to drink from, to wash in, to wade in, and to fight in unto the death. Dominating everything was the sand-covered ground. It lay before one like the benign universe, its golden colors changing with the night, enveloping all the action, reminding one of its mysterious essence.

In the spectacular war episode, hundreds of arrows were hurled through the air in choreographed motion; flags flew down from the mountaintops; armies were poised high on the rocks, their primitive weapons ready for the kill. Warriors were choked, knifed, strangled, disemboweled, and decapitated. Characters fought with knives, axes, poles, arrows, clubs, and tree trunks. They screamed and grunted and howled, they sank into the water, and were covered with filth, their mud-streaked faces unrecognizable. Finally, in a coup de théâtre, the divine secret weapon blew off half the mountain. The end of the world was before us.

The horror was counterpoised by lyrical moments. In an exquisite court scene, one saw princesses dressed in scarlet, rich maroon, and vibrant yellows. Lying on elevated couches, they listened to sweet music and watched a show featuring delicate handheld miniature puppets, while lotus flowers floated on tiny sparks of fire in the pond. In another scene, the melancholy Krishna played the flute on a hilltop and the proud god Shiva showed off his powers in an amusing dance.

Then there was the sensuality of the princess married to the Pandavas: her long black hair against her corn yellow garment recalled Indian miniature painting. Other lovely young women passed by: The river goddess, Ganga, dressed in her finery, walked through the waters after giving birth to one of the heroes; a jewelry-bedecked princess, on her way to marry the blind king, was carried on an elephant's back created by the bodies of the actors. And throughout, there was the innocence of the young boy listening to the storyteller, watching, questioning, searching.

At the end of the performance, many in the audience, like the boy, were full of wonderment and awe at what they had seen. For them, Brook's theatrical magic had worked, evoking the possibilities of live theater with grand themes in the hands of a master magician.

—————————— • ——————————

Q: How did you choose your material? Why *The Mahabharata*?

PB: I think that everybody in the theater and cinema knows that around each thing one chooses, there are about fifty things that, at some point or another, you've thought about, talked about, and perhaps for several weeks were even excited about. But something filters away, and then you feel one thing is infinitely more important than the next thing. I do think that more and more today one has to develop and follow a certain sense of responsibility, for when you put on a play, when you make a film, you are expending a large amount of people's time, devotion, and energy. I think one has to take this into account. That's what makes one eliminate subjects that one thinks aren't worth the investment of one or two years on the part of people who are doing everything to create a beautiful result. If you can choose, it is better to focus on a subject that contains something that can mean a lot to other people.

Q: How do you judge what can mean a lot to other people?

PB: Only by taking yourself as a guide, telling yourself that the subject you've chosen seems to be irresistibly rich. For example, Jean-Claude Carrière, the writer, and I encountered *The Mahabharata* through a Sanskrit student in Paris one night, who began to tell us this story; he went on night after night, until he had told us the whole vast story. We came out into the street in the middle of the night, and said, "We've had an experience for which we now must find forms that we can share with other people." And I told Jean-Claude that we would stage it no matter how long it took. Because this was something that we immediately wanted other people to hear. And in that way, we chose *The Mahabharata*.

Q: Did you know what you were searching for when you chose *The Mahabharata*?

PB: It came out of *US* quite directly. When we were doing *US* in the 1960s, we tried to have a completely different approach to political theater.* Which excited a lot of people and offended a lot of people, because I refused to take any of the approved lines about the Vietnam War at the time. I was not trying to make a polemical piece, but hoping to get an English audience to enter into the suffering and dilemma of the Vietnam situation. *US*, the title, meant not only those with anti-American sentiments, which the British love, but those sitting in the audience who felt the same sort of contradictions about a global mess, the Vietnam situation. I wanted to question any person living among the ruins and destruction, wherever it might be taking place. There isn't a person who can say that he or she is not part of this world—in all its destruction.

US was an experimental work depicting the tragedy of the Vietnam War.

Q: And this destruction has always gone on. Is this what interested you in *The Mahabharata?*

PB: Yes, it has always gone on. But what does it mean when you constantly see that a large number of human beings are willing to destroy other human beings? The real question is, What is the meaning of these conflicts? While we were rehearsing *US*, all kinds of people would come around during our lunch hour— journalists, political people, people who had just come back from Saigon, all the contacts we had. At the time, someone sent me a copy of the Bhagavad-Gita and the central image that emerged was of a soldier asking himself why he should fight. Much later, we opened the Bouffes with *Timon of Athens*, which was very timely. In Paris, it seemed not to be a classic, but a play very much concerned with things at the moment. We were also preparing *The Ik*, and, at that same time, we were looking ahead to our future, and thinking about how to explore the subject of conflict.

Q: Was the subject of conflict and of the soldier who doesn't really want to fight the determining factor in your interest in *The Mahabharata?*

PB: Well, yes, that got into our thinking about the whole *Mahabharata*. Later, we were well aware that once the choice had been made to start *The Mahabharata*, all the groundwork had already been prepared.

Q: Do you mean that once it is just an idea, even a fleeting one, in your mind, it is sort of in the air and will later emerge?

PB: Well, yes. You don't choose. Something drops into place; it comes along.

Q: What were some of the problems working on the nine hours of *The Mahabharata*—the logistics, the casting, the international aspect of it all? Was it different in New York from the way it was in Paris? Or the same?

PB: The same, because the actors—ever since we started at the Center with all our journeys—have always stressed the fact that they are very, very close to storytelling. When a storyteller relates to an audience, he tries with everything at his command to lift the audience to an imaginary world—without disappearing himself.

Q: But isn't it considered great acting when the actor does, in fact, disappear and the audience is presented with a different person?

PB: In the nineteenth-century theater, everything was done in order for the actor to disappear completely. By the time an actor goes through the stage door and reaches the dressing room to put on wigs and makeup, he will be someone else. And if one meets the actor backstage or on the street, one will be surprised by seeing this beautiful woman who played this shriveled-up old woman, or seeing a young man who played an old codger.

Q: Isn't that the remarkable thing about good acting, that the actor can, in fact, be so disguised that he is unrecognizable after the performance? Are you saying that the actors at the Center never need to wear makeup or assume characters other than what they are?

PB: At the Center, the actor doesn't need to disappear; he is like a storyteller. One of the things that keeps the story alive is that the audience sees the man who is telling the story as himself, and the audience is having a nice warm relationship with that person. In different ways, we are trying to preserve this so that you are carried along through the play with a good, friendly relationship with the audience. In relation to that, an international group is special because the audience can see so many different types and backgrounds working together, telling the same story, but through different physical instruments. I'm not saying this is better or worse. But this gives a very different impression to the audience than if an actor hides behind characterizations like makeup and wigs, et cetera. What the audience would be looking at, then, is basically a characterization. That's why more and more we are not interested in virtuoso acting.

Q: But you have worked with some very great actors who did give virtuoso performances.

PB: That's true. But it is a long time since I have worked with stars. However, I have never had anything but good experiences with them. For example, the work I've done with Paul Scofield has been memorable, as well as that with John Gielgud.

Q: How does *The Mahabharata* compare to other works—those of Shakespeare, for example?

PB: *The Mahabharata* is the richest material I have come across.

Q: Is it richer than Shakespeare?

PB: I would say that *The Mahabharata* would not compare with a single play by Shakespeare, but with the entire work of Shakespeare. They say that everything that exists is in *The Mahabharata*. If it isn't in *The Mahabharata*, then it does not exist. Because it touches on so many levels, from the practical to the most spiritual and metaphysical, all in one living world. This is what makes the material so dense; in comparison, other material seems thin. It poses not only intellectual questions but deep questions rarely addressed. The moment we came across this, we decided there was no better way of spending a long time.

Q: You seem to be comparing it somehow to Shakespeare.

PB: Yes, although it came almost two thousand years before. One of the great advantages of *The Mahabharata* is that it is fresh. I have always believed that being in the theater, it is necessary to do things continually, freshly. The theater is not a form for repetition. With *Marat/Sade*, we were the first to place a nude bottom on the Broadway stage. Whereas today the nude bottom is common. It is difficult to find fresh material.

Q: I can see why you directed *The Mahabharata* the way you did—getting these opposite forces on stage, which is very hard to get in one production. The production has it all—the rough, the holy, and the poetical—elements you have mentioned in one of your books and in interviews. What is the underlying story in *The Mahabharata* and its actual significance for you?

PB: *The Mahabharata* is a story told to a young man who is just entering into life in order to teach him all he needs to know to become a really good king. Now, if you just take a tiny step back, you realize that to be a good king means to be a fulfilled man—a complete man. And the story tells this not in abstract philosophical terms, nor in terms of fruitless practices, but in relation to any aspect of the life process, so that in the complete *Mahabharata*, there are whole vol-

umes on the politics of being a king. Some volumes
are about the relations between the king and his
wife, the morality of using spies even, and so forth.
The essential story is about how a young man finds
his way through one of the darkest and most tor-
mented periods in human history, three thousand
years ago. They were very conscious that they were
living in one of the darkest ages. And how you live
through a dark age without being destroyed, without
becoming cynical, how you can become reconciled
to the inevitable. That is the great eternal question.
What is destiny? And what isn't destiny, and can you
be free within destiny? These vast questions are eternal questions, which are relevant today. Any young
person—or even an older person—who wants to
know how to live through the next year, or the next
day, and who is faced with this mountain of conflict
and war, and wants to know how to go through it by
evolution and not by decay—these are the great
questions and the great material, which naturally
cannot be codified. *The Mahabharata* is a very revolutionary work, one that continually takes set ideas of
morality—what is right, what is wrong—and puts
contradictory characters in play so that on the good
side there are bad characters and on the bad side
there are good characters. And it turns these questions into human actions and therefore cannot be
cataloged or pigeonholed. Like in Shakespeare, there
is a lack of linear thinking. I have never respected
any formal ideology or formal morality. Whenever I
have been confronted with a play that shows only
one point of view, I have been unable to see that that
represents the truth. The basis of the Elizabethan the-

ater made something unexpected appear through the contradictions. And in this way, *The Mahabharata* does the same thing.

Q: Well, people do wonder why you undertook such a gigantic and esoteric project.

PB: One of the things that attracted me about *The Mahabharata* was that it is not a linear work. It takes set ideas of what is right, what is morality or immorality, and through contradictory characters who intermingle, great questions are turned into human material. Again, like the work of Shakespeare, *The Mahabharata* is not a piece of ideology. The telescopic effect that comes from many views seen in the round is the basis of Shakespearean theater, where roles are constantly intertwined in a way that makes something unexpected happen.

The Mahabharata touches many levels, from the practical to the spiritual and metaphysical. Besides, *The Mahabharata* is fresh, and in theater, it is necessary to do things freshly continually.

Q: You said there was a modern analogy in *The Mahabharata*. Do you want to explain this?

PB: Since the epic takes place in the Indian era of Kaliyuga, the time of destruction, where demonic forces are in the ascendancy and threaten the cosmos itself, a modern analogy is obvious. Of course, the basic themes are contemporary. One of them is how to find one's way in an age of destruction. Through *The Mahabharata* runs the story of a noble king. The leader of the Pandavas was searching for the right way, his dharma—the Hindu concept of moral law—and the trials he must suffer to find it. This kind of search is for every man, king or not. Every man is potentially king of himself, if he manages to get himself together. His country is himself. In that way, everyone can put himself firmly into the story, which is essentially a quest for morality.

What is brought out in *The Mahabharata* is that there is a certain world harmony, a cosmic harmony, which can either be helped or destroyed by individuals. And so one must try to discover what his place is in the cosmic scheme and how he can help to preserve the cosmic harmony, rather than destroy it, knowing that the cosmic harmony is always in danger and that the world goes through periods of lesser or greater danger. We, too, are living in a time when every value one can think of is in danger. What is the role of the individual? Must one act, or withdraw from the game? *The Mahabharata* comes out of Vedic times, and what was interesting about India is that you had a highly developed civilization artistically, and at the same time you had a civilization very close to nature, and although Indians have created great works of art, this was in no way an indoor civilization, like the Renaissance. Their work had constantly to do with images from the natural elements.

Q: How did that influence your overall design?

PB: Well, we could not stage such a work with a couple of chairs and everyday costumes. The epic contains the most luxuriant poetic writing and the energy of the imagery in the writing is the only way of telling the story. I had to find the appropriate form, the necessary language to tell such a story.

Q: How did you find the form?

PB: These different conventions and techniques evolved slowly, out of much study and discussion and intense experimentation.

Q: I understand you, Jean-Claude Carrière, and the company traveled to India a number of times. What of India did you actually use? What was your preparation?

PB: India was no longer a dream; it became a reality—infinitely real. Each day in India, it was a surprise, a discovery. We saw all the many possibilities, the colors, the textures of the clothes, the movements of people, the various religious rituals, the essences and subtleties of each particular element, the endless details of the objects, the traditional ceremonial forms of popular performance, including dance, mime, narration, song, and music. We met sages, professors, villagers who were happy to share their knowledge with strangers from the West. All along, we were touched by the love that Indians had for *The Mahabharata.*

   When we returned from India, we knew that we could not, and should not, imitate Indians or Indian art, but suggest it. We did not pretend to reconstruct ancient India of three thousand years ago. We did not pretend to present the symbols of the Hindu philosophy. In the music, costumes, and movements, we tried to suggest the presence of India . . . It took twenty-five weeks of rehearsal—it had taken twelve years to write—and we used authentic objects as much as possible, like the wheel.

Q: How did all the images fall into place?

PB: We did not make a chart or anything. But from our journeys to India—personally I never take notes—I just absorbed. Then one came home and one distilled this and that, and pragmatically we began to talk with people in the company. We discussed whether it would be interesting to have a wooden floor or a stone floor or what, and we tried different things, and then it all became self-evident that the story on wood was not as appropriate as earth, and suddenly it occured to us that you could have water in the front and in the background. It became quite clear to us that if there was one Indian element that was as important as earth, it was water. Then afterward, I could rationalize it and say that one can't think of India without thinking of the Ganges, and if you think of the Ganges, you think of the Himalayas, so that you are into rocks and sand.

Q: What about the costumes?

PB: The costumes started from a variety of shapes in India. Some were regional costumes and adapted to the European body. The fabrics were silk, cotton, wool; we didn't want to end up with something standard. Chloé Obolensky, the costume and set designer, went to India for one or two months at a time to get the feel of it. Costumes were discussed and begun four years before it all happened. There were endless conferences, rewrites with Jean-Claude Carrière and Marie-Hélène Estienne, who collaborated on the production. Chloé and Toshi Tsuchitori met with scores of Indians on our many trips to India to get a feel for the people. We knew we could not reproduce the Indian way. Our costumes look Indian, but actually they are variations on Indian colors and designs. Chloé not only dyed the fabrics in India but dragged around tons of sacks and cartons of artifacts to choose from—fabrics, props, costumes, accessories. Later, the company went there, too; watched Indian rituals; met actors, musicians, and religious people; did improvisations with Indian artists; and immersed themselves completely in Indian life. It all boiled down to a rehearsal time of two months per play, which is very little. The enterprise was wild and crazy for a tiny organization. Everything that we have undertaken fits into the scope of a major national theater on every sort of physical level.

Q: Tell me about the music.

PB: Toshi Tsuchitori spent a year working on the music. It is neither Indian nor non-Indian; it really isn't the true Indian theater music, but our way of interpreting it. What we were doing was refracting the Indian work through the many nationalities of our company. We needed a variety of music, especially for nine hours. The musicians were present, visible, and incorporated into the piece. We looked around a long time at the work of different composers. The musical listening of various types was based on the research and work of Toshi. Various Indians came for a period of work, and various musicologists came, too. And, of course, musicians came from around India, and they just played and discussed and so forth. The musicians, like the rest of us, were able to look at what India suggests without going literally into imitating Indian music. You can't do that. Not only do you not want to but you can't do it well. These are styles that have to be done marvelously or not at all. The final form of the music came very late. Like the rest of the work.

Q: What held it together for so long? Ten years in the making is a long time.

PB: Something in *The Mahabharata* pushed us. It was something very special. *The Mahabharata* documents a culture, a society, its dramas, mores, fables, a view of nature. I had always been aiming for this, although I did not stop other work. I was determined to do it once I heard of the work in 1975 and began to read it. I told Jean-Claude Carrière, who wrote the French text, that we would stage it and take as long as was needed.

Q: How did you actually choose what to put on that stage with such an enormous story?

PB: We had to separate the secondary stories from the main action. We wanted to maintain the flow of action. We chose to concentrate on the most dramatic part of the story, the part that presents the direct conflicts—but Jean-Claude did manage to include two aspects of Krishna, as a god and as a human, and the various elements of the Indian doctrine of dharma, which is the heart of Hinduism. He also had to use a restrained, precise language and avoid the tone of French classicism. Another problem we had was that the work has an epic quality and covers a long period of time, so the language had to be concise, but not modern or familiar slang.

Q: Can I ask you a little bit about your cast? One of the most striking elements in *The Mahabharata* is the barrage of accents and physical types among the cast members. Did you deliberately cast certain roles with certain ethnic or racial elements in mind? Or did it basically depend upon the actors you knew? Was it a big problem for the Westerners in the company to assume characteristics of Indians?

PB: Well, first of all, the actors had to be terrific storytellers, with many different faces. But, more important, you ask a question that touches a fundamental principle of all the work done since we started the International Center in Paris in 1970. We set out to avoid two things. One was being a little United Nations, so that, you know, if we had a South Korean, we needed to have a North Korean. On the contrary, there's never been any geopolitical pattern in our choices. There are people from seventeen different nations—not only people whose talents naturally drew them together but people who were different from one another. So we've had a good deal of peace in our Center, because few of our actors ever think that they can play the next man's role. This is what dogs other companies: Everyone wants to stab another actor in the back. And I suppose you, as an actor, know, with pleasure and pride, how different you are, and that's why you're here. That's the basic principle: to have people who are as different as possible.

The next thing we try to avoid at all costs is storytelling by casting. We do not want to say that the white man is this, and the yellow man is that, and that the black man is something else. For instance, in the case of a number of parts in *The Mahabharata*, in different versions—in the stage version and then in the second stage version, which went from French into English—what was played by an African actor in one part was then played by an English actor. For instance, the part of Karna is played at the moment by an actor who was born in the Caribbean and is half of African origin and half of Indian origin, and was brought up in England, the product of English Shakespearean theater. He is playing the same part that a British actor played in the French version. We have gone from a purely English actor to a Caribbean actor simply because of some new shuffling. And so we have avoided stereotyping.

Q: In what way is *The Mahabharata* an Indian story? What is specifically Indian about it? Or what is really transcultural about it?

PB: I think that this is a very, very interesting question, because for something to be interesting in the first place, it has to be specific. And if you write a story about somebody who is no one and lives nowhere, it's not very interesting. And *The Mahabharata*, which is a very great story, arose at a particular moment, in a particular culture. And so at the outset, it was a purely Indian story. And there are millions of Indian stories, but *The Mahabharata* is remarkable, like the works of Shakespeare are remarkable, like Shakespearean tragedy is remarkable, because it has a depth and width and a grandeur that makes it universal. Now, the moment it's universal, it is possible to interpret it in different ways. I'd say that the most extraordinary *Oedipus* that I've ever seen was in an African village, played entirely by Africans. And they had, in fact, taken it as their own story. And that was our *Oedipus*, something that we think of, perhaps, as being closer to us than anything else. I've seen a marvelous Shakespearean *Measure for Measure* played entirely by Tunisians. And so on and so forth. That happens when a work can transcend something. And what is very interesting is that every one of the people from these seventeen different nations who eventually played a part in *The Mahabharata* recognized and felt they could play this with intimate reality because it was their story—that this was one lot of people. The moment you accept that as the lot of people, whether in the theater or the cinema, you are accepting it for what I think it is—a story common to all humanity. Even great experts on the subject maintain, truly or not, that the whole of *The Mahabharata* began not nearly three thousand years ago in India, but prior to that, somewhere in Scandinavia. And that this typically Scandinavian legend was carried by Aryan conquerors halfway across the world, and so we're not doing much worse than they did.

Q: You speak of the dharma in *The Mahabharata*. How does that become part of the plot? Can you explain that?

PB: There are two dharmas, the dharma of right behavior and the dharma of personal morality in a given situation. The king is called by his personal dharma to try to avoid being a shit—that is, to be just a person. Most of the drama for the last hundred years has been individualized, but in most of the work, even in Sartre's existentialism, the characters are trying to find the right thing.

Q: What is the difference between so-called individualized dharma and what we find in *The Mahabharata*?

PB: *The Mahabharata* is related to universal dharma— that man must use all his efforts to discover what the universal pattern needs from him. In other words, what is his place in the cosmic scheme? What is his role as a living organism?

Q: Is there actually a cosmic scheme? If so, how does one fit into it? How does that relate to *The Mahabharata*?

PB: What is brought out in *The Mahabharata* is that there is a certain world harmony, a cosmic harmony that can either be helped or destroyed by individuals. And so part of the demands on an individual who is trying to realize himself in life is to try to discover

what role he can play in helping to preserve the cosmic harmony, rather than destroy it, knowing that the
cosmic harmony is always in danger, and that the
world goes through periods of lesser or greater danger. One can see that we are living in a dangerous
period now, a time when every value is threatened.

Q: The setting, then, for *The Mahabharata* is in an era
of universal destruction?

PB: Yes, all values and physical life are in danger. Now,
what is the role of the individual? How to be right in
one's own actions? And right in fulfilling one's role in
keeping and preserving universal harmony? That is
what *The Mahabharata* is also asking. The first challenge given in life is, Do you want to know yourself,
or do you want to remain asleep, blind, like the blind
king in *The Mahabharata*? Do you want to live blind,
or do you want to achieve the capacity to open your
eyes? To open your eyes means knowing yourself.
Knowing yourself well is inseparable from accepting
the fact that one is programmed, which is the modern word for destiny. Now, you can be nothing more
than your program, or you can go beyond your program. Of course, you have to know what your program is or what your karma is, and then you will
know how to fit in with dharma.

Q: How does the Indian notion of karma play a role in
dharma?

PB: Karma is what no tradition can get away from; knowing yourself, whatever tradition you are a part of,
whatever direction you take, you come back to
this first basic challenge. We don't know ourselves
deeply; we don't really understand ourselves.

Q: I don't know if these characters really know themselves. They seem very conflicted. Is there a clear line that one can follow?

PB: What you have to do to understand the characters is to follow them step by step, without relating it to any system of moral judgment. The game of dice is as multifaceted as the image of Oedipus; it has haunted the Indians for two thousand years. What is the relation between chance and nonchance in the game of dice?

Q: Why did the so-called good king lose in the game of dice? Why did he bet away his kingdom? What was the purpose of that? Of course, there was also the chance that he could have won. But he loses. Why?

PB: Why does he lose? There is no simple explanation; the whole of this is food for thought. What is the role of chance, and destiny, and the role of the gods?

Q: Aren't these the same questions the Greeks asked? The irony of life—and its meaningless absurdity. Maybe this story is not very new.

PB: These are characters; they are not epic figures. They relate to what's in their nature. All the psychological problems take place in a certain context—in the context of chance and destiny. Now, what is chance and what is destiny? And there the whole thing opens up like an enormous fan. The Indians' destiny was prescribed, like the Greeks'.

Q: What is the responsibility of the individual, then, if his destiny is fixed? That has always been a question. Besides, if destiny works, perhaps it is because Krishna is at the center of all things. Isn't he provoking each person in the play to action all the time? And doesn't he take sides, very much like the gods in the *Iliad*?

PB: Krishna is helping each person by offering a deeply compassionate provocation. He holds up a mirror to the person and pushes the person to the point where his own programming is much more visible to him than it would have been without Krishna.

Q: But as the god-guru, he advises Arjuna to kill his cousins. He even runs the chariot for Arjuna. Krishna is full of contradictions, more man than god. "Be a warrior and kill desire," he tells Arjuna.

PB: Yes, because as he says, it gives him no pleasure, but it gives him a deep joy when he sees that the person who is an obstacle or a menace to humanity is no longer there. Krishna does judge, but not in accordance to a fixed morality; it is judgment that has to be constantly renewed. What is the real aim of the war in *The Mahabharata*? If the war is the preserving of dharma, then it is justified; if the war has any other aim, then nothing is justified.

The Mahabharata is telling two stories at once. It is telling you the story of the battle in relation to the problem of dharma. The only story in relation to us— the Krishna story—is in one's own battle, and the question raised by Krishna's story is, How far is one prepared to go? Is one prepared to go all the way, or is one going to stop, give up, cop out, cheat at some moment? Either one cheats oneself and one compromises and one doesn't go to the end of the battle, or one recognizes that at a point within oneself, one can be as merciless as Krishna is for the sake of that essential battle being won. If you look at the outside battle, you can use all sorts of arguments, but if you turn it inward, it is very simple. Am I at this moment, any moment in the day, understanding myself?

Q: There seem to be many themes in the work. Do you think the audience gets all these philosophical points?

PB: Of course, the basic themes are contemporary, but to reduce *The Mahabharata* to an analysis of its themes may destroy it. But okay, one of the basic themes, as I have said, is how to find one's way through an age of destruction, and the whole of *The Mahabharata* is in the form of an answer given to a young king who wants to understand how to become a fully developed king—how to get yourself together on every level.

   The question is for everybody, king or not. As I have said, a man is potentially king of himself if he manages to get himself together—his country is himself. In that way, everyone can put themselves firmly into the situation of what we have in the story. We have a child who is told a story, by which he can understand better on all levels—the simple human level, the practical level, and the level of inner understanding—what it means to live through an age of destruction. Every play has a question. The question here is, How to be king, if to be a king means you have enemies and need to kill and so forth?

Q: Some people think that *The Mahabharata* is the climax of your work.

PB: I don't see it that way at all. It is *The Mahabharata*, that's all, the work we are doing at the moment. I really don't see it in terms of accomplishments or achievement. Looking back, talking like this, I can see how one thing can lead to something else. But it doesn't interest me to wonder about accomplishments.

Eleven

The Tempest

After *The Mahabharata,* Peter Brook's work took a different turn. In 1990, he returned once again to Shakespeare, directing a minimalist production of *The Tempest.* The play was translated into French by his longtime collaborator Jean-Claude Carrière. This was followed three years later by *The Man Who,* an adaptation of Oliver Sacks's book *The Man Who Mistook His Wife for a Hat.* Both productions represented what seemed like new vistas for Brook: Both were small, simple, unadorned, and totally different from *The Mahabharata.* But, as always, from the moment one entered the Bouffes du Nord theater, one was unmistakably in the domain of the Peter Brook style, however different these productions may have seemed from his other works. A Brook production has certain characteristics: a certain signature, a certain aesthetic, easily identifiable not only by the sheer simplicity and clarity of the work but by the unusual casting and unorthodox interpretations. Brook doesn't just stage a play; he is forever looking for something more, some quality that might reveal what he calls "the invisible world beneath the text," a world not easily fathomed and not easily reproduced in theatrical terms.

For this production of *The Tempest*—his fourth—Brook had chosen the simplest of forms. The stage was empty except for a large rock and a rectangular sandbox. The doomed ship was simulated by the actors, all in black, who manipulated an assortment of bamboo sticks while accompanied by shouts, screams, and eerie music played by two musicians sitting at the side of the stage.

The first shock for the audience was Ariel. Expecting the usual young girl in a flimsy tutu or white tights, one saw instead a heavyset black African (Bakary Sangaré), who was carrying a toy ship with red sails on his head to tell Prospero, also played by a tall black African (Sotigui Kouyaté), that he had created the tempest.

Soon Caliban appeared, working his way out of a paper box. Another shock: He was a small white boy (David Bennent) with enormous blue eyes and a dwarflike body, dressed in sackcloth. Although he spat, screamed, bit, and climbed on ropes, he was more a pathetic, almost helpless wild child than a full-fledged monster.

In this *Tempest* everything was suggestion and whimsy: Butterflies swung on sticks carried by fairies; clothes for the two drunken butlers (Bruce Myers and Alain Maratrat) were thrown from the wings; forest sounds were evoked by music; Miranda's wedding gown was a gauze veil; the fairies played with sandpiles, hoops, and ropes to irritate the lost crew; characters jumped, skipped, and romped in the sandbox and climbed at the side of the theater. Images flowed one from the other; the action was continuous, and the comic scenes were not set pieces, but an integral part of the action. Here the zany business of the drunken butlers paid off; entirely inventive and played very broadly, almost like Marx Brothers antics, their scenes with Caliban made a lot of sense.

The extraordinary casting gave the production a fresh, youthful quality and provided a way of telling one that preconceptions about *The Tempest* should be discarded. Those looking for the darker psychological issues or lavish costumes and spectacular theatrical effects generally associated with *The Tempest* would be disappointed. Not only was this production the epitome of minimalism but it was conceived by Brook to resemble the world of the child's imagination, where fairies dominate reality with amusing games, clever charades, and supernatural magic to create a fantasy island, a primordial natural habitat, or, if you will, a landscape of illusion. The action, with its cleverly acted comic scenes and numerous bits of inventive business, which were typical of Brook's humor, was so swift, breezy, and whimsical that the two and a half hours without intermission passed like a sudden, exhilarating dream.

——————————————— • ———————————————

Q: What made you go back to Shakespeare again to direct *The Tempest*?

PB: It's a marvelous play, a beautiful play, and one that I never, never felt I had done well, although I had done it three times. I thought that our group, our international group, would have something to bring to *The Tempest* that would be different. In Shakespeare's time the liaison between nature and culture had not yet been broken; ancient beliefs survived. Sentiment of the marvelous was always there. Today, modern actors have the ability to explore contemporary issues, but they are not able to find the images of an invisible world because they are not present in our ordinary day-to-day experience. Nor are they preserved in our living culture. For an actor brought up in a climate of ritual and ceremony in a culture that leads to the invisible world, playing witches, fairies, and goblins is natural. And this goes back to experiences in 1968, when we did fragments of *The Tempest*. Then Yoshi Oida [the Japanese actor in the group] revealed another culture—one that included the world of the supernatural. Also, his theater culture—Noh—made his playing ghosts and spirits and gods and goddesses something natural.

Q: Why is that?

PB: They are metaphors of reality that the actors are trained with in Noh theater from the beginning. Modern characters, such as university presidents, truck drivers, businessmen, are the characters you don't learn about in Noh theater. So at the time, Yoshi came to us totally unprepared for playing those kinds of people. But he was totally equipped to play something from the supernatural world. On the other hand, the actors I worked with at the Royal Shakespeare Company were marvelously trained to play realistic characters, but nothing had prepared them to play fairies and witches and goddesses. For Shakespeare, it was perfectly natural to write about these things; it was part of his culture.

Q: Did you learn something concretely from Yoshi, or was it just his presence that gave the work a certain quality, perhaps the quality you were looking for?

PB: My experience with Yoshi showed me that people from cultures that still have a natural contact with nature could bring some illumination to *The Tempest, The Mahabharata, The Conference of the Birds. The Tempest* completes that whole cycle. And for personal reasons, it was a completion.

Q: Why was this a completion of a cycle?

PB: For years, we were going to do *The Magic Flute* at the Bouffes. While we were doing *The Tempest,* I got three offers to do *The Magic Flute*. And I refused each time. I recognized that personally I could not once again—after *The Conference of the Birds*, after the whole of *The Mahabharata,* and then *The Tempest*—find a way of doing gods and spirits. I couldn't continue using the same images, or deliberately *not* using them, both of which would be artificial. I couldn't touch that imagery, so *The Magic Flute* was over. I can't do it today. Maybe in five years, I'll suddenly get the impulse. I can't see myself sitting in the theater and trying to find a way of showing a religious ceremony or a ritual. The *Tempest* production expressed all that I can do with that now. That's the end of that. People ask if that is, therefore, my farewell to the theater, as it was Shakespeare's farewell to the theater. That's ridiculous. First of all, there's no reason to say that it was Shakespeare's farewell to the theater. He didn't write about himself in it. He wrote about Prospero's story, not Shakespeare's.

Q: But is this a farewell to the classics, as you once said, and to the notion of "culture"?

PB: I have always hated the idea of "culture." The whole notion that culture, as such, has to be taken seriously and respected. That's why we formed a group and did what we did in 1970. I don't believe in culture in its normally accepted university and social sense of the word. I feel that it's a dead hand that is put on society, one that is best expressed by state theaters everywhere and other institutions. I've written about the relation of deadly theater and culture enough. If I have directed Shakespeare or Chekhov, it has been to try to break away from the cultural modes—to find the central line, and break away from culture. But today, I find that what I need—particularly after all that I have done in the last few years, including *The Mahabharata* and now *The Tempest*—is to try to attack, once again, what we had in *US* in the sixties. And that is to find how to open the same areas with a different imagery—so that we get away from classical imagery.

Q: What do you mean by "classical imagery"?

PB: I mean to touch on the invisible, which is all I'm interested in touching, through an image. In Shakespeare, unless one artificially uses modern dress, which has now become an out-of-date convention, one uses the imagery of kings and queens and gods and goddesses—imagery that comes from the past. When one uses remote images from the past, one is free from present-day associations, so you can receive the images more strongly, and yet they don't seem real because they come from the past. When you are confronted with everyday images, you are so close to them because of newspapers and television that you can never penetrate very deeply with them. And that is a problem. And I want to reexamine that problem.

Q: Is this why you are doing Oliver Sacks's book *The Man Who Mistook His Wife for a Hat?**

PB: Yes. It seems to me that there are areas in the brain, the subject of *The Man Who,* where the contemporary image is not necessarily cliché. If I were to do a play about politics, terrorism, ghettos, drugs, it would be virtually impossible to find a palette of images that wasn't deadened by television. Last night when I came in, I put on the television. And what did I see? The same old images deadened by repetition. In other words, I wanted to find modern contemporary images that had some deeper meaning.

Q: To get back to *The Tempest*—what is your method of work? How do you begin?

PB: I simply have to sit down and read the play and see what is in it, just as I would read a newspaper article. It's interesting to see how far people have drifted from what is actually in the text. For instance, the accepted idea that *The Tempest* is a play about colonialism, that Caliban is the native and Prospero is the imperialist. That's one of the contemporary theories about the play. The other is that Caliban is a pure monster. Another theory is that Caliban represents the wicked nature of man.

Q: How do you see the play?

PB: Nothing in the play is heavy or serious. Shakespeare tells it very lightly. We can see it is not a tragedy, and it's not a philosophical play in the Western tradition, like Goethe's *Faust,* which is how the Germans always play it. Shakespeare wrote it exactly like a fable—

*Later the play was called *The Man Who.*

charming, light, easy, and quick. If you listen carefully, you can see there is great depth, but it is not the depth of *Hamlet*. Like *The Winter's Tale,* it is a tale. For that reason, it's all of a piece—light. In this light way, Shakespeare put these conflicts in, but he never showed these conflicts brutally and heavily. He did it as a fable. Shakespeare tells the story through a language of theater games. Someone described it as a playing field, a playground.

Q: But Caliban is hardly a character in a playground. Nor are his actions very playful.

PB: Caliban is like a nascent man, a person who maybe thousands of years ago was an uncontrollable personality—naïve, angry, competitive—but who had the seeds in him of a Prospero. Shakespeare created this wild, uncontrollable adolescent who is not a real monster—he looks like a puppy; he looks like a fish—so that one doesn't need a great big monster type there. What Shakespeare wanted to show was how this ferocious creature could be led by the nose. He chose to show him in a comic way. Caliban chooses a butler as a god; he picks a comic character, a drunken butler. And he is almost a sympathetic character because of his mistaken choices.

PB: And Prospero, what is your feeling about him?

PB: Prospero needn't explain himself; he is not a psychological character. The whole point of the production is to avoid the psychological aspects and heaviness. Shakespeare was at the height of his powers. He didn't need to spell everything out.

So many books have been written about the so-called inconsistencies of Prospero. It is a play of suggestion. The story must have a simple line. What matters is what is happening under the surface, and under the surface you see something different.

Q: And that something is?

PB: The way you see the word *freedom* all through the play. And it can mean so many different things in so many different ways. Prospero spends all his time in dreaming unrealistically, and he is a poor politician. Objectively speaking, he deserves to be thrown out by his brother; he didn't pay attention to his dukedom.

Q: You say the play has a lot to do with freedom. Do you want to elaborate on that?

PB: Caliban wants freedom to have the island to himself. The drunkards yell that thought is free. But what kind of thought? The young man is shown as young and pure, with no psychological hang-up. His freedom is to love completely.

Q: What is Prospero's way?

PB: He has acquired all the powers a magician can have. But he realizes at the peak of the play that to be a magician is to jump the goal of being a normal man. When he renounces his magic, he renounces his superman qualities. To be a master magician doesn't make him free. His last speech is regarded as Shakespeare's farewell—a totally idiotic idea, for Shakespeare never betrayed his characters. When Hamlet makes his soliloquy "To be or not to be," it is not Shakespeare contemplating suicide. *The Tempest* is as light as a feather, but it becomes serious in the last few words, when he says his ending is despair. Having gone through the heights and the depths—to do the right thing, to forget his enemies—[thinking] that his ending is despair, [he realizes] that he can be "saved" by prayer. And that prayer can only happen

if you—the audience—release him; he has to be par-
doned by the people who have watched him—the
audience—to be set free. He is finally dependent on
others. Freedom is something shared—freed by love.

Q: But that's pretty serious—not something light, no?

PB: It is light—a droll game. There is no realism; there is
no island. You can't place it historically. Any attempt
to localize it is fruitless. That's why for years and
years it has been done as a spectacle in the English
tradition, with lots of changing scenery, pretty costumes, and masks. This is understandable because it
is entertainment; you can do it that way, but at a
price. If you don't do it that way, if you try to make
it very light, you get a better play. If you go for spectacle, or you go for philosophical drama, you get a
lesser play. But if you take a lighter touch, always in
the world of the imagination, but with absolute seri-
ousness in the last moment of the play, then you
have the play.

Q: What about the comic scenes?

PB: The comic scenes are not separate; they are part of
the action, not comic relief. They are part of one texture. This is not a heavy play with comic relief. Ariel
is a shock. One thinks of Ariel as a light ballet dancer.
Instead, a big black African plays the part.

Q: Why did you cast this large African in the role of Ariel?

PB: When did you last see with your own eyes a spirit?
There is no real image attached to it. Once you realize that, then the whole notion of putting a gold ballet costume on the spirit is ridiculous. You can ask
yourself, Why should a spirit whom no one has ever
seen look like a girl from a dancing academy? It has
been played by girls in white tights. Horrifying. Sen-

timental. Or it's played by little fellows. A little fellow is lively and small, so you look around in the company and say, "Who's small? He's the one to play Ariel." Did you ever see *The Sylphides*? Have you ever been underneath the stage? It's an interesting experience. On the stage, you see dancers trying to be as light as possible on their toes; you go under the stage and you hear loud clumping. You hear the real genuine heaviness of the pirouetting. So there you can imagine the spirit world. What, therefore, can suggest a spirit? It is not really an image. What is left? What do we know of spirit? *Esprit* means "spiritedness." High-spiritedness. Being lighter than ordinary. Lightness and dexterity. What I looked for was a quality of spiritedness, and this particular actor has that, and that he was so much heavier than the little fellow had no bearing. What was important was that he should show a wit and humor and drollery that correspond to the sense of spirit.

Q: And how did you cast Caliban with this little fellow? Was this a deliberate piece of mischief on your part?

PB: Caliban had to have energy plus purity. The actors playing Caliban have always been stereotyped. It's foolish to do Shakespeare for the sake of doing it differently, but to get away from the stereotype, to find the real life, is the aim.

Q: People talk about the Brook touch. Do you want to tell us about that? What is the Brook touch?

PB: It comes about through hard work; we work together. Style emerges when you stop thinking about yourself.

Twelve

The Man Who

After *The Tempest,* Peter Brook continued to stage pieces in a minimalist style and in 1993, he once again surprised audiences. Discarding all prior theatrical forms, he mounted a four-character piece, *L'Homme Qui* (*The Man Who*), inspired by Oliver Sacks's book on neurological problems, *The Man Who Mistook His Wife for a Hat.* The shabby, unadorned Bouffes du Nord Theater in the working-class section of Paris was still Brook's playing palace. But instead of having the visual beauty and complicated mise-en-scène associated with earlier Brook productions, this piece was staged on what looked like a sand-colored platform six inches off the ground, so that the setting was totally incongruous with the ancient arches of the theater and its crumbling, faded walls.

This time, Brook used squares—not circles, as he had in *Carmen;* square white chairs and tables on wheels, actually ugly in their way. Despite the two television monitors onstage, this was a hospital—sterile, sparse, and functional. There were no adornments on stage, no colors, no special images. Clearly, the hospital setting was intended to deliberately contradict the nineteenth-century architecture of the theater and emphasize the clinic-like ambience onstage. Yet despite its austerity, there was an uncanny Noh-like beauty to the work, which served to humanize its dour subject matter and provided the audience with a truly moving experience.

At the start four actors and a single musician entered. The musician went to the side of the stage, where he remained for the entire evening, while the others took their seats on the plain white chairs. Three men wore white doctor's jackets. The fourth, dressed in ordinary street clothes, was presumably a patient; he was given an injection in the skull, which instantly affected his body. One was about to witness a play—without a structural story, without theatrical trimmings—about human beings with severe neurological problems: damaged people.

For a brief ninety minutes, four actors—the African, Sotigui Kouyaté; the Japanese, Yoshi Oida; the German, David Bennent; and the Frenchman, Maurice Benichou—played both doctors and patients in a work about people in extremis, those whose neurological problems signified not only their particular afflictions but also the dysfunctional aspects of ordinary people. A succession of scenes in which the patients described their conditions followed without intermission.

What carried this production were the brilliant actors, who doubled as patients and doctors. They portrayed with extreme sensitivity brain-damaged people in a way that was free of stereotypes of madness or patronizing sentimentality. Yoshi Oida played a man who could not feel the left side of his body and knew it. In an amazingly quiet performance, Oida captured the interior of a man in all his silence and loneliness: He lived in a world he could not grasp. Maurice Benichou was an amnesiac who had been living in an institution for the past twenty-seven years; for him, time had stopped, for he still thought he was twenty-three years old. David Bennent played an autistic child who, when confronted by two doctors, told the story of his day, showing his obsession with numbers; he counted everything from his footsteps to the number of pens in the doctors' pockets. Totally self-absorbed, he could not see anything through someone else's eyes. Maurice Benichou, in another role, was a patient with a tick—he suffered from Tourette's syndrome—who was fully conscious of his illness. In rapid-fire double-talk jargon, Benichou delivered a monologue in which he proudly described his syndrome's various manifestations. Though the speech was a brilliant tour de force and highly amusing, the scene was immensely sad nevertheless. Then there was Sotigui Kouyaté, a tall, noble-looking African, playing an epileptic patient who, when his brain was stimulated, recalled scenes from his past, particularly his childhood in Africa. Yoshi Oida, doubling in the role of a man who continually heard certain music in his head, was tortured by memories of his mother. He struggled to get the tune out of his head but couldn't, and so he relived the past over and over. Some of the patients knew they were ill; they had moments of comprehension and sometimes acute realizations about their illnesses, but were nevertheless bound by their conditions. The cases demonstrated the rupture between thought and action, between moments of lucidity and forgetfulness, between moments of awareness and complete derangement.

There was a certain nobility to the performances, almost

a sense of heroism, without any displays of grandeur or exhibitionism, yet a certain innocence, too. It was as if the actors were not acting, but simply existing onstage. As such, this kind of performance was a rare example of acting in the here and now. The quietness of the actors, the economy of their movements, the authenticity of gesture, and the serenity of the playing suggested a meditation on the fragility and vulnerability of all human beings—all damaged souls.

At the end, the message was clear. A giant brain flashed on the TV screen—in itself a strangely effective image, and, in its own way, a coup de théâtre. For the brain, staring out at the audience, looked gorgeous, mysterious, and wondrously complicated. Indeed, it was the ultimate work of art, the primary source of all action, of all thought, of all accomplishment, of all memory—everything that links mankind together. No wonder Brook undertook this project, for what could be more challenging?

———————— • ————————

Q: How did you work on this piece?

PB: We did our own research in the mental hospitals of Paris and London, met with various inmates, and found equivalents of the cases described in Sacks's book. In hospitals, we saw vast numbers of videos and for the first four months studied cases and extracted the material. After almost two years of research and experimentation and after consulting physicians and neurologists, and Oliver Sacks himself, the group [together with help from playwright Jean-Claude Carrière and Marie Hélène Estienne] forged a script. And so the authors of the work became those who worked on it.

Q: Did the writing of it come from the company entirely?

PB: The writing was entirely a product of the company distilling the original material. We in no way introduced anything that would make it literary. We didn't even talk about the theatrical shape.

Q: Why did you choose this subject?

PB: True, it is not what one would call a subject for the theater, but everything that touches on what it is to be human is appropriate for the theater. But how to represent the abnormal, the dysfunctional, how to show this onstage? That was the problem.

Q: This piece seemed to be a departure from your usual pieces, which have always had strong story lines, or at least storytelling aspects.

PB: I deliberately chose not to have a story line or costumes. After *The Mahabharata,* I wanted to see where one could go without leaning on any of these things, something strictly contemporary, recognizing that contemporary is an artificial image—like doing a play about terrorism: If you have a man with a gun in his hand and a hood on his head, it is the same as doing an Elizabethan drama in costume and having a man with a sword. There is, it would seem, an array of cultural clichés with which we live. But someone who cannot recognize anything on the left side of his body, for example, is a man who cannot recognize that anything on the left exists. A man who cannot recognize his wife's face but sees a lot of dots and lines is absolutely precise.

Q: Did you feel that these images would be theatrical?

PB: We were in very clear territory when we began to work. I wanted to move away from recognizable cultural theatrical images and see what would happen. I wanted to see if we could make a direct connection

with the audience without leaning on anything whatsoever. I wanted to work within the most basic reality
and recognizable conditions possible—the function
and mystery of the human brain.

Q: How did it all begin?

PB: When I read Sacks's book, and knowing Sacks and
talking to him about it, the idea was already there. I
had already discussed with Jean-Claude Carrière the
use of science as the essential basis for contemporary
life, and we were wondering how one could actually
touch the world of atoms, and we were sure that we
could not humanize an atom. But the working of the
brain involves not just chemicals and the electrical
activities of neutrons. The working of the brain is revealed in human behavior. And from this starting
point, I began to think that neurologists are unique in
medicine, in that their treatment is minimal, but they
can enter into the hidden parts of the brain when the
patient's behavior is suppressed and his condition
makes him behave in an unexpected way—and that
unexpected behavior enables the neurologist to discover something that is hidden.

Q: What do you mean?

PB: Well, if the behavior is normal, you can't see what's
going on—not even with a scan. The moment something goes wrong, you begin to see what's happening
in the mind. Which is what the whole of neurology is
based on. And in that way, we can enter the mind
through jokes, distortions, and abnormal behavior.
And then one sees that everyone has these distortions of behavior to some degree. And people with
neurological problems have them to a degree that
shows itself at once from the outside.

Q: What was your method of work in theatrical terms?

PB: We were in very clear territory when we began to work, which lasted over a year. Sacks came over. We had two weeks of workshops with him. Our first work was, naturally, work based on the Sacks book. And gradually, we discovered that with something as precise as this, work from a writer's description of cases was already secondhand. In the case of *The Ik*, we had already been to Africa, and so we had the experience in us; only after that were we able to use Colin Turnbull's book. Here, we saw that we had to start from the beginning to find the equivalents of the cases in Sacks's book. Each of the cases you see onstage is parallel to something that Sacks experienced in his hospital in New York. Sacks describes a woman who manages to move only by using her eyes. We found this same condition in England. For example, a man had become like a rag doll but he was able to do everything. Neurologically, he was someone who couldn't cope. But it was amazing that he could come to Paris and behave in a normal way, and yet he was described as a neurological case. We based our story on "A Disembodied Lady," which is in the Sacks book. In each case, we had to find the equivalents; the actors could not work merely from the Sacks text.

Q: How did you select the cast?

PB: We began with a group of twelve, but that proved impossible. We couldn't go into a hospital with such a crowd. We had to be a tiny group. Then we went into hospitals. We didn't even talk about the theatrical shape. We used Sacks as a metaphor and found the source out of our own experience.

Q: What were you searching for? These people had

neurological problems. You couldn't have been interested only in that? What were you searching for?

PB: The human being inside. Every one of these cases represented just an exaggeration of what is called "normal" behavior. The normal control that prevents you from imitating someone, for example. We are all on automatic behavior all the time. The only thing that interests me in the theater is bringing to the surface the invisible side of man's behavior. When we did *Marat/Sade,* there was this enormously theatricalized form that gave us strength as well as posing limitations. After *Dream*—not that we did theatrical acrobatics in that work—we tried to depict spirits that one does not see in normal behavior—and that's what led to acrobatics. It was not acrobatics for the sake of acrobatics; we were suggesting what is meant by *spirit,* which is something quicker, people doing unexpected things with virtuosity and lightness. And therefore suggesting what Shakespeare meant by *spirit.*

Q: You told me once that you had exhausted the images related to great classics. Did you hope to find fresh images in the Oliver Sacks work?

PB: It isn't that I'm tired of imagery, but I am searching for something more essential, something deeper, which can touch people beyond the imagery. This doesn't need to be explained; it is self-evident. Here one is encountering the human being. The fact that the actors are both doctors and patients, one senses, is a variation on one theme: the human being who is at the center of all that.

When Jerzy Grotowski started, I thought it—the idea of a gesture that has a pristine quality, with no associations to everyday life—was totally relevant to what he was looking for. The purpose was to crack through all the clichés and the photographic view of life, and the fact that human beings' every movement is associative. Research of this kind has led to abstract art: the pure gesture, the pure sound, the equivalent of Miró, Picasso, Braque, and Matisse—paintings that were pure abstraction and pure language. Of course, all research carries its own limitations, and there comes a point where it is dehumanized, when the abstract nature goes too far. Then the audience is no longer thinking that we are talking about you and me, and can no longer relate to what it sees.

Q: How does this work relate to your concept of the invisible theater?

PB: For a long period, I thought that invisible forces have to be harnessed with something that is a story. In this case, the piece *The Man Who* is not gorgeous, the lifeline is not the story, but it is totally recognizable nevertheless. But the story is there; it is the inmates' story that comes to life.

Q: Is this an attempt to find a new way? Is this a new cycle for you?

PB: When we did *The Conference of the Birds,* this cycle was already beginning. *Birds* was the first step to *The Mahabharata.* So was *Ubu.* The aim then was to amalgamate that into one pattern, and that was the beginning of *The Mahabharata.* This piece is the beginning of the first sketch, which will come in two or three years. And that is the beginning of something else. The whole purpose of research work is to find a visible shape.

Q: What does this mean exactly?

PB: Something very simple. There is basically no difference between working on *Carmen* and doing an experimental project. Once the work starts, it is all research. The next project is about the nature of the theater experience. How to put that on the stage. To find the essence of the theater experience through very strong personalities and what they were looking for and what they could capture and failed to capture—that is something we are interested in.

Q: Oliver Sacks talks about preserving the identity of people. How does that work with damaged people?

PB: There is only one story: What is a human being? How does he live his life? Different people approach this theme in different ways. It is always the same question. In *Oedipus,* you have the same thing: Why does he do what he does? In all the great spiritual ways, the images, like those in *The Conference of the Birds,* are just trying to penetrate more essentially into exactly the same theme. Sacks is the same. He is not blocked purely by clinical and technical medicine— he is a deeply feeling human being. I've often compared him to Dickens and Chekhov. There is no difference at all between Chekhov, who looked at people with damaged lives, damaged by pride and prejudice and frustration and boredom, [and Sacks]. Sacks is looking at lives damaged by brain injury, and he sees that inside each person is a totally valid human being, living as much as he can, moment to moment, as fully as possible, what life has given him.

Paris, 1993

Thirteen

The Tragedy of Hamlet

In the fall of 2000, Peter Brook returned to Shakespeare to stage an eagerly awaited *Hamlet*. A Peter Brook production is always an event to be reckoned with, whether it be his nine-hour epic, *The Mahabharata;* a depiction of the dysfunction of the human brain, *The Man Who;* or an adaptation of Bizet's *Carmen*. In his seventy-fifth year, Brook mounted yet another amazing work: his own, very streamlined version of *Hamlet*. It first opened in Paris at Brook's Bouffes du Nord. Performed in English—itself a startling event in France—it quickly sold out the entire run, then went on a world tour, starting in New York with performances at the Brooklyn Academy of Music.

Brook's *Hamlet* (which he called *The Tragedy of Hamlet*) was a streamlined skeleton of the play, cut down to an intermissionless two hours and twenty minutes, with eight actors and with a third of the original play eliminated.

Moreover, Brook had rearranged the text, reordered scenes, and excised certain characters and material—for example, Fortinbras, and the famous Polonius lecture to Laertes ("to thine own self be true"). What was left was the central theme of Hamlet and his dilemma.

True to the Brook style of interracial casting, this Hamlet was played by the black British actor Adrian Lester, who startled audiences with his audacious, dazzling characterization and his eloquent delivery of Shakespeare's text. But it was Brook's signature style—the transparency, the simple staging and uncluttered setting, the impeccable color sense, the essential beauty of the mise-en-scène—that attracted the most attention: It was all there, visible the moment one entered the theater.

The space at the Bouffes is in itself beautiful. Despite the obvious seediness of the theater, with its shattered old terra-cotta walls, the stage seemed enveloped with a warm rosy hue that magically took on a special, courtly quality. There were no sets, just an open minimalist space with a few pillows and small benches carefully and cleverly arranged geometrically by Chloé Obolensky. The floor was covered with a single blood orange–colored carpet, its six cushions—green, yellow, and indigo—spread around the stage and moved about by the actors themselves. Sitting in a small area at the side of the stage, the musician Toshi Tsuchitori played his exotic instruments. Most of the company doubled: Bruce Myers played Polonius and a grave digger, and Geoffrey Kisson played the Ghost and Claudius; Natasha Parry was Gertrude. But the concentration was on Hamlet, and Adrian Lester dominated the stage, though there were intriguing performances from Natasha Parry and Bruce Myers.

Ms. Obolensky, Brook's longtime designer, imagined

the costumes neither as Renaissance nor modern, neither African nor Asian, neither Parisian nor Danish, but as unidentifiable in origin. Yet she achieved a universal regal quality, even though the colors were extraordinarily subdued—black, white, and gray tones. The actors wore no makeup, and they maintained their modern hairstyles— Adrian Lester sported dreadlocks, for example.

Perhaps the most interesting aspect of the production was its ability to suggest a certain elegance and royalty without any of the scenic accoutrements; there were none of the court scenes one has been accustomed to seeing in *Hamlet,* and no elaborate trappings of a kingdom. Also fascinating were the English-speaking actors, who captured the imagination of the Parisians. Lines formed every night in front of the theater in Paris (as well as in New York), and once inside the Bouffes, the audience seemed mesmerized: People were totally immersed in the language of the play, as if it were being performed in their native tongue. They were particularly intrigued by Adrian Lester's Hamlet, with whom they apparently identified. Mr. Lester's radical rendition—the speed of his performance, the dazzling control of his body, and his commandingly youthful vigor—earned him a standing ovation every night.

Although most of the critics in Paris gave Brook splendid reviews, a few were bothered by what they considered his meddling with the text and his daring to alter Shakespeare. But Brook has never been seen to waver, or change his mind, because of the critics. Possibly no other director in the Western world has had the nerve or the confidence and daring to contest commonly held views, views that have influenced a generation of theater artists. He has always been on an undaunted search for new meanings, for greater insights, for a taste of what may be beyond the naked eye. Never satisfied, striving to find a more refined aesthetic to express the mysteries of the human spirit, Brook is unfazed by challenges, hardships, or criticisms that may arise because of his unorthodox endeavors—even his cutting down a Shakespearean masterpiece. Peter Brook goes his own way—and, to his credit, has always done so.

— — — — — — — — — — • — — — — — — — — —

Q: How did this adaptation of *Hamlet* come about? This is not your first effort with *Hamlet,* is it?

PB: We did a play, *Qui Est La?—Who Is There?* (the very first line of "Hamlet")—made up of fragments of *Hamlet.* In doing these fragments, I got the taste for developing a concentrated version of *Hamlet.* A long time ago, when I was sitting in the audience during the *The Man Who,* I looked at the set of one table and a few chairs on a very small stage. I thought, How curious—that's all one needs to do *Hamlet.* A couple of years later, we did a project about the influences of pioneer theater directors, and we needed raw material to work with, so we took some scenes [from *Hamlet*] just for the purpose of having extracts. In doing these excerpts, I saw something fresh and strong come to the surface just because of this pruning. And I thought that one day it would be interesting to study the play and make it into a complete concentrated form. Then I met Adrian Lester, and I asked him if he would like to be in an English version of *Qui Est La?** But rather than this, we did a condensed *Hamlet.*

*Qui Est La? was a short-lived experiment dealing with theatrical techniques in playing scenes from *Hamlet.*

Q: Why did you choose Adrian Lester?

PB: I saw him play the part of Rosalind in *As You Like It,* and I thought he was marvelous. He is extraordinarily versatile. He came out of the Royal Academy as the most promising student and went on to do *As You Like It* and then went on to do *Company* with Sam Mendes. He has extraordinary range. He sings, he moves beautifully, he dances, and he is an adorable person. I thought he was a natural for our work.

Q: What do you say to those who find all these changes in *Hamlet* are something of a shock, that your vision doesn't fit their conception of *Hamlet?*

PB: I would say that it is good news if it's a shock. That's part of the aim. The reason for doing *Hamlet* is for people to receive it as a new experience. And the first thing was to break the disastrous habit that exists with *Hamlet.* People come to the play humming the tune, as they say on Broadway, before they enter the theater. I've seen it many, many times, and one can't help listening to the words heard in one's mind, and comparing the production one is seeing with thousands of other versions. I remember, when I was eighteen or nineteen, seeing John Gielgud in his very mature *Hamlet,* where you could see that even he, while playing, was taking into account fifty footnotes that a thousand editors had stuck onto this play. The first thing I had to do was cut through the enormous superstructure of prejudices and do away with the various conceptions of *Hamlet.* If this production broke through expectations, that is already good news. Under layers and layers of superstructure is a great play.

Q: Why did you change the order of the play, like putting "to be or not to be" in a different place? And you changed the ending?

PB: For the audience—and, above all, a critical audience—to look at this and try to understand from direct experience what this order tells, or what, in fact, it tells not. Why has this gone there? Of course it is all for a very precise reason. The question is very much like making you see a new play. When you see a play by Pinter, for example, the critic asks himself or herself, Why is this there? What is the meaning of this? What is the link between them?

Q: Well, what is the link?

PB: It's for you to tell me. Look, you were there in the theater last night and you saw the audience, which had a very rich experience. Did you get that impression?

Q: Yes, they were truly enraptured. They didn't make a sound. Their attention was astonishing.

PB: They made a powerful sound at the end, didn't they?

Q: Of course. There was plenty of clapping and shouting. And a standing ovation. I was particularly impressed by their attention—no coughing, no shuffling around, no whispering.

PB: You saw that the impression is very powerful. Even the English who came felt it. And Adrian Lester, this Hamlet—I've never worked with an actor who has had such an acute sensitivity toward words and their meanings. And when Richard Eyre [then head of the National Theatre] came to see the play, he told me that of all the Hamlets he had seen in his life, this was the first time he had seen an actor who seems as intelligent as the character he plays.

Q: Why did you change the title?

PB: I call the play *The Tragedy of Hamlet,* just as I called *Carmen La Tragédie de Carmen,* which brings out more strongly what is in the full five-hour play. Even though the king, the queen, and Laertes have many more words in the full-length play, they are more related to Hamlet in this production. If you take these characters away, Hamlet does not exist. The tragedy of Hamlet is in his interrelations with those forces around him. If you play it five hours long, you will find that the interest is held only because of Hamlet. There has never been a production in which you find, for example, that the king is more complex than what you see in this cut version. The interrelations are always between those forces inevitably impinging on Hamlet. That's why *Hamlet* is unlike *King Lear,* for example. *King Lear* is, by chance, called *King Lear.* But it is not only about Lear. All these changing forces in Lear come together, whether it's Goneril, or the Fool, or Edgar, or Gloucester. All this complex network is called *King Lear.* And in *A Midsummer Night's Dream,* there is not *one* single central character. The whole network is *A Midsummer Night's Dream.* But *Hamlet* is uniquely a centralist play; there has never been a network. Which doesn't mean that the others are not important. But the feel of it is *The Tragedy of Hamlet.*

Q: You cut out Fortinbras. Are you not interested in the political aspects of the play?

PB: I deny that that exists. In the sixties, starting in England and in America, the reaction against a whole complacent bourgeois theater was to rediscover political implications that had been forgotten for centuries. And it was very fashionable, like all intellectual movements, to say that Shakespeare had not been considered a political writer but, in fact, Shakespeare's plays are deeply political. And in this light, Peter Hall did his great *Wars of the Roses** and one also sees that there are plays like *Coriolanus* and *Troilus and Cressida* that are political. But with *Hamlet*, it is just a sixties throwback that says that if you take out Fortinbras, where is the political dimension? In fact, if you look at it very coolly, there is nothing in the whole story of Hamlet and the reason for his tragedy that makes a link to political questions. Only on the crudest levels is there a court, and in a court, naturally, there are court plots, and there is a king who is suspicious about a potential rival. All that doesn't make it a political play like *Coriolanus,* where the protagonist is involved in choices that are political.

Q: But why did Shakespeare put in the character of Fortinbras?

PB: No one can answer that. In pruning the play, I took out Fortinbras because, for me, he is not relevant to the central tragedy. If you look at Shakespeare, you will find that the man was endlessly pragmatic and was working for a living theater, where he did many, many things for the needs and taste of the times. And one of the conventions of the Elizabethans was plot and subplot. And saying things over again so that the audience got it and so on. There are plays like *Lear* where the subplot is totally integrated and is insepa-

---

*The Wars of the Roses (1963) was Peter Hall's production of a number of Shakespeare's history plays: *Henry VI*, parts one, two, and three, and *Richard III*. In 1964, he did *Richard II, Henry IV,* parts one and two, and *Henry V*.

rable from the main plot. In *Hamlet,* Fortinbras is somebody you don't see. You are told at the beginning that Hamlet's father had a quarrel with Fortinbras's father. It is not dramatized. It's just told. In an Elizabethan setting with a queen, before parliamentary democracy in England was even thought of, Shakespeare made his hero someone who puts the whole country back in order. The implication of the Fortinbras story is that life goes on, what Shakespeare always wanted at the end of his plays. Here you have a country in a state of confusion and chaos, like in a certain election, when a strong, decent young fellow comes into view, and is put into power to straighten things out, only to become a dictator. To end the play on someone not close to the action during the whole of the play is not exactly relevant today. This, my ending, is closer to us, and healthier than to convey, in a major play, a message that when your country is in turmoil, get a young leader, a young good-looking soldier, who can take over. He suddenly becomes a dictator. This to me is the political aspect that I wanted to change. And put something else in its place. Instead, Horatio ends our play and carries the whole meaning of our play and the future with him.

Q: But Horatio says at the end of the play, "Who's there?" which is the first line at the beginning of the play. One wonders what that means. Why that change?

PB: How can one define anything as simple as that line? "Who's there?" is a question. How you take that question is your business.

Q: Okay. Why cut out the Laertes scene with Polonius?

In fact, Laertes doesn't appear until the end of the play. How do you justify that?

PB: Laertes is a key figure, not in the scene where Polonius gives him advice, but in contrast to Hamlet. Here we have Hamlet, an enormously talented young man, who is not neurotic at all, who is full of energy and passion and observation and self-doubt, like every human being should be, who does not rush like a madman to revenge. He asks himself, What is the meaning of this? In contrast to him is this fine young man, who asks no questions. Father killed; I kill the killer—demonstrating the present-day image of the cycle of the revenge motif and violence. He enters into a sordid plot and dies knowing that he has been used. This contrast between the two changes the view that Hamlet is incapable, that he is weak, that there is something wrong with him. Hamlet is a strong, humorous, poetic, intelligent man who is trying to put his life together. Laertes is the opposite. Hamlet is the example of what one would call a true human being. This contrast is more important than that of miserable Fortinbras, who represents the good soldier needed to set the country right.

Q: You have written with a certain disdain about people who would modernize or change Shakespeare. How do you reconcile those views with your own production, which plainly changes various aspects of *Hamlet*?

PB: Nothing is more disastrous today than to have false gods. And even the text is a false god. I have written a thousand times that my goal is to try to penetrate what is behind the text, what the author was truly trying to say. In our version, the modernizing was done with the deepest respect. As I have said, the only way to discover Shakespeare is to forget him. To rediscover Shakespeare was why we did the adaptation. Making *Hamlet* is not adding modern gimmicks. Fifty years ago in England, there was the first production of *Hamlet* in modern dress. And everyone was amazed. It was a great event. But today when one does the external modernizing—fascist uniforms in the Roman plays, or people playing Shakespeare in jeans and bringing motorbikes on stage—everything is being modernized by external use. This has become a new cliché.

Modernizing, as I see it, means making something from the past live in the present—representing. And representing demands different things in different plays. Representing *A Midsummer Night's Dream* required the particular invention that went with it. It didn't require touching one word of the text, because of all the plays of Shakespeare, *Dream* is the most Mozartian in the sense that there is perfect marriage at every moment between form and content. But actually, Shakespeare was not like Racine, who looked for a perfect union of form and content. Shakespeare's theater was like Dickens and Dostoyevsky, in which the form is loose and rich and in which passionate rhythms flow. Nobody has ever thought of Dostoyevsky as an example of exquisite formal structure. Dickens certainly was not, because he wrote for serialization. *Dream,* however, is perfect in form and content. But not *Hamlet.* It is not like *The Marriage of Figaro,* a work of absolute perfection, in which every detail comes together, so that if anyone today does a cut version of *Figaro,* they will do less well than if they did it exactly how it stands, because the form and content are one and the same thing. On the other hand, Bizet, a beautiful composer, wrote *Carmen* according to the needs of the Opéra Comique. He took the Mérimée story, which was beautifully structured and in which form and content were perfectly captured within a short story. But the Opéra Comique needed a chorus and a children's chorus and processions with even a horse onstage. So they put a horse onstage. All that superstructure had nothing to do with the beautiful form, which was hidden and came from the original story.

Modernizing *Hamlet* is not bringing in gimmicks, but digging deeply into the text to find the level where one touches the fibers that have been buried through the years and have led people to think that the text is sacrosanct.

Q: You wrote in one of your lectures about the metaphysical aspects of Shakespeare. Can you elaborate on that?

PB: Shakespeare carried inside him at every moment an interrogation about every aspect of life. Shakespeare was questioning everything, but on another level. It might be, what is the level of passion in a human being? Is it better to be without passion, or should a human being have passion, and how far should one follow its lead or resist it? And then you have the questions of whether there is a heaven, or hell, and are there invisible forces that have names like devils or spirits? Do these devils and spirits cover up something infinitely more mysterious and unknown? This is in the whole of Shakespeare. One cannot approach Shakespeare without realizing that he himself was living through an interrogation that one calls metaphysical. One tends to forget that Shakespeare was not only a writer but a human being, a person. And as a person, Shakespeare carried inside him everything he wrote, so that all strands of meaning and feeling are there, and if one denies the metaphysical, one is cutting out some essential part of Shakespeare.

Q: How is this manifested onstage?

PB: That depends entirely on the person watching it, how he or she is feeling. Two critics wrote interesting reviews of my *Hamlet,* about what they considered to be the metaphysical aspects of the play. It is not for me to claim anything. It is for the people who see it to respond.

Q: Doing this play in English for a French audience must have presented a problem. How did you work on the language?

PB: The pure sound and texture of the words carry an enormous weight of meaning. Ninety-five percent of the French viewers followed the sound, the movement, and the rhythm of the language, even though they didn't speak English. The actor must be sensitive to words and appreciate the taste and sound and imagery of a word, even a simple word. Many modern actors, especially American actors, tend to speak the way that they do in everyday life. What the actor needs to work on all the time is finding the thought behind each word. When you do that, you find that there is a music in thought. When King Lear says, "Never, never, never, never, never"—if you try to analyze this in metric terms, you can never say it truly.

When Paul Scofield said it in *Kinglear* every single night, he said it differently. Every single time, it had music and different music. The music was the thought and feeling that led from one to the other so that the beat was not regular. The beat is the human beat, which can only be found by the actor discovering more and more deeply the true thought and feeling that comes not just from his own thinking but from the actual texture of the words themselves. In Shakespeare, there is such a compact thought in each line that if you take the line as a whole, it would actually be beyond the human being to think so elaborately. If you listen to the texture of the work, you can discover the sense of music and link it to meaning. It is the difference between Western music, which is all based on a predictable structure given by bars that the composer has set down, and Eastern music, which is based on an awareness of the irregular rhythms— there is no regularity. When the thought and the feeling are right, the music returns, but it isn't a music that comes from starting with the external structure.

Q: How did you come to select costumes in mostly gray and black?

PB: I have always had an enormous need to have strong colors in my productions. Either we could have had a gray or black or neutral floor and very colorful figures or the other way around. In the end, the joy of color is there in the cushions and on the ground. When we started, I said I did not want contemporary clothes—that would have been a cliché. When I first started Shakespeare productions, it was common to put the play in another period. But today if you do it Victorian, or you do it medieval, or anything like that, it is something that has been seen a hundred times. And it has become a cliché. So we started with what is not contemporary and what is not period. That's a very fine tightrope. This is a tragedy, and we needed simple clothes so it would be impossible to say what period they represent. The actors wore no makeup. No wigs. Adrian Lester's dreadlocks were his; that's the way he is. We wanted his natural self in the part. We tried to make our everyday life a natural link to the past. Adrian Lester is a young man who wears what is natural and comfortable to him—dreadlocks. If someone told him that in playing Hamlet, a Danish prince, he should look less like a black man, that would be appalling.

Q: The ending of your *Hamlet* led many people to think that your interest in the Gurdjieff work influenced the ending—the so-called questioning on a metaphysical level: Who am I? Who is there? What is death? And so forth.

PB: I rigorously, one hundred percent, avoid ever using anything of the Work. [The Gurdjieff teaching is known as the Work.] Where the two do come together working within this field, as in the work of Grotowski and Joe Chaikin, there are certain exercises and working principles, such as sitting in a circle, listening, doing exercises with the body, that have a natural relationship to elements in the Gurdjieff Work. But I would never ever use a method, a principle, an idea from the Work and say that this is a structure or a formula that we can use in the theater. Obviously, no one can be involved in an inner search without increasing something in one's own capacity to respond. It makes you more sensitive; it doesn't make you better, but it does make you a little more open. I don't sit down and do a rehearsal thinking about Gurdjieff theory. Certainly nothing would be more horrendous than if I had called the actors together and told them that they were now going to have a religious experience, that we were going to take this play and look for its spirituality. Can you imagine anything more terrible?

Q: But the Gurdjieff Work has affected you. So something has to come through.

PB: What comes through, comes through. There is nothing deliberately conscious that I do.

Q: What do you consider your most memorable achievements?

PB: I never think about it. I never look back. I have no sense whatsoever of pride or achievements. Quite truly. I work, and at the same time I am very realistic and know that if things go well with the particular work I am doing, it helps to do the next thing. If you have a bad flop in the theater, it makes it difficult to do the next thing. And if you have a success, it is indeed more pleasant for everyone.

Q: How do you feel about your fame?

PB: I don't feel it. I don't take it seriously. I don't think it has any deep justification. Of course I am grateful to those who have helped me. I have to earn my living, so I go on working. I have no pension. To support my family, I have to go on working. It's a practical thing.

Q: You have had the golden touch in your life. How do you feel about that?

PB: I don't think people can take credit for themselves for what happens to them. It is either genetic or life's circumstances, largely due to help or hindrance coming from other people. And from what one is born with, something evolves. And gradually one looks back and sees that one has gone on a certain path. But to take credit for oneself and to say, "I did that" is something one can never say.

Q: Why not? You did direct that show and all the other great productions. It is quite clear that this is a Brook production. It has your signature all over it.

PB: But I can't take credit for that.

Q: Who else should take credit?

PB: Because there is no credit to be given. You go to a concert and there is someone playing a piece of music that you love. And it happens to be a marvelous performance. And for the pianist to go away and think that he or she must take credit for it is wrong, because, at that moment, where does the credit go? To the event, to the music, to the combination of circumstances, or what? The one thing I do have regrets about is when an actor who works with me for the first time feels intimidated. My job is to try to dispel that. I can only do the best I can with the group of actors and not make declarations. *The Tragedy of Hamlet* is presented as best we can, so that the interested spectator can find something in it. It is all up to what the audience sees. And feels. That's all.

Paris, 2000

Fourteen

Looking Back

During the thirty years that I've known Peter Brook, we've had all sorts of conversations. Often they were related to a particular work I was covering for the *New York Times,* but just as often, there were random discussions about this and that—informal talks between friends.

In the following pages are samplings of Brook's reflections on acting, his method of directing, his family—and whatever else happened to come up. As always, a sophisticated mind is at work: a searching mind, unafraid to take on any challenge. These lively talks convey once again the energy, vigor, and optimism of the masterful Peter Brook.

———————————— • ————————————

Q: Let's talk about acting. You've worked with big stars like Paul Scofield and John Gielgud. And then you've worked with young actors in a group situation. What's the difference between the two?

PB: True, I've always worked interchangeably with many different types of actors. And it was interesting. Paul Scofield, for example—no one could predict his incredible depth. That's the most rewarding thing. On the other hand, when one works with a group, it's something quite different. It is the unity of a group that is most important. What one's looking for is more transparent acting; in other words, the opposite of the virtuosity of acting. It is acting where, in the end, you can no longer be sure that the person is acting at all.

Q: You mean he just exists onstage, as it were?

PB: Yes. This is one of the big differences between the best European and the best Third World acting. I've seen different sorts of African actors in our work, sometimes just within our own private researches, actually go further than the greatest European actors. It is so organic that you don't get the impression from any angle that the actors are acting. Every fiber of the person is totally transformed.

Q: Can you remember a specific actor or incident where this happened?

PB: I remember one of the greatest things I've ever seen was an African actor in an exercise playing a blind man. And with no preparation, he just suddenly stood up and there was a blind man. Normally, you can actually see an actor making a characterization. You can see the thin line, the division, but here it was completely transparent. And this, as you rightly have said, is what we were looking for, for example, in *The Ik*. We had reached the point where I was delighted when someone would say, "Have these people ever acted before?" Which of course the actors hated.

Q: The greatest thing about *The Ik*, as I remember it, was that it was seamless; the actors just existed as people—as though they had reached a state of being. Is that what you were looking for? Is that what you mean by "transparent" acting?

PB: Yes.

Q: Do you need very special types of actors to withstand months of exercises and the long period of rehearsals that you demand?

PB: Yes. There's a natural selection. There are some people who are right, and some people who can't stand it.

Q: How do you select the actors? How do you know who will be pliable and have the required strength? Do you look for the most experienced actors?

PB: There has to be a balance. Experience with openness. That's a very particular person, because there are people who are young and open, and ready to do anything. And because they have no experience, what they bring isn't personal. Something becomes personal through experience. On the other hand, there are people who, through experience, have lost their openness. In between the two, are the people who are truly balanced.

Q: Who in your theatrical career, or in your life, influenced you the most?

PB: I think that one exists to receive and give influences. And nothing is worse than to try to deny that. I'm influenced and influencing. But specifically, when I started work in the theater, the English theater, I thought was just dreadful. It was deadly theater.

That's where I got the image of deadliness. It was lifeless, sometimes skillful, but deeply uninteresting, deeply boring, but with one exception: Tyrone Guthrie, the first director whose work I thought was marvelous. He brought a sweeping energy to everything. He loved doing crowd scenes and operas and creative Shakespeare. And I was very excited by that, because I like doing that, too. In his work, there were great, rushing movements of people sweeping across the stage and moving into one lightning shape and another. He drove everything—even the smallest part—with tremendous energy. Everyone was bursting with life and excitement. And when I started work, he was the model, a director whose work I loved enormously.

Q: What about other masters, like Stanislavsky? And Brecht?

PB: I stayed clear of all theories. I hardly read Stanislavsky or Brecht. Only years later did I ever look at them, because I didn't feel that I could be helped, or interested, by theory.

Q: But you did hear about Artaud?

PB: Years later, I read Artaud, of course. Mainly, it was his intensity that interested me. I thought that his theories were absolutely useless. We tried out a few of the things that were interesting. What everyone in France admired enormously was a very unique and extraordinary man, a wild, extraordinary human being—but the work he did, for the people who saw it (in France, few people ever saw his productions, or took part in them), was never very interesting or very good. His intensity was extraordinary, but I didn't find anything practically useful in Artaud.

Stanislavsky, I never really read. And by the time I first met Brecht and the Berliner Ensemble, I had done a lot of work already. And I was into my own way of work. So apart from liking and constantly being influenced by about fifty or sixty different films or film stars—no, I'd say the greatest influence—what we won't talk about—

Q: Are you referring to Gurdjieff?

PB: It's common knowledge in a sense. You've written about *Meetings with Remarkable Men,* so that you can say that one of the most powerful influences in my life was Gurdjieff.

Q: But who in your youth influenced you before Gurdjieff?

PB: I always look back to a Russian music teacher I had when I was a child. After suffering with very dull, boring, prosaic English piano teachers, I encountered this Russian lady who, from the first lesson, put me in front of things that nobody else had. One was that you don't play with your fingers; you play through listening. The quality of the note you play depends on the quality of the note you've heard in your mind just before playing. In a way, you could say that about the writer—who doesn't write a word on paper. Your hand only follows a word after it has appeared in your mind. You think of something, and then you write it down. Your hand doesn't write; it writes what it's told to write. So the first thing she taught me was the value of listening. There's an acute listening, through which you become aware of the exact sound, and then the body follows and implements that sound.

She taught me the nature of just playing simply,

of repeating it, and of playing dynamically. There's no point in playing a musical phrase unless it is to bring out its most vivid dynamics. From the very first, you should bring out the crescendo and the decrescendo, the passion, and the dynamics immediately—not after you first learn the steps, but right away.

She taught me that, even as a beginner, if you learn to play, you must play for other people. Every few months, she would get an audience. She'd hire a hall, and we all had to play in public constantly. Right from the start, I saw miracles: She would take on middle-aged businesspeople who, as children, had dreamt of playing the piano and had never had time. People at the age of fifty or sixty would meet her at a party and say, "Oh I've always dreamt of playing the piano." Then I saw a businessman who after six months was playing Liszt for two pianos at a public concert. Do you know why? The difference was that children who had to learn the piano because their mothers paid for lessons would learn it in a dour way, which had nothing to do with the life of the phrase—it's just learning because it's there and your fingers have to do it.

Q: Did any of this apply to your work later on?

PB: These things are the basis I've applied to my work ever since. The sense that if you learn something, it has to be put in front of an audience. The audience is what gives you the necessity. You know it has to come out in its most dynamic way because there are people there. And that powerfully transforms one's wish to play. The recognition of an audience was one thing. The other was that listening is more important than doing, that doing is the result of good listening. Which is what I drum into our actors all the time. As I say, my greatest influence—when I was twelve—was this teacher.

Q: You did a film, *Meetings with Remarkable Men,* a film about the spiritual teacher G. I. Gurdjieff, and you did *The Conference of the Birds.* People associate you with mysticism—or something akin to that. Do you want to talk about that?

PB: I think that one has to face the fact that crudely put questions can only be answered in a crude way. Anybody who talks about mysticism obviously can't know what they mean. Otherwise, they wouldn't be talking about it, and therefore they are talking about something they dislike because they don't know. So that's why I say crude questions can only be answered crudely. I could put this exactly the other way around. I think every human being, if he stops to reflect for a moment, would recognize (as I do) that 99.9 percent of universal experience is completely outside one's own possibilities of understanding. I don't believe for one moment—and I think only very blind and pigheaded people can believe—that one can know or experience everything, or can be firmly in the right. I think there's only one simple starting point for anyone at any point in life, which is to say, I know very little—I've had some experiences, but I can't think I know all that is not evident. The moment you realize that—which I've put in the crudest, simplest way once and for all—you realize that many things in heaven and earth are beyond our understanding. I could only communicate with someone who, like myself, believes that there are many things more than we ourselves understand. Having reached that point, let's say that therefore any field in which one works is potentially a field in which one can increase one's understanding. I've been very fortunate in working in the theater, a field that is, in every way, a miniature of many, many aspects of human life—in relation to the individual, in relation to the group. Almost all these elements come into the theater situation and therefore become practical questions.

Q: Would you say that your beliefs or your discoveries have been useful in your work in the theater?

PB: I have rigorously avoided applying to the theater anybody else's discoveries. But what I've been very, very conscious of is that discoveries that I've made quite simply through working are the discoveries of certain basic patterns and principles in human beings and in human relations. I have found discoveries matching those made by other people in other fields. And, by intuition and empirically, I have discovered in theater groups that the growth and decline of energies within the theater context have been known and understood much more fully and richly in certain ancient traditions.

Q: Can you be specific about these traditions?

PB: People within these traditions have very precisely studied the relation between apparent human behavior and little-known, long-forgotten laws that human beings encounter. When I was twenty-one or twenty-two, I first encountered mathematical laws of proportion—what's called the golden section—that explained the relations between different shapes and between harmonious and unharmonious proportions. This was known in classical times and related directly to certain things, the reason one made something so high, or why one would have three columns instead of four. And so I've always been interested in turning toward sources where the very things that we know as empirical turn into principles in our work. They are reflections of what, in traditions, go way beyond the theater and encompass human life as a whole. So in that way, there is a parallel that makes me, from a practical basis, completely confident that what is crudely called "mysticism" is actual reflections of truths that we know very little about.

Q: But Peter, didn't you say that you had read Ouspensky—Gurdjieff's first pupil—and you became interested in him when you were twenty years old? Or you met people who were interested in these philosophies?

PB: Well, no. In fact, what I was talking about first was not Ouspensky. It was before Ouspensky. It was a book by a certain Russian, who wrote a series of books about mathematical proportions, which I found later developed in Ouspensky. Having been interested in all the different forms of Middle Eastern and Oriental practice and philosophy, I find that, in the twentieth century, a certain person has brought ancient science into an understandable form for the West, and that is Gurdjieff.

Q: Well, why not come out and say that? After all, you did choose to make a film about Gurdjieff.

PB: What I do *not* want to say, simply by knowing how harmful this can be, is that one has to put up a very strong barrier against anything to do with this. Especially in America.

Q: Why in America? Should this barrier be put up in France, or elsewhere?

PB: In America, more than anywhere else, there are a vast number of shady and phony groups going by every kind of name and involved in every sort of thing, so I would only talk about the Gurdjieff Work to somebody really serious. To me, the most interesting person of all the different explorers and teachers, the most comprehensive, and the one with the most scientifically developed view—which is constantly confirmed by our own discovery in our work—is Gurdjieff. I find that you can certainly say that very firmly.

Q: I know you don't like to talk about this, but the logical question is, Are you a follower? True, I have asked you that before, but . . .

PB: Your question is, Am I a Gurdjieff follower? I can say that one of the tragic aspects of any really difficult teaching that's ever brought into the world is that it is rapidly stolen and cheapened. And today, at every street corner, there are people selling Gurdjieff on the one hand, Zen, yoga, Grotowski . . . Take Grotowski, for instance. I know [this] from very close experience with Grotowski—he is my dear friend; I've followed and known him now for thirty years. I've seen better than most people how his work is only meaningful for eight people, or perhaps only five, who are around Grotowski, working with him. By the time it gets to be secondhand, it's already pretty useless. I mean, there are seven people—whose names we won't mention, whom you know—who are already using Grotowski secondhand. But by the time it has got to the fifth hand at the street corner, anybody is doing Grotowski work.

Q: Well, isn't this a natural development? New ideas or novel ideas take hold, become popular, and then fade. Everything is merchandised, especially art.

PB: This applies to our work at the Center, too. I know that there are people who've happened to come to the door, or want to eat in the café next door, when we've been there . . . people who later are printing programs saying that they are teaching the methods of the center in Paris.

Q: So what you're saying is that even talking about the Gurdjieff Work might cheapen it?

PB: One of the central aspects of Gurdjieff's Work, he said, was that his "great specialty is treading on people's corns." By which he meant that he was provoking people. He was not trying to make followers. He was not trying to make believers. "I am trying to provoke people to follow the first principle, which is everything must be verified by oneself," he said. And the street-corner proselytizers who easily use Gurdjieff or Ouspensky—because anybody can; they're not copyright names—they are actually trying to produce followers for the same terrifying reasons that sects all over the world wish to hypnotize, encapsulate, and exploit people. The one essential, and I'd say unique, fact of any serious Gurdjieff group is that it's doing everything to prevent—whether by boastful claims, publicity, or proselytizing of any sort—making people into followers. The relation of our own work is not that there are principles here, or teachings that I try to bring into our own work, but exactly the opposite.

Q: But if Gurdjieff's Work is important, why keep it for a select few?

PB: It's very simple. The meaning of *Meetings with Re-markable Men,* the reason that we made it at the time—and I talked about this all the time when the film came out—was to try to capture a sense of what is meant by the word *searcher.* And so you asked me a question, which is, "Are you a follower?" And I'd say, "No." It's a contradiction in terms. But a "searcher"? I hope so.

Q: But it implies that you—

PB: No, that's nobody's business. There is a point where one's under no compulsion to answer. I feel that one of the great misunderstandings of our time is that people feel, when confronted with the television camera, or the journalist, that you have to tell all. And you don't. You tell just so much.

Q: All right. Let's get back to talking about the theater. You say you let everything go when you're rehearsing. You don't make decisions too quickly. You say you have no preconceived notions about what the end should be. You keep changing. I heard actors complain that you change even on opening night. How does a production get on with that procedure? Don't the actors go crazy with all of that?

PB: They survive—and productions have gone on. And most of the actors come back for more. So, obviously, the actors, our actors, come back, and have been there for a long, long time. None of our old prominent actors, those close to us, have ever left. I mean, some have evolved. Some of them have gotten film work, but none of our real actors have ever left.

Q: But let's say that if some of your old actors are not available and are doing other things, you will need to cast other people. How are you going to work with actors who haven't been in your group and are not used to the way you work?

PB: Directing involves many different things. You have to try to make rehearsals interesting. You have to make it more exciting for a person to work this way than to work another way. It's obvious that I also wouldn't take somebody who I felt was so frightened, and so anxious, and needed security so much that if you changed anything, they'd be demised. I mean, there are lots of actors—the old-fashioned sort of English actors whom I know—who, if you changed anything after the first day, would be paralyzed with fear, or blazing with anger. But I don't work with those. I mean, right from the start, somebody like John Gielgud or Orson Welles would be throwing things out every second and changing and starting again. They would have felt appalled if I'd come up with a rigid plan and said, "Well, even if you've got a new idea, it's too late, because I fixed that scene yesterday." Can you imagine how John Gielgud or Orson Welles would have reacted?

Q: You used the expression in one of your books that one needs a "sense of direction." Can you explain what you meant by that?

PB: Yes. I've done things that haven't worked out. And I've tried to find what's the difference between something I've done that's come together and something that hasn't. And this relates to what I call the "formless hunch." The usual directorial conception is that there is a blueprint that a director works out before he starts. And then he directs people to implement his blueprint. That's the opposite of what I do. What

I do, on the other hand, is to prepare, to study, until something grows, which is a sense of direction. What that means is exactly what the words say.

I'll give you an example. I was once in a broken-down Jeep in the desert in Afghanistan with an incredible crazy guy, an Afghan driver. He had, in the middle of the desert, this uncanny sense of direction. There were car tracks going in five directions, and nothing to show which was the right one. And unerringly, he would swing there, swing here, and eventually find the right direction. And in doing a play, if you haven't done your preparation, or somehow you're not touched deeply by the subject—it's happened to me when I've taken on something in a way for the wrong reasons—that sense of direction is either weak or not there.

Q: If you've taken it on and later realize it didn't really appeal to you, how do you work with that?

PB: I'll try with all my means to do good work, to think of things to try, but it's very difficult, and sometimes impossible to find the way. Then, one listens to everybody's suggestions, and then you get in a muddle. Because you listen to one person and he says this; you listen to another person, who says that. And if the result isn't good, it's the bad effect of democracy, that everybody has put their finger in the pot. But the opposite of that is autocracy, where the director knows what he wants to do, and he's not going to let anything, or anyone's suggestion, take away from what he wants. This is the autocratic way of direction, in which he says, "I'm very sorry, but while you made a very good suggestion, it's not in my plan. And my plan is this." He is like a general.

Q: How do you avoid all this?

PB: By the "sense of direction." This means that I know that what I'm looking for is over there, on the other side of the mountain. And it takes exploration. One might try to go to the north, and someone says, "Let's go due south, or to the east." And you say, "Ah, that could be very interesting." And you explore that.

Q: Is that what happened in *The Mahabharata*? I was told that you had some kind of a "foggy vision." What was your hunch there?

PB: I had, in theater terms, an overall sense that *The Mahabharata* should unfold with great fluidity in a space so free that it would be possible—no, I won't take *The Mahabharata* because it's too involved. Take *Carmen*. Much more simple to explain. In *Carmen,* I had a hunch that the great values in this particular work were very human and very realistic. That was a hunch. Thirty years ago, among the operas that I would have liked to do was *Carmen*. And the formless hunch I had at the time was something that was a kaleidoscope of moving colors. And when I asked for *Carmen,* the opera people would say, "Next season." And again: "Is there an opera you would particularly like to direct?" And I'd say, "*Carmen*." And they'd say, "Well, no, you can't do it this year, but perhaps another time." To me, *Carmen* at that point was something of light and color and movement—Spain as brilliant colors, as heat and energy. Had I done a production then, it would have had dazzling costumes, a chorus that I would animate, get them to rush around the stage continually, and it would have been something perhaps very colorful and very brilliant. Brilliant in the sense of dancing and choreography, say thirty years ago. But I never did that production. When I came back to it years and years later, something had crystallized through hearing the music again—there is a very tense, powerful inner story that is very naked and very human. And not at all fantasy, but very much rooted in the earth. Which is related to the best music in it. Now, that was a formless hunch. I started working with Marius Constant, and Jean-Claude Carrière, and gradually we three came to the conclusion that, indeed, if we concentrated the piece on the small number of characters and just developed their music, something much more powerful would emerge. And we could throw away everything that related to that colorful spectacle show that thirty years ago attracted me. There was a day when, in the Bouffes du Nord, our theater, we looked at the concrete floor we were rehearsing on and said, "Now, are we going to do this on a carpet?"—which had been our tradition. In all our famous carpet shows, we put down a carpet, and on a carpet you can conjure up everything from a palace to a desert. "Should we do this on a carpet? And not even have an audience, just have a grand piano and a big carpet?" There were people on our team who were very passionately for that. And I went along with it and said, "Yes, let's try it." I measured that with the formless hunch, with the sense of direction, and the sense of direction said, Yes, but there is a grit that is fundamental in this. And a carpet is alien to that sense of grit. It's obvious that under the people's feet should be neither the boards of the theater nor the concrete that's natural to the theater—nor a carpet. What should it be? It should be earth. It should be sand. Because these people should be standing on a sandy soil. And then we started doing different things . . . and then we found a ready mixture. Out of that, the formless hunch took form.

In the same way, the general feeling of *The Mahabharata* defined itself equally. But *The Mahabharata* on a carpet would make no sense. Not only did it have to be on earth but these characters had to be in contact with water and fire. When we started, we didn't know that we were going to have a river over in back and a pool over in front. We just thought of water, and then one day, by trial and error, Jean-Claude Carrière, Chloé Obolensky [the designer], and I said we could put this here, until we found the right place—where the action was more to the back, and another body of water was in the front. At first, we had a river at the back, and I had a whole canal of water separating the audience from the stage, all the way around; it was a whole circle; the actors were on earth in the middle. We tried that out, looked at it, and decided against it because that would break the contact with the audience. Then we reduced that to the little pond in the front . . . so that one had the water where one needed it—in the front—and yet we had contact with the audience, so that the audience and actors were all on the same earth. And that's how that gradually evolved. That's how a sense of direction makes it possible for a million things to be explored, everybody's ideas to be brought into the pool, and yet there has to be the guiding factor that enables you to say yes or no at the last moment.

Q: And it is you who makes that last decision?

PB: Yes, of course. All the time. That's my job. That is directing. If you quibble over words, you can say that directing is pointing, not imposing. That's how you direct. Somebody asks you the way; you direct them. People think of directing in terms of a company director. If somebody asks you the way, you direct them—in plain English. And if they set off, misunderstanding you, you stop them and you say, "No," and you actually point the way. Which is very different from the theory of the company director.

Q: But you have to have some idea of the way.

PB: Yes.

Q: Have you ever been dissatisfied with any of your productions, or is that a question you'd rather not discuss?

PB: Oh, yes. Constantly. But in a very definite way. Basically, I am dissatisfied in different degrees and constantly think that one can do better and differently. But at the same time, I recognize that there is a very curious phenomenon. It's another one of these things you see as the expression of certain laws. There is an analogy between a production and cooking. At certain times, when the process has gone well, as the time goes by, the heat increases like the intensity of rehearsals. Sometimes you really like making omelettes and scrambled eggs, so that, in stirring, you try many different things, and after trying again and again, there comes a moment when something actually crystallizes. And when that shape crystallizes, you can't change it, even if you want to.

Q: Why not? Is this the reason that so many shows actually fail, because they can't be changed at a certain time?

PB: Well, even if you let time go by, and do a completely new production, it can't be changed. Things reach their final shape for that production. What I try to avoid is to think that any production should live too long. And I really think that about five years is the longest for any work.

Q: Have you ever revived a play after a few years?

PB: We just revived *Carmen* last year. But the shape of it had crystallized. In casting new people, I did everything to bring in new personalities. But actually, I didn't change the shape of the production. I didn't want to change it at all. That doesn't mean that it can go on indefinitely. At a certain time, it certainly becomes old-fashioned. It's for somebody else to do it. And I could even do it myself in a completely different way. But today, for instance, I don't think I could do a production of *King Lear* even if I wanted to, because if I tried to reproduce the old one, even with documents, exactly as it was, it would be old-fashioned. And if I tried to do it in a new way, too many things would have crystallized.

Q: I've noticed that in your productions, the tempo and rhythm are extremely important. If one actor lets down even for a moment, the scene, even the entire production, can lag. What's the most important aspect of a production? Is it this rhythm? Or tempo?

PB: What is important is what you say. There is something I talk to the actors about every single day. Which is this energy and rhythm. But when it's good, it really is natural. In other words, it does come from the group playing together like a team. And there it's like in a football match: The rhythm is there when everyone is playing well. For that reason, it can't be imposed. Like with a farce, you can rehearse a very strong rhythm just by saying, "Now, quick, c'mon, quickly now, run." You can pick up your cue. You can work that out with comedy and farce. That's an imposed rhythm that's good for that sort of thing, but it isn't a subtle one. The subtle rhythm is when the whole group really is playing together as a team. Then you get something much more satisfying.

Q: How do you get that to happen?

PB: It has to be worked on, because it is, of course, more fragile. So that it can vary. On the other hand, the actors realize because of that variation that each performance is a new event. And it makes the actors more aware of the need to try to find that rhythm and energy, and they are unhappy when, for one reason or another, that energy isn't there.

Q: Is that why your actors do some exercises before the production?

PB: Oh yes. Everyone does them. I mean, there are exceptions.

Q: Are you more interested in the here and the now? Is that what keeps you from looking back?

PB: There is no separation from the past; it's just a natural development. We just hope it's better.

Q: People have said that you had deliberately broken with the past when you moved to Paris.

PB: There is no truth in that whatsoever.

Q: But you do live in Paris, not in London.

PB: Yes, but I've had a flat here in Paris for twenty-five years. I did the film *Moderato Cantabile,* and the play

Cat on a Hot Tin Roof. There is no reason that people in the States, for example, should know what I have done, because of the small number of things I've brought to America. If you have three hits, and one failure, people say, "Aha, he's going over to experimental work." The truth is that I've done experimental work all my life. The break in 1970, when I started the Center, was no bigger a break than in the sixties when we started the RSC, or the break with *Lord of the Flies,* and my early Shakespeare productions. They were, all in their time, radically experimental, as well. The nature of the work developed but the aims were not different. But what has no bearing is that I changed in a different direction. There really has been no shift at all.

Q: You have talked about your search each time. You have said that every production you've done has had a certain meaning in itself. And I presume that it is connected with something you are searching for. May I ask what answers you have found in your search?

PB: I've known since long ago that there are no answers. The very first thing I learned in connection with any sort of work or teaching or searching is that there are different qualities of awareness. There is a low-level awareness and a greater awareness in more directions. And a greater awareness is the only kind of answer one can ever have. One wishes to know something, but the answer is in a form of being more aware—of being open to a richer level of experience. This is endless and this is the aim in any production. My capacity for awareness is absolutely inseparable from other people. And with people in a group. And with the audience. If the work increases awareness, I am as much sustained by it as is a member of the audience.

Q: Does that answer why you are in theater?

PB: Yes. And that's why there is no abrupt difference between this, my work, and what one is looking for in life.

Q: Is this why you can sit through performances so many times, because of the double vision you may have—you're the audience, you're the director, and you're the actor? Is there a more profound attention that you are involved with?

PB: Oh yes. Which doesn't happen all the time. When it happens, it's very rewarding. I would say the only fundamental difference with all the work I had done before the Center is that once a production took shape, usually on the first night, I then felt that I had dropped out of it. I had done everything to that point and I didn't feel any longer connected, so that it was very difficult for me to go back to the production. I would go back only if something had gone wrong, but not otherwise, which is the normal way of the director: It is finished.

Q: Is this one of the reasons you left London and started the Center?

PB: When I started the Center, I saw the possibility of creating different conditions where the work would not reach its final shape at the first performance. On the contrary, the first performance was just one step in a continuous process. This was only possible with the group, because we had done many, many improvisations while working on a piece (like *Timon of*

Athens, for example), before the piece was finished. Having done a hundred or more improvisations with the same people, I wanted to make this kind of work more structured, so that even if it took a shape, that shape would not be so definite, so that I could feel that after one performance it was not over. But on the contrary, that performance was meeting the next performance, and so on. And so each performance had the possibility of being more than a single event, and therefore it was natural for me to be there, rather than go away.

Q: One of the things you've often said is that you wanted to work toward creating in your theater "the invisible world." And how does this invisible world manifest itself? Does language play a part in the invisible world?

PB: Language can cover a great number of things. There is a point when the real experience happens in between the words. Language can carry it to a certain point, and then the actual reality of the experience is neither this nor that. It is somewhere just in between. And that's rare. Sometimes just a word or sentence, or the slip of a word, may catch or miss the essence.

Q: How does one really know what the essence is? It is so abstract.

PB: Well, take the whole of music. You can write a hundred words describing the experience of a piece of Bach, or a Mozart quartet, or a piece of jazz, and you know that the essential experience—this mysterious underground world of human emotions—can give you something that is there, out in the open, and experienced by millions of people through music. In terms of the real forces that come into play with human beings in the theater, the actual acting out of something fills in the gaps.

Q: Are there examples of this in any of your productions?

PB: In *A Midsummer Night's Dream,* you have a generalizing word, *love,* but not a generalizing word for spirits. In writing and describing, you can go just so far. In *A Midsummer Night's Dream,* you actually bring out interweaving threads. You know they are there. You, as an audience, have lived with them, and see them as they are. In *The Conference of the Birds,* there is something in Arabic that they talk about—an inner experience that no one can describe poetically. You try to find an image for this through the use of myth. In trying to play this, one thinks that the audience is ostensibly watching a children's story. They are being made aware of certain things they are unaware of. This, to me, is clearly and simply the feedback one gets from an audience when they say, "Something in me is touched." They experience something that, without this work, they would not have experienced. Suddenly—in place of the word *invisible,* substitute the word *abstract*—the abstract becomes concrete while you are in the theater. Concrete in the sense of its being there, and you can actually taste it. Take *Marat/Sade,* which is the other end of the stick. While you are in the theater, you might say, "I don't believe that madness and violence really exist." When you live through that in the theater, you have a taste of what it's like to be caught up in that tremendous surge of energy and passion of a violent nature. You can really experience this. Cruelty is an abstraction, but it has become real. And the fine shades, or the finer shades, are coming through in a concrete fashion. This is the difference between reading a play and seeing the play, if it is played properly. In playing, it must be more concrete than in reading.

Q: Are you saying that the audience cannot see the invisible but that they feel it, that there is a certain density, a certain indescribable feeling in the atmosphere?

PB: Of course. Something that is only an idea has become material. When I talk about the invisible, I am talking about the subtlest currents. There are finer forces in all human interactions that are easily felt and recognized, but only on certain occasions. On certain occasions in everyone's life, one can actually come in contact with this part of the richness of the human being. The theater and all its aspects—increased perception, increased intensity, concentration, elements that are part of the spectrum—can be experienced. And that is what is potentially life-giving.

Q: What do you consider the most important question in theater?

PB: We all expect far too easily that the most profound contact—that of the author, actor, and audience—can somehow happen by itself. Every shade of theater today, from the most traditional to the most popular to the most committed research theater, all tend to put this question as though it were a secondary one, as though it didn't need to be faced with the same intensity and purpose and depth that one encounters in other explorations. To me, this is where the whole question of the future of theater lies.

Q: You've been in the theater all your life; you've done more than fifty shows. How do you face getting older?

PB: I welcome it. All I can say is that every natural process has its meaning, and the process of getting older is a very good process. One can benefit from experiences of the past. I would be horrified to think that I wasn't older today than when I was younger.

Q: Do you think you're reaching a stage of wisdom—a word that has become a cliché? People say you are still searching and that you have the interest of a child—that everything is always new to you.

PB: Those are two sides of the same coin. The only way that something can grow and develop all the time is if it is irrigated by constantly seeking new impressions, so that those that you have inside do not wither. Of course, the two things go hand in glove. It's very difficult, but it's very necessary to perceive the world in a fresh way, to remain, in that sense, young and open. "Young" is not connected with years and "old" is not connected with years. And you know how terrible it is when you meet young people and they are closed.

Q: Do you feel you can do all that because you're always working and can achieve everything in a fresh way through your work? If you were an ordinary person reaching a certain age, it would be a different matter, wouldn't it? Since you are a creative person, there is always that stimulus, isn't there?

PB: I always think about how one is always mystified by what one is and who one is, and what one is doing— even in an imaginary way. It is pointless to think of oneself as someone else. If I were someone else— but I'm not; and if someone else were in my position—but they are not. You can only understand things when you recognize what happens to be your condition. And one must grasp hold of that as a fact. At this moment, I'm in Paris and nowhere else, and talking to you.

Q: Did the fact that you were very well brought up enable you to deal with all kinds of people, and remain supremely yourself at all times? Most people have different facades for different occasions. But you seem to remain the same for all occasions. Is that due to your family upbringing or your education?

PB: The most powerful thing in my life comes straight from my father. My father was everything to me. And that was a tremendous security. I look unhappily, regretfully, upon people who have resentments toward their parents; I know they can't help it. At an early age, there was the confidence and fidelity of my father and mother, and that was a permanent element. My brother had the same solid base.

Q: I thought you had learned it all at Oxford, but it really was your family life? Were both your parents Jewish?

PB: Oh yes.

Q: Were you more British than Jewish? Did your parents tell you anything about being Jewish?

PB: Oh yes, but that was not something that interested them. My father was an intellectual, and intellectuals at that time were freethinking, liberal, progressive people. My father was a big revolutionary. He was involved with the Russian Revolution before he came to England. By the time he came to England, England seemed to him a marvelous country, a free country, a great institution, and he became naturalized. Jewishness to him had to do with religion and rabbis, and he was a modern, assimilated Englishman. We were brought up in a completely secular atmosphere. We were not hiding that we were of Jewish origin, but it was not more powerful than in families where the grandparents were Spanish. It was a hereditary fact, but not an emotional influence producing feelings of guilt, or worry, or concern. In the milieu in which we lived, there was never, at any point in my life, any friction.

Q: Your father was financially secure?

PB: He made money, yes.

Q: How do you look back at your career? You were twenty when you became successful. How do you view your work? Are you satisfied with your choices?

PB: I don't look at it at all—as though that is something one can do. I don't see it as my work, in those terms, or as an accomplishment, or as a turning point. People ask me if *The Mahabharata* was the climax of my work. I don't see it that way at all. It is *The Mahabharata,* that's all, the work we were doing at the moment. I really don't see it in terms of accomplishments or achievements. Looking back, talking like this, I can see how one thing can lead to something else. But it doesn't interest me to wonder about accomplishments.

Q: People have said you overwork, that you should do less. You take on too many projects. Why?

PB: Why? There's a simple answer to that. I like it.

Acknowledgments

The first one to thank, of course, is Peter Brook, for his hours of talk, for his friendship and help in many different ways, for his energy and drive, and for principles that influenced my own life. Nina Soufy, Brook's office manager, has been of enormous help in securing vital information about photographs and for carrying messages with goodwill, courtesy, and charm; she has been a good friend. Thanks, too, to Marie-Hélène Estienne, who has always been supportive of my comings and goings in Paris; I also appreciate her conversations with me about Brook's work. Micheline Rozan, Peter Brook's longtime manager, now retired, was instrumental through the years in arranging time with Brook and arranging for me to see his productions in Iran, Stratford, Avignon, London, Belgrade, and Paris. And I thank Natasha Parry Brook for her sweet telephone calls to me at a certain important time. I owe special gratitude to the late great Jerzy Grotowski, who introduced me to Peter Brook and knew we would all become lifelong friends.

I want also to acknowledge the talks I had in Iran with the late Ted Hughes, who explained his work in *Orghast* to me and who, in a memorable and nostalgic meeting later in London, spoke about his work with myths and the English language and his life as the British poet laureate, while also reminiscing about his experience with Peter Brook.

I appreciate very much the professional work of my agents, Fifi Oscard and Carolyn French of the Fifi Oscard Agency. They not only sold the manuscript quickly but helped with many details and were always available for advice and consultations. Thanks also to my editor at Farrar, Straus and Giroux, Linda Rosenberg, and her assistant, Sarah Almond, whose attention to the manuscript was first-rate; I appreciate their gentle ways and their accessibility.

A wonderful helper has been Burke Hilsabeck, who transcribed the tapes quickly, and helped me put it all in order. I wish also to thank William Coco, a true friend, who read the manuscript and gave me many suggestions. And thanks to Jean Sulzberger for finding the photographs of *Meetings with Remarkable Men*.

Parts of the interviews with Peter Brook were published in the *New York Times* when the late Seymour Peck was editor of the Sunday "Arts and Leisure" section; I remember his advice and support. Arthur Gelb, then the managing editor of the *Times*, was also instrumental in publishing my pieces in the Sunday "Magazine" section, and I thank him for his help. *American Theater* magazine carried some pieces on Brook, and Jim O'Quinn, the editor, was a pleasure to work with.

Finally, my deepest thanks go to my cousin and lifelong friend Phyllis Dain, who, as always, read parts of the manuscript, edited some of it, was always ready with advice, tolerated my many questions and apprehensions, and gave me much encouragement. Her love and deep interest in my welfare made my task tolerable, even enjoyable. I am forever grateful.

New York City, 2002

Selected Chronology

1925	Birth of Peter Brook in London
1945	Graduated from Magdalen College, Oxford University
1946	*Man and Superman*, *King John*, *Lady from the Sea*, Birmingham Rep; *Love's Labour's Lost*, Stratford; *The Brothers Karamazov*, Lyric Hammersmith Theatre, London; *Vicious Circle*, Arts Theater, London
1947	*Romeo and Juliet*, Stratford; *Men Without Shadows*, *The Respectful Prostitute*, Lyric Hammersmith Theatre, London
1948–1949	*Boris Godunov*, *The Marriage of Figaro*, *The Olympians*, *Salome* (operas), Royal Opera House, Covent Garden, London
1950	*Ring Round the Moon*, Globe Theatre, London; *Measure for Measure*, Stratford; *The Little Hut*, Lyric Hammersmith Theatre, London
1951	*Death of a Salesman*, Belgian National Theater, Brussels; *A Penny for a Song*, Haymarket Theatre,

	London; *The Winter's Tale*, Phoenix Theatre, London; *Colombe*, New Theatre, London
1953	*Venice Preserv'd* (opera), Lyric Hammersmith Theatre, London; *Faust* (opera), Metropolitan Opera, New York; *King Lear* (with Orson Welles in title role) (television); *The Beggar's Opera* (film)
1954	*The Dark Is Light Enough*, Aldwych Theatre, London
1955	*The Lark*, Lyric Hammersmith Theatre, London; *Titus Andronicus*, Stratford; *Hamlet*, Phoenix Theatre, London
1956	*The Power and the Glory*, *The Family Reunion*, Phoenix Theatre, London; *A View from the Bridge*, Comedy Theatre, London; *Cat on a Hot Tin Roof*, Théâtre Antoine, Paris
1957	*The Tempest*, Stratford; *Eugene Onegin* (opera), Metropolitan Opera, New York
1958	*The Visit* (starring The Lunts), Lunt-Fontanne Theater, New York; *Irma la Douce*, Lyric Hammersmith Theatre, London, and, later, at the Plymouth Theater, New York
1960	*The Balcony*, Paris; *Moderato Cantabile* (film)
1962	*King Lear* (starring Paul Scofield), Stratford, and, later, New York State Theater, New York
1963	*The Physicists*, Aldwych Theatre, London; *Serjeant Musgrave's Dance*, *The Representative*, Paris; *Lord of the Flies* (film)
1964	*The Screens*, *Marat/Sade*, premiere, LAMDA, London, and, later, at the Aldwych Theatre, London, and Martin Beck Theater, New York
1965	*The Investigation*, *US*, Aldwych Theatre, London
1968	*The Tempest*, Roundhouse, London; Seneca's *Oedipus*, National Theatre at the Old Vic, London; *Tell Me Lies* (film)
1970–1971	*A Midsummer Night's Dream*, Stratford, and, later, at the Billy Rose Theater, New York
1970	Establishment of the International Center of Theater Research
1971	*Orghast*, Persepolis, Iran

1972–1973	African Voyage
1974	*Timon of Athens*, Les Bouffes du Nord, Paris
1975	*The Ik*, Les Bouffes du Nord, Paris, and, later, at the Roundhouse, London, Avignon, and La Mama, New York; *The Conference of the Birds*, Les Bouffes du Nord, Paris
1977	*Ubu*, Les Bouffes du Nord, Paris, and, later, at the Young Vic, London, La Mama, New York, and Latin America
1978	*Measure for Measure*, Les Bouffes du Nord, Paris; *Antony and Cleopatra*, Stratford, and, later, at the Aldwych Theatre, London
1979	*Meetings with Remarkable Men* (film)
1980	*L'Os*, *The Ik*, *Ubu*, *The Conference of the Birds*, La Mama, New York, and Australia
1981	*The Cherry Orchard*, *La Tragédie de Carmen*, Les Bouffes du Nord, Paris
1982	*La Tragédie de Carmen*, Vivian Beaumont Theater, Lincoln Center, New York
1985–1987	*The Mahabharata*, Les Bouffes du Nord, Paris, and, later, Zurich, Los Angeles, Glasgow, Australia, Japan, and the Brooklyn Academy of Music, Brooklyn, New York
1988	*The Cherry Orchard*, Brooklyn Academy of Music, Brooklyn, New York
1990	*The Tempest*, Les Bouffes du Nord, Paris, and, later, Glasgow
1993–1995	*The Man Who*, Les Bouffes du Nord, Paris, and, later, Europe and the Brooklyn Academy of Music, Brooklyn, New York
2000–2001	*The Tragedy of Hamlet*, Les Bouffes du Nord, Paris, and, later, Chicago and the Brooklyn Academy of Music, Brooklyn, New York